TREES FOR THE SOUTH

DON HASTINGS

LONGSTREET PRESS, INC.
Atlanta, Georgia

Published by
LONGSTREET PRESS, INC.
2140 Newmarket Parkway
Suite 122
Marietta, GA 30067

Printed in the United States of America

1st printing 2001

Library of Congress Catalog Card Number: 00-111988

ISBN: 1-56352-596-8

Cover design by Burtch Bennett Hunter
Interior page design by Jill Dible
Cover photo of Live Oak by Chris Hastings

To my dearest love,
Betsy,
my blessed wife and companion for 33 years,
who has exhibited eleemosynary character while I have been writing this book,
especially when responding to my many requests like,
"What does *eleemosynary* mean, and how do you spell it?"

and to my son,
Chris Hastings,
for all his advice and help with the text and especially for the use
of his photographs, which add so much to this book,

and my deep appreciation goes to
John Yow, my editor,
who has been kind, gentle, and long-suffering,

and to
Jill Dible,
whose design has made this a beautiful book.

This topographical and zone map of the South delineates the three growing regions referred to throughout this book:

LOWER SOUTH: The areas of the South that include the Coastal Plain from Virginia south to Georgia and west through Alabama to Texas.

MIDDLE SOUTH: The areas of the South that include the Piedmont region extending south from Virginia to Georgia and west through Alabama to Texas.

UPPER SOUTH: The area of the South that includes the western Piedmont and mountain regions from Virginia and North Carolina west through northern Tennessee and Arkansas.

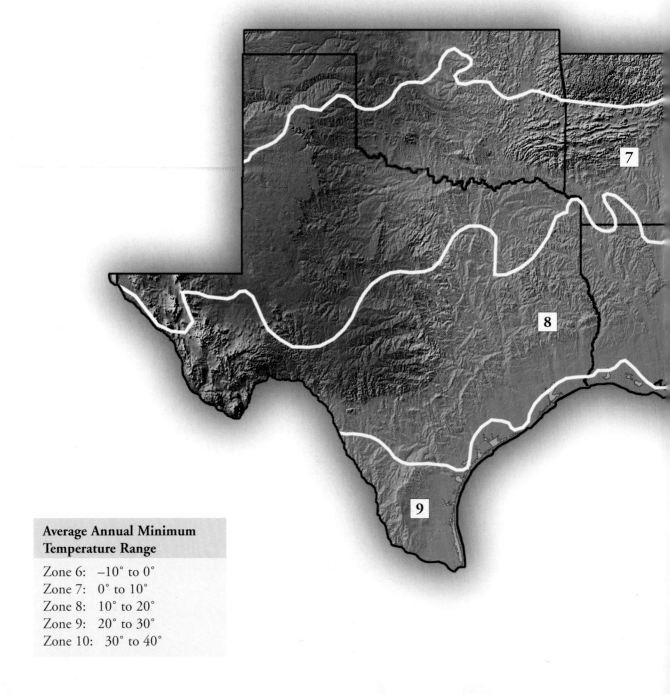

Average Annual Minimum Temperature Range

Zone 6: −10° to 0°
Zone 7: 0° to 10°
Zone 8: 10° to 20°
Zone 9: 20° to 30°
Zone 10: 30° to 40°

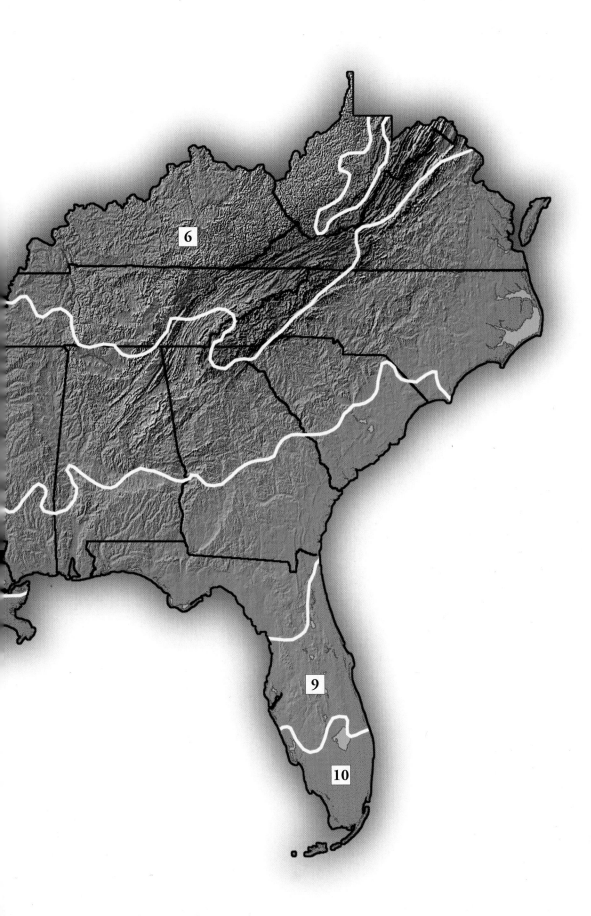

TABLE OF CONTENTS

Introduction vi

Historical Time Line 1

CHAPTER 1: HISTORY (by Chris Hastings) 2

CHAPTER 2: TREES AND TREE NAMES 4

CHAPTER 3: TREES FOR SOUTHERN LANDSCAPES 16

        TREES FOR SPECIAL PURPOSES 172

CHAPTER 4: TREE PLANTING AND CULTURE 174

CHAPTER 5: SEASON-BY-SEASON TREE ACTIVITIES 182

CHAPTER 6: INTRODUCTION TO TREE PROBLEMS 194

References 207

Index 209

Introduction

Trees are the most important part of any landscape. They are the upright pillars and outreaching beams upon which a landscape is built, like four-by-four and two-by-four pieces of lumber are used to hold up a house. A landscape can be acceptable without shrubs, vines, annuals, and perennials, but without trees it is barren and evokes a feeling of desolation. I know because I once helped build and direct a project in the desert in Egypt where there were no trees, except a few we planted for windbreaks. When I see a subdivision where all the trees were removed before houses were built, I think of our farm in the desert.

I grew up in a house on a hill covered with trees, so maybe I'm prejudiced against homes without them. My father also liked trees and wanted as many as possible around the house he built. I am glad he did, since a child finds comfort in the protection they give and the fun they afford a youngster who wants to climb high in their limbs to see the world. Whenever I hear wind blowing through a pine, I remember lying in bed at night and listening to the wind in the large pine next to my bedroom window. It sounded like angels singing to me, soothing the hurts of the day and calming the fears of the night.

Above: *Deserts are lifeless and hostile places without trees.* Top right: *Trees make a landscape pleasing.* Right: *Many modern subdivisions look lifeless until homeowners plant and nurture new trees.*

Few places on earth have as many kinds of native trees as we have in the southern United States. Some, like Live Oaks, are magnificent in size and age; others, like Flowering Dogwood, have no peers when in bloom. Oak, magnolia, hickory, beech, dogwood, ash, and a myriad of other species inhabit forests and landscapes all over the South. Facing untold hardships, early plant explorers from other continents discovered trees here that they had never seen before in their native lands. The seeds they carried back to their homelands developed into valuable additions in their landscapes, and now our expatriate trees beautify parks, botanical gardens, and home landscapes all over the world.

Trees are everywhere around us except in the caverns made by the concrete buildings in our large metropolitan areas. Go just a few thousand yards outside of these man-made jungles, and you'll find homes, parks, and buildings blessed with these extraordinary members of the plant kingdom. Some of the better specimens are older than the cities that have built up around them; some once offered shade for the Indians who dwelled here long before outsiders settled the South. Older

southern cities like Charleston, Mobile, New Orleans, Richmond, and Savannah are more conscious of trees and their value than our newer, highly commercialized cities, where concrete and steel measure success more than preservation of these great natural resources.

There is a park near where I lived when I returned to Atlanta from college. Back in history, a spring-fed stream wound its way between groups of huge American beech, hickory, Tulip Poplar, and oak. Indian families camped on the flat ground underneath the protective arms of the largest beech tree. I would sit beneath the same branches and dream of the past – a time when life might have been hard but the surrounding sounds came from birds in the trees, not

from irritated motorists raging at each other. The stream ran clear and fresh, unlike the foul-smelling liquid flowing there today, suitable for neither man nor beast. I don't want to give up indoor plumbing or central air conditioning and heating, and I'm not against progress, but I hope we mature quickly enough in the New South to save these cherished monuments given us by nature.

Planting a good tree is leaving something for the next generation and hundreds more to come. Maybe if

Above: *Older southern cities protect their trees.* Right: *Before settlers arrived, this huge American Beech in mid-town Atlanta provided shade for Indian families.*

Trees help neighborhoods look mature.

the bulldozers stay away, the tree you plant will live a thousand years – or at least a hundred.

Learning about trees for the Southern landscape takes us on a journey to far-off lands where many had their origins. Just as seeds from our native trees have enriched landscapes abroad, so have many foreign trees taken welcome root in the South. We go to the Holy Land where a cedar of the Bible, *Cedrus libani*, still grows as it did when the prophets lived and John was born. It's hard to comprehend that a 3,000-year-old *Ginkgo biloba*, a fabulous tree whose ancestors are seen throughout the South, still grows by a rice paddy in China. Flowering Cherry trees came from Japan, and Crape Myrtle, a tree we think of as typically southern, is originally from China. While I'm thankful for these imports, I believe that nowhere on earth is there a tree as beautiful as our Flowering Dogwood or one as magnificent as Southern Magnolia. I, for one, think we have given more fine trees than we have received.

The history of trees we see every day is interesting, but this book is really about trees to plant in your own landscape – as well as those already growing – and how to nurture them. Sometimes you, your landscaper, or your nurseryman might disagree with my assessments. But I am like an umpire behind the plate in a baseball game: I calls it like I sees it.

I have seen too many chopped-off tall-growing trees planted under power lines. I've seen too many fast-growing miracle trees break apart in windstorms. I have lived long enough to watch fad trees suddenly develop serious problems and fade away. I want to help you to avoid mistakes that might be costly when you have to remove a bad tree or repair a roof damaged by a weak-wooded tree's limbs falling on top of your house.

We cannot go back to the days when William Bartram traveled through the South in the 1750s describing the magnificent oaks, magnolias, dogwoods, hickories, and many other beautiful trees growing with ease. But we can do our part by planting trees in the landscape that will grow equally well and last hundreds of years for the enjoyment of our families and those who follow.

Historical Time Line

3000 BC	Malee and Huon Trees Australia, Tasmania, 5000 years old
2600 BC	Pyramids constructed
2000 BC	Cypress, Chile, 4000 years old
1000 BC	Ginkgo biloba, China, 3000 years old Baobab, South Africa, 3000 years old Kauri Tree, New Zealand, 3000 years old Cedar of Lebanon, Lebanon, 3000 years old
900 BC	Athens founded
753 BC	Rome founded
525 BC	Buddha begins teaching
400 BC	Plato teaches
356–323 BC	Alexander the Great
100–44 BC	Julius Caesar
AD 1	~~Birth of God~~ Jesus! Sherman Redwood, USA, 2000 years old Cypress, Mexico, 2000 years old Yew, Great Britain, 2000 years old
AD 500	Douglas Fir, Canada, 1500 years old
AD 570–632	Mohammed, founder of Islam
AD 1000	Linden, France, 1000 years old
AD 1095–1270	The Crusades Middleton Oak, Charleston, SC, 800–900 years old
AD 1492	Columbus discovers America
AD 1585	Founding of Jamestown Colony
AD 1750	Horse Chestnut, Kilfane House, Ireland, 250 years old White Oak, Alpharetta, GA, 250 years old
AD 1775	Beginning of the American Revolution
AD 1776	Signing of the Declaration of Independence
AD 1781	General Cornwallis surrenders to General George Washington
AD 1788	American Constitution adopted
AD 1861	Civil War begins Tulip Poplar, Floweracres, Lovejoy, GA, 125 or more years old
AD 1890	Champion Fraser Fir, Cashiers, NC, planted
AD 1898	Spanish American War begins
AD 1900	Twentieth century begins Numerous 100-year-old trees continue to grow
AD 1941	Japanese bomb Pearl Harbor Numerous trees planted prior to World War II are still growing well
AD 2001	Third millennium begins New trees planted. How long will they last in our environment?

Chapter 1

History

By Chris Hastings

Shortly after Christmas in 1700, a young English immigrant by the name of John Lawson left Charleston on a reconnaissance tour of the interior of what was then known as "Carolina." His journey lasted 59 days and he covered 550 miles, most of it on foot. During the trip, he kept a journal that was soon published in London under the title *A New Journey to Carolina*. It was eagerly read by prospective immigrants thirsty for news and descriptions of the unknown interior of America.

In his journal of 300 years ago, Lawson describes the trees of the South as they stood before European colonization. One of my favorite descriptions is that of the Tulip Poplar or Tulip Tree, *Liriodendron tulipifera*:

> The Tulip-Trees . . . grow to a prodigious bigness, some of them having been found one and twenty foot in circumference. I have been informed of a Tulip-Tree, that was ten foot diameter; and another wherein a [fat] man had his bed and household furniture, and lived in it, till his labor got him a more fashionable mansion.

Another giant tree Lawson felt compelled to describe was the Bald Cypress, *Taxodium distichum*:

> Cypress is not an evergreen with us, and is therefore called the Bald Cypress, because the leaves, during the winter season, turn red, not recovering their verdure till the spring. These trees are the largest for height and thickness, that we have in this part of the World; some of them holding thirty-six feet in circumference.

Early settlers quickly learned from the Indians that the giant Bald Cypress of the South could be fashioned into dug-out canoes, ideal for transporting themselves and their supplies inland along our many Southern rivers. Among these early travelers were explorers like Mark Catesby, André and Francois Michaux, and John Bartram, who sought new and interesting plant and animal life previously unknown in Europe. Their mission was to catalog new plants and animals, as well as to collect and retrieve as many live specimens as possible. Many of these new discoveries included trees that were returned to Europe as seeds, where they were cultivated as exotic specimens in the most fashionable gardens of the day.

In the latter part of the 18th century, William Bartram (the son of botanical explorer John Bartram) set out for the Southern colonies on a journey to locate and document native plants for his English patron, Dr. John Fothergill. Bartram visited forests untouched in the years since Lawson's journey, and, as he recorded in *The Travels of William Bartram,* he was just as amazed as his predecessor at the sight of a 100-foot-tall Southern Magnolia, *Magnolia grandiflora*, or the magnificent Bald Cypress, "lifting its cumbrous top toward the skies."

John Lawson and William Bartram explored the South some 100 years apart but found virtually the same native forest, characterized by an incredible diversity of plants and plant sizes. For every giant Bald Cypress, there were 10 other plant species filling every nook and cranny of the woodlands. And for each 10-foot-in-diameter Bald Cypress, there were 10 waist-high Bald Cypress growing to replace it when it died of old age.

In the years that followed Lawson's and then Bartram's travels, a growing number of colonists spread into the interior of the South and tapped the rich resources of the Southern forests. Trees were not only a commodity, but a source of building supplies, food, and medicine. Lawson had described the marvelous grain of the Sweet Gum, *Liquidambar styraciflua*, suitable for "fine tables, drawers, and other furniture"; the acorns of the Live Oak, *Quercus virginiana*, "sweet as chestnuts"; and the bark of the Pink flowering Dogwood, *Cornus florida*, which, "infused, is held an infallible remedy against the worms."

air of pollution by using the carbon dioxide that animals, man, and machines produce and give back oxygen, our breath of life. They reduce the heat reflected by man-made objects in cities. Their roots keep the sides of mountains from crashing down on us and the seas from eating away the shores. Without trees, mankind's survival would be in doubt.

Yet we take trees for granted over and over again. Man can destroy in minutes what Nature took years to develop. A 100-year-old Tulip Poplar has no right to existence when a developer wants a parking garage that will come and go in half that time. Developers, bulldozers, highways, and cost considerations are sovereign, not a tree's longevity, beauty, historical significance, and role in making our planet habitable.

My father was a great believer in conservation, the mid-20th-century term for environmental protection. He often lectured that conservation starts in the backyard. You and I can't change the world, but we can help by planting trees on our land and protecting those that have escaped the bulldozers. By the time the oak or maple you plant in your landscape sees the beginning

of the 23rd century, maybe it will be appreciated for its maturity as much as you appreciate its part in making your surroundings more beautiful.

I must hasten to add, however, that trees, just like all living plants and animals – including man – can be good or bad. Trees don't mean harm but they can be harmful anyway. There is an old saying that a weed is a plant out of place. A tree can also be a weed when growing where it shouldn't. Oaks and maples are fabulous trees for the landscape, but only when the right ones are planted in the right spot. First choose the right species; the wrong one can be disastrous. Plant it with the future in mind or its limbs may ruin your roof and its roots undermine your home's foundation. I can assure you that in such battles, the tree will win.

Some trees have other problems: insects, diseases, unsightly fruits and seeds, weak wood that breaks in high wind or ice and snow, or even too much or too little growth. Consider power lines when choosing a tree. Nothing is more disheartening than seeing a magnificent tree butchered or topped to keep electricity flowing into a home, when a smaller-growing tree would do just as well.

Unlike annuals planted for flowers and vegetables that finish their cycles in eight or nine months, trees last much longer, often hundreds of years. They can't be replaced in the middle of a growing season like annuals, then allowed to develop and produce before frost. Unlike most other garden plants, trees are for the long haul. If you plant the wrong tree or even the right tree in the wrong place, it may be several years before you realize your error. Tree mistakes can be very costly, especially when you lose two, three, or more years of growth before starting over.

Choosing the right tree depends on knowing what is needed for each spot in the landscape. Consider a tree's size, shape, leaf and flower color, rate of growth, strength, longevity, insect and disease resistance, fruits, seeds, and your own personal taste before choosing what to plant.

Better developers take pride in protecting native trees on the lots where they build houses. One such development is close to me, and a drive through the area is a delightful experience. Native Sweet Gum,

Top Left: *Another forest disappears to make way for buildings.*
Left: *Bulldozers destroy in a few hours what Nature took many years to grow.*

Tulip Poplar, Chestnut Oak, Red Oak, White Oak, Red Maple, and seldom-seen species like Bigleaf Magnolia protect homes from the blazing sun and make landscapes more natural and mature. Nearby is a slash-and-grade development. A quick look from the main road shows the stark difference between the two.

In older sections of Southern cities and towns, homeowners are fortunate when they have large, handsome trees already growing. The question for new homeowners and older residents alike is how to treat trees already in place. My best advice is to keep them, nurture them, and relish them. However, to reiterate, not all existing trees are equal. Take an inventory of the trees on your property to know in advance what problems might arise sooner or later.

Many years ago, my sister and brother-in-law moved into an old, tree-filled residential section of

Top: *Avoid planting trashy, weak-wooded trees like Empress Tree.* Above: *Don't plant tall-growing trees under utility lines.*

Atlanta. Some trees on their property are 75 years old or more and growing well, but an Empress Tree, *Paulownia tomentosa,* gave them serious problems and had to be removed. The rest are oaks, mainly Water Oak and Willow Oak, not noted for their longevity, strength, or desirability. Over the years their limbs have broken and crashed down. They drop small acorns that sprout in their lawn and shrub borders, and they slowly shed their small leaves, making leaf removal a long-term chore. Still, though, who wouldn't rather have handsome old oaks in the landscape than a bare lot dotted with new plantings?

When you are fortunate enough to have mature trees on your property, keep all you can and remove the potentially dangerous or messy ones like the Empress Tree in my sister's backyard. Study your tree inventory as if you were buying new trees. Knowing what might happen to existing trees and giving them extra care or removing them is an insurance policy against future problems or disasters. We keep an eye on my sister's oaks and try to remove dying limbs before they fall through the roof.

Heavily wooded lots with new homes also benefit from a tree inventory. Builders seldom finish off a landscape by thinning groups of trees, especially pines. Your inventory should consider spacing as well as identification. Remove the small and weaker trees, but be sure you are not removing an unusual or interesting tree that grows slower than less desirable shorter-lived trees like pines. Know and protect your keeper trees and other native woody plants as if you had just purchased them at great expense. A good landscape architect or designer will always help you decide which existing plants to keep.

Your inventory should include a tree's common and botanical name, size, and distance from other trees, drives, structures, power lines, and underground utilities – like drain lines, water lines, and gas lines.

Many years ago in my early days after college, I ran across a puzzling situation with several older Sugar Maples in a large front yard. One was bright yellow every fall while all the others were flame-colored, even though the trees were about the same size and equally vigorous. My tree mentor, Nelson Crist, asked the homeowner where the water, sewage, and gas lines were. The man didn't know, so we figured it out by finding the connections on the street and the meters at the house. It looked to us like the gas line traversed the outer root zone of the unusual maple, and Nelson asked the homeowner if his gas bills seemed high. Yes,

they did, he said, and he had wondered why.

"Get the gas company to check for leaks near the tree," Nelson strongly suggested.

The homeowner called later to thank us. There was a small leak, which was a hazard not only to the tree but to the home and family. It took several years for the tree to regain the same fall color as the maples nearby, but the homeowner remained grateful to the tree for warning them of danger.

In many ways, existing trees are a valuable asset. They are usually larger than any you can purchase and they go a long way toward making a landscape look mature. Knowing your trees and how they should perform is asset protection at its best.

In the end, how a tree appeals to you is the final step toward making the right choice. Living things are seldom perfect in every way, and trees are no exception. Choosing the right tree is up to you, the person who will live with and nurture it.

Different kinds of trees that you can choose:

Shade Trees
Deciduous trees that lose their leaves each winter
- Broadleaf shade trees (e.g., oaks, maples, and elms)
- Needle deciduous shade trees (e.g., Bald Cypress and Dawn Redwood)

Deciduous trees like Red Maple cool homes in the summer and let the sun warm them in the winter.

Evergreen trees whose leaves remain year-round
- Broadleaf Evergreens (e.g., Southern Magnolia and Carolina Cherry Laurel)
- Needle evergreens (e.g., Balsam Fir, Norway Spruce, and Indian Cedar)

Flowering Trees
- Spring-Flowering Trees (e.g., flowering crabapples, flowering cherries, and dogwood)

Dogwoods are our finest spring-flowering trees.

- Summer-Flowering Trees (e.g., Golden-rain Tree, Chaste Tree, and Crape Myrtle)

Evergreen trees like Southern Magnolia keep their beautiful foliage all year.

Crape Myrtle trees blossom though most of the summer.

Important Characteristics to Consider When Choosing a Tree to Plant:

Size, Breadth, and Shape:

The size and breadth a tree grows is of prime importance when choosing what and where to plant. The small, straight, almost limbless tree you find in a nursery looks like it will never be as large as 50-year-old specimens or mature trees in parks, botanical gardens, and estates. But it will, often in less time than you think.

In general, because outward-spreading limbs can cause myriad unforeseen problems, a tree's breadth is a more critical consideration than its ultimate height. When it comes to height, after all, "the sky is the limit." The one important exception here is planting beneath utility lines, which obviously impose a barrier. There is nothing uglier than a tree butchered by power line crews into a hideous-looking creature whose limbs look like the flailing arms of a drowning person. And don't be fooled: the first butchering may not look too bad since the tree is still young. But the tree's continued growth, and subsequent butcherings, will inevitably result in ugliness.

Plant a tree where it will continue to fit comfortably for many years. Pyramidal, fastigiate and upright developing trees, like Fastigiate European Hornbeam, Japanese Cedar, and Leyland Cypress, are more narrow than tall. Upright oval trees, like Tulip Polar and European Linden, may spread about half as far as a tree's height. Broad oval and wide-spreading trees, like White Oak and Red Maple, may be as wide or wider than tall.

Remember, though, that trees are living and variable, especially when grown from seeds. Natural variations,

Pin Oak has a tight pyramid form until it is older.

Red Maple has a broad rounded canopy.

White Oak limbs grow upward and outward like a vase.

Choose a tree with a strong central trunk for restricted areas.

Sugar Maple has a tall oval to round canopy.

Choose low-growing trees for planting under utility lines.

mechanical damage, insects or diseases, soil quality, and drainage may cause a species to grow differently from its normal habit. A tree listed as upright might become wide-spreading on its own.

Cultivars of a species are generally propagated by cuttings or grafts to prevent the wide variations found in seedlings. Those with a desirable characteristic will have a much higher probability of being like their parent than a seedling-grown tree. However, we are dealing with living things, so don't shoot the messenger when some external factor causes a cultivar to grow different, from the way I describe it.

Growth Rate:

Fast-growing trees seem like the best choice when sun beats down on a house or boils through a picture window. But remember: fast-growing trees, like Catalpa and Siberian Elm, have weak wood and short lives. Medium and medium-fast growing trees, like Katsura Tree and Red Maple, are ideal for home landscapes. Slow-growing trees, like White Oak and American Beech, are definitely for the long haul and work best for parks, large open areas, and people who plan to stay put for a long time.

Leaves:

Leaf size, shape, color, and retention in the fall should all be taken into consideration when choosing a tree. The small leaves of some oaks and elms, for example, can be a real pain to remove from lawns and shrub borders; on the other hand, the extra large leaves of trees like the Bigleaf Magnolia may not be as hard to rake up but require quick removal to keep a landscape neat. Needles of pines and other evergreen trees have to be raked up when they drop because most contain high amounts of resin, which keeps them from decaying rapidly. Fortunately, pine needles make excellent, long-lasting mulch.

Leaf shape is important when considering texture contrasts with other trees and shrubs, as is your tree leaves' shade of green. Also, since leaf raking is a job few of us relish, you might think about how fast your trees drop their leaves. Ginkgo, for example, is noted for its quick leaf drop, while the larger leaves of oaks can't seem to let go. With beeches, however, prolonged leaf retention isn't such a bad thing, since their light tan leaves can be attractive on a bleak winter day.

Fall Color:

Many deciduous trees seem to have a sixth sense about when winter will come by saving a spectacular display for their last gasp before dormancy. A fall visit to the mountains of the South or New England is a must for many of us. Maples, oaks, beech, hickory, Black Gum, and many other deciduous trees have better fall color where the nights are very cool and the days aren't too warm. But don't belittle fall color in your own yard,

Dogwood fall color is a brilliant maroon-red.

which can be as spectacular as it is many miles away. Learn which trees have the best fall color and factor that into the equation for choosing which tree to plant.

Fall color is an important characteristic to consider. Reds and yellows are the most popular fall colors.

Flowering trees like Okame Flowering Cherry make spring our most colorful time of the year.

Flowers:

Shade trees seldom have flowers worthy of consideration when choosing which one to plant. Sometimes noticeable flowers on a shade tree can be a drawback because of the seed formations that follow. Empress Tree and both Catalpa species grown in the South have unattractive seed formations that can be a real bother. On the other hand, Red Maple, *Acer rubrum,* is one of the earliest flowers to brighten forests and landscapes.

Flowering trees are chosen for their flowers and not necessarily for their qualities as a handsome tree. There are no perfect flowering trees. Most have specific times during the year when they bloom. Be aware of spring-flowering trees whose blossoms come so early that cold or frost might kill them. Spring-flowering trees generally blossom before leaves appear, which makes them more spectacular, but those that blossom after their leaves appear, like Chinese Dogwood, can add a month or so of color in the landscape. Remember also: the time when a flowering tree blossoms determines when you prune it. Study bloom-season, color, mass of flowers, and length of time in bloom before choosing the one best for your landscape.

Also, before making your choice, be aware that some flowering trees are prone to debilitating insect and disease attacks.

Red Maple flowers brighten landscapes in early spring.

Fruits make Chinese Chestnuts a dual-purpose landscape tree.

Fruits:

We seldom grow shade or flowering trees for their fruits, though some, like Indian Cedar, have attractive and ornamental cones. Delicious nuts are an extra bonus when you plant a pecan, but they can also be a nuisance to pick up if you don't like pecans or don't want a raft of squirrels. The same is true of walnuts, hickories, and chestnuts. I don't mind the large acorns that form on a Chestnut Oak, but the tiny ones dropping off a Water Oak or Willow Oak drive me nuts.

Insects and Diseases:

If you study insect and disease manuals, you'll find some kind of problem listed for almost every tree. Fortunately, shade trees are tough and most survive many years with relatively few problems. They are not likely to require special care unless a sudden and catastrophic insect or disease attack occurs, which has never happened at my house. I see leaf spots, worms every now and then, cankers, galls, and all sorts of things I have to look up in a book to identify, but my trees keep on growing and performing.

In crowded urban areas, however, trees can become stressed due to pollution, heat from asphalt and concrete, moisture shortage caused by over-engineered drainage, and the dense planting of one species or cultivar, which leads to rapid build-up of pest populations. Even so, well-chosen shade tree species and cultivars reduce the insect and disease problems to a point of little concern.

Flowering trees are a bit different. Most are closely kin to a fruiting counterpart, making them susceptible to a wider range of insects and diseases. Fireblight, borers, scale, and leaf spots of various kinds plague some flowering forms of fruit trees. Also, flowering trees are often planted in groups, either on your or your neighbor's

Most diseases like Maple Tar Spot are not a problem, but avoid trees with severe insect or disease problems.

property or up and down the street, which allows insects and diseases to spread rapidly when conditions are right.

Choose species and cultivars known for their resistance to pests, and plant only a few in one area.

Landscape Use:

Some trees look best when standing alone, while others are most attractive when planted in groups of the same or contrasting types. Others do well in tight corners, next to the street, along driveways, or between properties. Try not to be swayed by a pretty picture in a book, or a beautiful tree in a friend's yard. Instead, think of your own individual landscape, and choose a tree that fits in every way.

The purpose of planting a tree or shrub is to visually please those who live with it day after day. All the king's horses and all the king's men – or, to be more accurate – all the architects, designers, horticulturists, and passersby cannot put together a landscape plan without knowing what you and your family like and dislike.

Longevity:

I mentioned longevity when discussing fast-growing trees, which is entirely appropriate since they seldom live very long. However, longevity deserves more than a mere mention. It is important in our own lives and the lives of those who follow. There is something very special about a tree that has a history. When I see two names carved on a beech tree, how can I not wonder what happened to those two youngsters who bound themselves together in 1922?

Tree Names

My name is Donald Madison Hastings Jr. When I was a very small boy, my family called me Donnie to distinguish me from my father, Donald M. Hastings. After college, the diminutive form seemed inappropriate, so someone on the farm started calling me Mr. Junior. Fortunately that name didn't last very long. Now my friends call me Don Hastings. Almost everyone has been called by more than one or two names during their lifetime.

Trees also have names: dogwood, magnolia, Red Maple, and tulip tree are familiar to most of us gardeners. But which dogwood am I talking about? There are many dogwoods – like Flowering Dogwood, Redosier Dogwood, Pagoda Dogwood, and Chinese Dogwood. Is the magnolia I am thinking about the evergreen one with big leaves or an Oriental one with beautiful spring flowers? Red Maple is one of our finest shade trees, but the smaller-growing red-leaf Japanese Maples are also called Red Maples. Tulip tree is better known in the South as Tulip Poplar, which might seem to keep us from confusing it with an Oriental flowering magnolia called Tulip

Magnolia, but it's not a poplar.

Bible readers are familiar with the story of the Israelites, unhappy in captivity, hanging their harps on willow trees by the waters of Babylon.

Actually, those were poplars, not willows. Tree names vary tremendously from place to place and culture to culture, making it difficult for travelers to know what they are admiring.

In the mid-1700s when our forebears were getting really put out with the British, a Swedish botanist, Carolus Linnaeus, introduced a system for naming plants. His name in Swedish was Carl von Linné but in those days science was taught in Latin; hence the Latin form, *Carolus Linnaeus*, became his pen name. All names in his system were in Latin, which turns out to be a good news/bad news story. It is good news because all names can be clearly understood in every language, including those like Chinese and Arabic that don't use the Roman alphabet like we do. The bad news is that few students in America are taught Latin, so botanical names are as foreign as if they were in Chinese or Swahili. I took Latin in high school where we Latin

Thomas Jefferson's Monticello became a home rather than a museum when I read that in the 1700s he planted the tree I was standing under. Monticello inspired Jefferson to write that "No occupation is so delightful to me as the culture of the earth, and no culture comparable to that of the garden." He obviously had in mind the cultivation of trees since many he planted are still alive.

I took a picture of my wife, Betsy, under the huge Middleton Oak at Middleton Plantation outside Charleston, South Carolina. She was dwarfed by the huge tree, which in itself made an interesting photograph, but when we read that the tree had stood in that same place since the Crusades, we were truly awe-struck.

Old trees may not hold the fascination for you that they do for me. If not, try to reconsider what you give back to Nature when you plant something that may still be alive when we have colonies on neighboring planets, or when some extraterrestrial visitor stands underneath and wonders what it is. Sound impossible or irrelevant? Maybe, but I think William Bartram and Thomas Lawson would have been just as amazed that an oak they saw would ever have flying machines roaring above them.

A tree's longevity is an important part of the future, not only for you but for subsequent owners of your home, who – if you have chosen wisely – will look up in its branches and thank you for choosing to plant such a magnificent tree.

Besides, long-lived trees don't usually break apart and crush your roof.

students, like generations before us, drove our teacher nuts with a great rhyme:

Latin is a dead language, as dead as it can be.
First it killed Caesar, and now it's killing me.

The truth of that silly rhyme is the reason Latin is used in science, including horticulture. It is a dead language, which means it is the same today as it was yesterday, and we can count on it being the same tomorrow. *Metasequoia gliptostroboides* may be a terrible name to remember, but at least you've only got to learn it once. Plus, its English name, Dawn Redwood, might translate into something unprintable in Urdu or Ilongo.

Plants belong to a number of different groups, like orders, which don't concern us except when we become interested in botany and taxonomy. A plant family is the first group of major interest to horticulturists. For instance, all maples are in the Aceraceae family. A genus in a family is the first group of interest to most gardeners, since it is the first word in a plant's scientific name. The second name is the species and, when applicable, a third name is a variety. The botanical name for Pink Flowering Dogwood is *Cornus* (genus name) *florida* (species name) var. (for variety) *rubra* (variety name), using the system devised by Carolus Linnaeus and still the accepted method 250 years later. A recent revision to the system prescribes that all species names be in lower case; hence the "f" in *florida* is not capitalized as it might be, since it is named for the state of Florida.

Research has shown that horticultural forms of plants are not botanically different from the species, a requirement for a variety. For instance, a horticultural form with a different color flower from those of the species would not be a botanical variety since its seedlings would not produce flowers like the horticultural form.

The method of naming a horticultural form is using the term cultivar instead of variety. A cultivar is indicated by enclosing the name in single quotes, like Acer rubrum 'October Glory'. The letters cv. can also be used to denote a cultivar, as in Acer rubrum cv. October Glory.

Confused? I understand how you might be. My first few weeks taking Taxonomy at Cornell were worse than Miss Minnie Barrett's Latin I class when I was 15. I lived through both and now spout Latin plant names easily. Give them a chance and you will, too.

In the meantime, please don't paraphrase our Latin rhyme:

His explanation is dead, as dead as it can be.
I'd like to kill Don Hastings, 'cause this is killing me.

CHAPTER 3

Trees for Southern Landscapes

Trees for the landscape are not all created equal. Some may grow too tall, others too short, and some may not grow at all. Choosing the right tree for your landscape is not difficult if you take the time to learn its characteristics. Height, spread, shape, density of limbs and leaves, growth rate, and longevity are important to you and your landscape designer; but how well it will grow in the spot you have chosen is the ultimate question. You might have a great place for a Crimson King Maple like you grew in Pennsylvania, but will it perform as well in your landscape here in the South?

Personal feelings are also important. Why buy a Purple Leaf Plum when you hate red or a Water Oak when your least favorite job is raking leaves? Choose a tree that fits all your criteria, not just one or two. My family and friends accuse me of being opinionated about a lot of things. I admit to the charge. Over the years I have seen too many trees grow out of bounds or start dying a few years after being planted.

My father was fond of saying, "Differences of opinion are what sell bad farm land." You might like a Crape Myrtle cultivar that I think is an ugly hot pink, but maybe pink is your favorite color and you want a pink flowering tree in your landscape. Your opinion, not mine, is what counts in matters of taste. But trees with inherent problems you might not know about are another matter. My purpose here is to warn you before the tree you plant goes into a tailspin and creates unforeseen trouble or, worse, dies in a year or so.

Trees are an extremely important part of the landscape. Unlike annuals and even perennials that grow and perform quickly, trees are an investment in the future as much as the present. A tree may take two or three years before its true character starts to show and many more years before you decide it is not the dream tree you wanted. Not only have you lost years of growth, but the cost of removal and replacement can be very high. You may have to spend a small fortune to replace a tree that has been growing in your landscape for only a few years.

In the previous chapters, I have described what to look for when deciding which tree to plant. The following descriptions focus on the important characteristics like growth rate, height, breadth, texture, shape, and longevity, plus special characteristics like fall color, insects and diseases, and leaf drop in autumn – all flavored with a considerable dose of my opinion developed from a lifelong look at trees in the South.

The South is larger and more diverse than many countries. A Live Oak is a great tree in Mobile or Savannah but won't live through the cold winters in Asheville, and the fantastic Fraser Firs you see in the Smoky Mountains quickly expire when planted in the heat of New Orleans, Jacksonville, or Charleston.

You may not find the tree you're looking for at the nearest nursery or plant outlet, but don't give up. Try several places before you accept a substitute that may lack the qualities you want in a tree.

Nursery growers are doing a fantastic job introducing new cultivars of many well-known species, like Red Maple. Some of these have wonderful qualities that make a good choice even better. When a cultivar has been proven over many years, I make special mention of it. Consider others only after they have succeeded in your locale and shown themselves worthy. A new cultivar has a great chance of doing well since it is a form of a proven species.

I have yet to see a new miracle tree from some place like Outer Mongolia prove to be better than a tried and true tree like Ginkgo biloba, which arrived from China hundreds of years ago, or our native Red Oak, which has been around longer than history itself. Ginkgo and Red Oak cultivars may fine-tune a choice and provide something very special, while a

White Oak is a strong long-lived tree.

new miracle tree may end up with insects eating its leaves in mid-summer.

To hold this book to a practical length, I have not listed every worthwhile tree that will grow in the South. But I daresay I have listed more than you can find in your favorite nursery. Not even the best nurseries can stock so many, but many specialty mail order nurseries' lists are broader. Unfortunately, the small trees generally available in catalogs may take many years to grow into a specimen plant, but the wait may be worth it to you.

The listings cover the most important trees for the Southern landscape, including trees you may find already growing on your property. Hickory and Black Gum (Tupelo) are two native trees found in urban wooded areas all over the South, yet are seldom found planted in the landscape, and you won't find them in many nurseries. They should be left standing if at all possible since they can enhance a landscape as well as many nursery-grown trees.

The tree you choose should outlive you, me, our children, and many generations to come, so choose wisely.

Special Notes

- I give the low range of height, not that of a hundred- or two-hundred-year-old National Champion. The tree should reach this height in 30 to 40 years or less.

- The habit is that of a mature tree unless otherwise noted. Younger trees will not necessarily conform to the mature habit until they become established and gain some age.

- The growth rate listed is under good conditions, not all conditions. I have seen medium or slow-growing trees develop much faster when fertilized and watered on a regular basis. Trees planted in a lawn usually grow faster because their roots benefit from lawn irrigation and fertilizer.

- Fall color may vary from year to year and location to location and is usually more intense in the higher elevations where fall nights are cooler.

- Cultivars abound for many species listed. In general it is good to buy a cultivar, but only when you are convinced that it is well adapted to Southern conditions. I only list cultivars that have a long record of doing well in the South. There may be better ones on the way – at least I hope so.

- Most Americans move frequently. Please choose trees that will also bring joy and happiness to those who follow.

Green Ash in the fall

Ash

Fraxinus, sp.

There is a large White Ash growing in our pasture, and I pass a huge Green Ash almost every day. Neither have the problems that often seem to plague these trees growing in groups in landscapes, subdivisions, and along streets, and I have always considered both to be suitable when you need shade fast.

A cousin of mine in the Midwest wrote about severe problems in her subdivision with the Green Ash lining the streets. Insect attacks reduced their vigor and made them unsightly. I have heard of others starting a gradual decline after many years of good growth.

I would not dismiss the idea of growing either listed below. However, I suggest using only one or two trees of a suitable cultivar, rather than using them in large groups or to line streets.

Cultivars of Green Ash and White Ash make wonderful, fast-growing, wispy trees in limited space and offer great shade over patios, decks, and other outdoor living areas. Native seedling-grown White Ash and Green Ash are planted in more open areas where they can develop into large handsome specimen trees with excellent fall color.

Marshall Seedless Ash

Green Ash
Fraxinus pennsylvanica

HEIGHT: 50 feet or more.
HABIT: Pyramidal to loosely open when young, spreading when old.
GROWTH RATE: Medium-fast to fast-growing.
BEST USE: In large open areas, but see cultivar information below.
LEAF COLOR: Medium green to rich green.
FALL COLOR: Yellow.
DRAWBACKS: May have serious borer and scale problems. Also Green Ash seeds freely, which may be a problem with seedlings sprouting where you don't want them.

Green Ash can be an impressive tree in a landscape. If you have one growing, nurture it, but if you decide to plant one, choose a seedless cultivar. Smaller-growing Green Ash cultivars are great for quick shade over patios, decks, and in small garden areas. There are better trees to plant for large specimens in the landscape unless you have a particularly severe sun problem requiring quick shade.

Cultivars

There are more Green Ash cultivars than you can shake a stick at. New ones constantly pop up, making evaluation difficult until they have been grown long enough to develop significant attributes, like better fall color and more defined growth habits. Unfortunately for us in the Deep South, northern nurserymen are more active in identifying new cultivars, which may not necessarily be bad, but always raises the question with a species known for problems specific to our area and not theirs.

Marshall Seedless Ash appeared on the scene many years ago and remains one of the better cultivars. Older plantings have survived quite well in Atlanta.

Leprechaun is listed as more dwarf and Urbanite is reputed to have a neat, broadly rounded head and dark green foliage.

White Ash
Fraxinus americana

HEIGHT: 60 feet or more.

HABIT: Spreading, with a number of large upward- and outward-growing limbs producing a wide tree.

GROWTH RATE: Fast in most of the South.

BEST USE: Large specimen tree.

LEAF COLOR: Rich green.

FALL COLOR: Yellow, but mine is not spectacular in most years.

DRAWBACKS: Subject to borers and scale and declines under stress; also seeds very freely.

White Ash is native to a more Southern range than Green Ash, which may be an advantage for us in the South. My native tree does well, though a native Red Maple close by outperforms it in almost every way. Still, I'm glad it's there because I like to add interest to my tree groupings with contrasting foliage and form.

The major reason to plant White Ash is that it grows faster than most other acceptable trees. Seeds are a problem in smaller landscapes. Mine is in a five-acre pasture where a bush hog makes quick work of the problem, even though my fence lines have a number of seedlings, which doesn't make me too happy.

White Ash

Cultivars

White Ash cultivars pop up every now and then, though not in the numbers of Green Ash introductions. However, most are from northern nurseries, which makes me a bit hesitant about recommending them for the Deep South until they are more widely grown.

Bay, Loblolly
Gordonia lasianthus

HEIGHT: Maximum 35 feet in cultivation, larger in the wild.
HABIT: Varied depending on circumstances from tightly upright and oval to loose upright. May have multiple trunks.
GROWTH RATE: Medium when nurtured.
BEST USE: In moist, well-drained locations with some shade.
LEAF COLOR: Evergreen. Darker above than underneath.

Loblolly Bay is native to the lower coastal plains where you often see it along with Virginia Magnolia, *Magnolia glauca.* growing in the swampy edges of highways. It is easy to distinguish from Virginia Magnolia, which has distinctive white undersides to its leaves.

Loblolly Bay is rarely seen in the landscape. What a pity, since it is a delightful evergreen tree with white flowers through much of the summer! It does well in the piedmont even though it is more common in the coastal plains.

The secret to Loblolly Bay doing well in the landscape is good drainage, without the soil being overly dry. Though they grow well in the swamps, they don't usually survive in heavy wet places in the landscape.

My friend, the late James Patterson of Patterson Nursery, in Putney, Georgia, became interested in Loblolly Bay, which grew in the wetlands around his nursery, and was the only nurseryman I knew who was growing it at the time. James gave us a tree that we planted on a cool bank at one of our nurseries in Atlanta, where it grew very well and gave rise to much favorable comment. We sold the company in 1976 and the tree continued to prosper until the new owner moved the nursery to another location. It was still a handsome tree the last time I saw it in the 1990s, but then the property was graded for a shopping center and the Loblolly Bay, along with many other fine specimen plants, was destroyed.

In my experience, Loblolly Bay is much easier to grow than its kin, Lost Gordonia, *Franklinia alatamaha*, made famous by William Bartram in the 1700s. Plant it in a cool, well-drained but not dry location with a low pH, then sit back and wait a few years for it to develop into a handsome evergreen tree with a smattering of blossoms during much of the summer.

Hortus Third lists its mature height as 90 feet. Maybe somewhere they grow that tall, but the largest trees I have seen in a landscape were only 25 to 30 feet and no more than 50 feet in the wild.

Use Loblolly Bay to add something more interesting in your landscape than the run-of-the-mill shade trees so often used.

American Beech

Beech

Fagus sp.

Few trees rival a Beech. They are tough, large-growing, and just plain beautiful when standing in a lawn or growing in a forest. Many fine specimens of our native American Beech, *Fagus grandiflora*, grow throughout the South and the European Beech, *Fagus sylvatica*, grows in the upper South. You can always identify a Beech in a forest during the winter by its attractive tan leaves that hang on until spring.

For some reason, nurserymen pay much more attention to the European Beech than the American Beech when selecting cultivars. I have not seen or heard about any cultivars of American Beech, while there are numerous European Beech cultivars including weeping and purple-leaf forms.

Plant Beech trees as much for the future as the present because they grow slowly. If you plan to stay in your home for only a few years, choose another tree to plant, but if you have settled down for the long haul, a Beech is an excellent choice.

American Beech
Fagus grandiflora

HEIGHT: 60-plus feet.

HABIT: Breadth about the same as height when unrestricted by surrounding trees.

GROWTH RATE: Slow.

BARK: Distinctive silver gray and smooth.

BEST USE: Specimen tree in the open or on the edge of wooded areas.

LEAF COLOR: Rich green in the summer.

FALL COLOR: Golden to bronze. Leaves stay on the tree during most of the winter.

Fruit of American Beech

American Beech is found in older urban areas where homes were designed to fit the topography and to nestle among specimen trees rather than sites graded to fit the desired structure. There is a sense of security and longevity in a neighborhood with a magnificent specimen beech growing so close to the street that you have to park your car carefully for fear of nicking something so beautiful and so old. Any tree that has survived so long and remained so magnificent deserves more than a quick glance, even when hosts are waiting for you. Contrast that with a huge Water Oak in the same type of situation, which barely raises more than a grumpy growl for being in the way.

To reiterate, American Beech is not for quick shade, but when you plan to stay in your home for many years, it is as magnificent as any tree. If your lot has one growing on it, do everything possible to save an American Beech, even if it is small. Lovingly nurture mature trees, knowing you are the owner of one of the finest trees in America.

American Beech

European Beech
Fagus sylvatica

HEIGHT: 50-plus feet.

HABIT: Pyramidal to broad-oval, often with low branches which may even touch the ground. Cultivars include many upright variations as well as weeping forms.

GROWTH RATE: Medium under best conditions, perhaps a bit slower in the piedmont South.

BEST USE: Specimen tree in open areas.

LEAF COLOR: Dark green above, lighter underneath. Cultivars include purple, copper, and variegated leaves.

FALL COLOR: Golden.

RANGE: The European Beech is happiest in cooler climates above Washington, D.C. and in the southern highlands, where I have seen handsome examples. That said, consider using the European Beech, not its cultivars, in the upper piedmont and farther north.

Cultivars

In his textbook, Michael Dirr describes over 40 cultivars while *Hortus Third* lists over 20. Most are not particularly suited to our climate and warrant careful investigation before you attempt to find one or plant one if you find it. I have included two older ones, which I have seen growing in parks and home landscapes, but these are just a taste of what might be possible to grow in the higher elevations and in northern Virginia, West Virginia, and Kentucky.

Copper Beech
Fagus sylvatica 'Atropunicea'

This is the common Purple Beech (sometimes called Copper Beech) seen all over England, Ireland, and much of Europe. Specimens can be found in many botanical gardens of the northern United States.

Purple Beech is magnificent when growing well. The leaves are dark purple-red when they first come out in the spring, gradually turning lighter with less color intensity as the summer wears on.

Its habit is similar to European Beech, though seldom growing as large in the South.

Use Copper Beech in the higher elevations.

Weeping Beech
Fagus sylvatica 'Pendula'

Weeping Beech is an extraordinary tree and a sight to behold. There is a gorgeous example at Biltmore Estates near Asheville, N.C. Ever since I visited Ireland and viewed a monster tree at Kilfane House, as well as a magnificent Copper Beech, I have dreamed of living where they grow, except where it snows too much for my Southern blood.

I was so struck with seeing one doing so well at Biltmore Estates that I took dozens of pictures of it. Later, Chris and his wife did the same thing. All of you in the upper South should try to grow this fabulous tree.

Old specimens will grow 35 feet or more and as wide if not wider than tall. The branches weep down to the ground, making a cascade of green from top to bottom. Its appearance is coarse and not as delicate as our common Weeping Cherry, but more interesting during the summer with its stronger foliage.

Weeping Beech

The beautiful Paperbark Birch does poorly in our heat.

Birch

Betula sp.

There is something mystical and a bit romantic about the white trunks of birch trees emerging from snow-covered New England forests or American Indians paddling their birch bark canoes on tranquil lakes and rivers. Poets and novelists often describe such scenes as a nostalgic slice of Americana.

Unfortunately, white birches are susceptible to the birch borer, which decimates these beautiful trees here in the South. Nurserymen once thought that the European White Birch was more resistant, and many were planted farther south than was thought possible. I planted one at my pond many years ago and it has never had a problem; its isolation seems to have saved it from birch borer attacks. More recently, I have seen a few young trees being planted near where we live, so I am watching to see how well they do, even though in my heart I doubt they will survive for long.

The answer in the South is to plant our native River Birch, which is resistant to the birch borer. It has the same peeling bark as the White Birches of the North without the risks. The bark is a pleasant tan, which in its own way is striking, though hardly in a class with the white-bark species. Since most River Birch plants are grown from seeds, there is a tremendous variation in the color of the bark, summer green leaves, and fall leaf color. New cultivars are being propagated that have uniformly richer green leaves in the summer and fine yellow fall color. 'Heritage' seems to be the preferred one, though I have not grown it.

River Birch
Betula nigra

HEIGHT: 40 feet or more.

HABIT: Pyramid shape when young but more oval as it matures, especially when multistemmed.

BARK: Exfoliating, salmon brown to lighter cream in new cultivars.

GROWTH RATE: Fast.

LEAF COLOR: Rich green.

FALL COLOR: Yellow and lasting in most years.

Our native River Birch is definitely the birch to plant in the South. It is a gracious tree in its own right with its wispy open appearance. It is most often used as a multi-trunk clump tree, enhancing its cool and fresh feeling.

I have seen beautiful old specimens along the Chattahoochee River that have survived heavy foot traffic quite well. River Birch is being used more and more in home and office landscapes because it is tough. Leaf spots and aphids may attack plantings in landscapes as well as in the wild, but I have never seen them become serious enough to worry about or to restrict the use of this attractive tree.

River Birch's bark exfoliates heavily, giving a papery appearance to the salmon-tan trunk. This outstanding characteristic is similar to the Paperbark Birch of the North, even though not as well-known or written about, nor as striking as if it were white. More importantly, River Birch survives in our climate while few White Birches live for long.

The ideal plant in the landscape is one with three or four equal or nearly equal trunks, giving an entirely different effect in the landscape than a single trunk tree. However, I must warn you that many of the clump River Birch you find in nurseries were not cut back and allowed to develop several strong shoots, like you see beside rivers and streams. What is most often sold in nurseries are three small plants grown together. Most of the time this is not a problem, but occasionally I have seen one or two of these seedlings die due to competition from stronger growing companions, leaving

Cultivars

Dura-Heat: A recent introduction whose whiter bark begins exfoliating at a younger age than the species. I have seen several new plantings of Dura-Heat which, so far, are surviving impossible conditions in shopping villages.

Heritage: A patented cultivar with excellent uniformity, good foliage cover, and attractive salmon-tan exfoliation.

River Birch does well in the South.

River Birch with its fall color

The peeling bark of River Birch is attractive.

a single- or dual-trunk tree that may not develop as attractively as you want.

There are a number of new cultivars of River Birch, which have been developed for better uniformity, bark color, and degree of exfoliation, but which retain the good growth and pest resistance of the species.

Other Birch Species:

The following birch species are best left out of the home landscape due to debilitating insect and disease problems. Occasionally you will find them in retail nurseries or on landscape plans, but be aware of potential problems before you plant one.

European White Birch
Betula pendula

European White Birch was once thought to be resistant to birch borers and birch leaf miner, and a good alternative to Paperbark Birch. The one I planted at our lake many years ago has survived without difficulty. Its bark is not nearly as white as the ones I've seen in New York State and New England and not in the class of Paperbark Birch.

Despite my own good luck, I hesitate recommending this tree, especially where other birch are growing or for an important place in the landscape.

Paperbark Birch
Betula papyrifera

Suffering hideously cold New England winters is made almost acceptable by the sight of Paperbark Birch groves arising from the snow. Otherwise, look at pictures of wintry New England scenes rather than trying to duplicate them in the South.

Our summer's heat, birch borers, birch leaf miners, and Paperbark Birch's antipathy toward our environment are too much for this fabulous tree.

Sweet Birch
Betula lenta

If you are a birch lover and want to expand your collection, plant Sweet Birch. Otherwise, I see no reason to plant this native, which is best viewed by the roadsides of the upper South. It has all the problems of other birches without any compelling landscape value, which is enough said.

Black Gum is an excellent native tree for the South.

Black Gum, Black Tupelo
Nyssa sylvatica

HEIGHT: 50 feet high and 30 feet wide.
HABIT: Pyramidal when young; spreading when old.
GROWTH RATE: Medium under good conditions.
BEST USE: In open areas or next to woods.
LEAF COLOR: Rich green.
FALL COLOR: From yellow to maroon and red.
Some leaves may be multicolored.
It is always striking when the leaves turn in the fall.

Two gum trees are common in the South: this one, *Nyssa sylvatica,* and Sweet Gum, *Liquidamber styraciflua,* which is described later. Most of the other gums you hear about are in the genus *Eucalyptus,* and Silver-dollar Tree, *Eucalyptus cinerea,* can only be grown in the lower South.

I grew up with a Black Gum and a Sweet Gum in the back of our house and have to admit that the Sweet Gum was my favorite because its branches are much better for a 10- or 12-year-old to climb. Since few of us are nimble enough to climb a tree when we are at an age to be landscaping and gardening, these prejudices are no longer worthy of consideration when choosing a tree, unless you have a young one who has the noble desire to be closer to the clouds.

Black Gum is one of our best native trees, despite its lack of easy climbing limbs. It is clean-growing with rich, dark green leaves and spectacular maroon or red fall color. I have seen some fall leaves that also have yellow mixed in, especially around the edges.

Black Gum may grow to 50 feet or more, though the one of my youth never reached 35 feet. When young, it is mostly pyramid-shaped but it spreads and becomes more oval after many years.

Black Gum isn't one of those trees to plant for quick

Black Gum turns a deep red in the Fall.

shade to block the sun since it grows rather slowly. A push with fertilizer applications or planting in a frequently fertilized lawn will increase its growth rate, but if fast shade is demanded, choose another tree, like Red Maple.

Cultivars

Black Gum has not developed enough of a reputation in the landscape for American nurserymen to search for outstanding cultivars. More are being found and grown commercially in England, where it seems to be more respected as a garden tree. There are a few cultivars being listed in grower catalogs, including some possibly interesting weeping forms introduced by English nurseries.

Bradford Pear in the spring

Bradford Pear
Pyrus calleryana 'Bradford'

HEIGHT: 30–50 feet.
HABIT: Pyramidal when very young but quickly becoming oval.
GROWTH RATE: Fast.
BEST USE: Unimpeded specimens in the open.
LEAF COLOR: Dark green.
FALL COLOR: Maroon.

Bradford Pear burst on the scene during my early nursery days as the greatest of all flowering trees. It supposedly had everything: heavy flowering in the spring, deep green foliage in the summer, and gorgeous deep red fall color. I planted one at our house as a result of the hype. About the time mine was growing well, complaints poured in over its tendency to break apart during rain, heavy winds, and ice. I carefully pruned away the limbs developing the bad crotches that induce the weakness and breakage. When my tree was growing like crazy and was indeed everything it was cracked up to be, we moved overseas for several years. By the time we returned, new tight branches had developed, and one day during a moderate rain with not-so-high winds half of the tree came crashing down over the power line. I traveled overseas again, and when I returned, the other half had come down during an ice storm. I am amazed that Bradford Pears are still being planted everywhere despite such scenes of disaster, which follow every high wind or ice storm.

Soon after I planted my Bradford Pear near the house, I planted two more on the edge of our pasture. One of these has survived and done quite well over the years, while the other one broke apart. In addition, we have dozens of seedlings planted by birds and deer all over the place. Unfortunately they don't flower as heavily or develop deep leathery green foliage, which is why you plant Bradford Pear.

Many such seedlings are being evaluated to find a new cultivar without Bradford Pear's problems. 'Aristocrat' was supposed to be the answer, but it seems to be more susceptible to fireblight and doesn't bloom as well. So Bradford Pear apologists keep looking. Since there are many other very fine flowering trees, why bother?

Somebody in my neck of the woods came up with the theory that heavy top pruning reduces the leaf weight and prevents or reduces breakage. However, these pruned trees bear no resemblance to anything you would want in your landscape. I have also noticed that severe pruning forces excessive numbers of succulent shoots, which are prime targets for fireblight. Besides, who wants strange-looking, half-dead trees?

Perhaps the combination of constant breakage and fireblight will curtail the trend of planting Bradford Pears in every nook and cranny of the South. Let's hope so.

Bradford Pear is covered with white flowers in the spring.

Bradford Pear is weak and can crash down, breaking walls.

Bradford Pear leaves turn a maroon-red in the fall.

A Bradford Pear demolished in rain and wind

Southern Catalpa is attractive when in flower.

Catalpa
Catalpa sp.

There are two catalpas grown in the South – our native Common Catalpa, *Catalpa bignonioides*, and Western Catalpa, *Catalpa speciosa*. Common Catalpa is all over the place and quite noticeable when in bloom in the spring. The large panicles of off-white flowers covering a tree are a pleasant sight, but that's about it for Catalpa. It is coarse in appearance and quite unattractive, especially while the long brown seed pods are hanging on forever.

Catalpa trees are well-known in the South because of the worms that feed upon the foliage during the summer and are harvested for fabulous fishing bait. Most of us old-timers grew up using "Catawba" worms at our fishing holes.

One of Chris's early horticultural ventures was to grow Catalpa trees from seed and sell them to fishermen to plant for a personal supply of worms. I never ask either of my sons for the financial results of their many ventures, so I can only say that the trees disappeared and he didn't buy a new car. I did notice several new Catalpas around our place, one of which has done quite well and supplies all the worms we need during "Catawba" worm season. The flip side is that the worms defoliate the tree, making it ugly as sin until new leaves sprout. Fortunately, Chris's landscaping instincts placed the tree behind a big magnolia, so we don't notice the bare branches during the middle of the summer.

Both Catalpa species grow rapidly and are weak-wooded. Be wary when one is near a house or other structure, since limbs can break and come crashing down during storms.

Neither our Southern native nor its Western counterpart hold anything important for a landscape. If you have one that neither threatens any structures nor detracts from your fine plants, keep it until something happens to it; otherwise forget it and find your fishing worms on Catalpa trees growing by the roadside.

Southern Catalpa
Catalpa bignonioides

HEIGHT: 40-plus feet.
HABIT: Broad oval, but not always defined well.
GROWTH RATE: Fast.
BEST USE: Out of sight as a source of fishing worms.
LEAVES: Large and coarse. Dark green above and lighter underneath.
FLOWERS: Late spring; huge panicles of white flowers with yellow and purple spots.
FRUIT: Long unattractive beans, dropping seeds that can be a nuisance.
FALL COLOR: Sort of yellow, but really more light brown.

Cultivars

Several cultivars are listed, including a yellow-leaved form and dwarf forms. Both add insult to injury, in my opinion.

Western Catalpa, Northern Catalpa
Catalpa speciosa

HEIGHT: 50-plus feet.
HABIT: More oval than Southern Catalpa.
GROWTH RATE: Fast.
BEST USE: See Southern Catalpa.
LEAVES: Large and coarse.
FLOWERS: Large panicles of creamy white flowers without the frequent spots found in Southern Catalpa.
FRUIT: Unattractive long brown beans that spread seeds freely.
FALL COLOR: Yellowish to brown. Not attractive or significant.

Western Catalpa is very similar in appearance to our Southern Catalpa. Its size may be a bit larger in its native range, but I don't notice the difference in the mid-South. Blossoms are also a bit later.

For practical purposes, plant either one. However, my comments about Southern Catalpa hold just as true for Western Catalpa. Neither is a tree to plant in a landscape. The only question is whether to keep either one if it is already growing well. Personally, I would watch it for a few years and remove it when excessive problems arise. The only exception is when it is growing close to a structure that might be damaged by breaking limbs.

Western Catalpa

An old Indian Cedar

Cedar
Various Genera

Cedar is the common name for a number of conifers used in the landscape that do not necessarily belong to the same genus. The genus *Cedrus* includes several handsome species grown in the South, though none are native. The Japanese Cedar is *Cryptomeria japonica*, while our native Red Cedar is *Juniperus virginiana*.

True cedars are beautiful specimen evergreen trees planted more in the past than now. The biblical Cedar of Lebanon grows well here in the South and is seen occasionally in older landscape plantings and parks. Japanese Cedars are often used as tall screening plants since their branches reach the ground when they are young. Older Japanese Cedars become tree-form, making handsome specimen trees. Our native Red Cedars grow wild and are found everywhere. Cedar chests and other fine furniture are made from its wood.

Large Red Cedars can be very attractive and should be left standing, though there are many better trees to plant. One severe drawback is a two-host disease, Cedar Apple Rust, which spreads from Red Cedars to nearby apples and crabapples, then back to the Cedars. The stage on apples and crabapples causes yellow spots and possibly severe defoliation, while the Red Cedar stage is a hideous-looking orange gall.

True Cedar
Cedrus sp.

True cedars come to us from such diverse places as Asia Minor and the Himalayas, yet all do well in the South. Indian Cedar has been here so long and used in so many landscapes, most people assume it is a native, but it comes from northern India, where it is an important timber source. Lebanon Cedar is from Asia Minor, while Atlas Cedar is from North Africa. All three have adapted well to the South. These great trees are good examples of how landscape fads come and go. They were widely planted in the 1920s and 1930s, which accounts for many older specimens around houses dating back 75 or so years. New plantings are common now, indicating a return of their popularity.

Cedar of Lebanon
Cedrus libani

HEIGHT: 60 feet in most landscapes, though century trees may reach over 100 feet.
HABIT: Pyramid when young. May be upright or flattened when old.
GROWTH RATE: Slow.
BEST USE: Specimen tree.
LEAF COLOR: Usually light green, but may be darker with age.
CONES: Showy, shaped somewhat like a barrel. May be as long as five inches.

I have mentioned Lebanon Cedar in previous chapters because of its historical and biblical significance. The largest I have seen was at the Royal Botanical Gardens adjacent to Kew, England. They were magnificent!

Two stately specimens, given as a memorial to a parishioner, framed the entrance to St. George's Episcopal Church in Griffin, Georgia. They were still pyramidal at the time, but must have spread too much over the years, and the last time I drove by they were gone.

Lebanon Cedar lacks the fluffy appearance of the more commonly grown Indian Cedar, but still has a place in a large open area. It is a great tree to grow when creating a landscape with character and interest to distinguish your home from those nearby.

Lebanon Cedar survives under a wide range of conditions. A 3,000-year-old tree in Lebanon proves my point.

For those of you in the higher, colder parts of the South, plant the hardier *Cedrus libani var. stenocoma*, which withstands temperatures to minus 10 to 15 degrees.

Gray Atlas Cedar
Cedrus atlantica 'Glauca'

HEIGHT: 60 feet but much larger with age.
HABIT: Upright pyramid shape until older, when it spreads into a wide and beautiful tree.
GROWTH RATE: Fast for a few years, then slow.
BEST USE: Specimen tree in the open.
LEAVES: One inch long at most. Blue to blue-gray.

An ancient Atlas Cedar

I drove through the Atlas Mountains in Morocco when I was preparing a study for an agricultural project many years ago. My Moroccan associate stopped at a roadside vista to show me some rock formations that weren't nearly as interesting as the view of the tree-covered mountains. Later at a ski resort I saw huge evergreen trees that made me think of the spruce you would see in a Colorado village. My associate said they were Atlas Cedars, which grow wild in the northern Atlas Mountains. This Moroccan and Algerian native has found its way into American landscapes, where it is considered one of our finest evergreen trees.

Gray Atlas Cedar is planted more often than the greener form, though both are excellent trees. Unfortunately, it has little form or character when young, being spindly and sparse. It fills out with age, and by the time it is 25 years old, it develops a beautiful spreading habit. Atlas Cedar is not for a homeowner who requires instant maturity, but if you have patience, it is worth the wait.

TREES FOR SOUTHERN LANDSCAPES

Its North African heritage limits its use to places in the South where temperatures seldom, if ever, reach –10 degrees.

Several cultivars with more uniform and better color and a weeping form are listed, but are hard to find in nurseries.

Indian Cedar
Cedrus deodara

HEIGHT: 50-plus feet.
HABIT: Pyramidal when young, broad-spreading when old.
GROWTH RATE: Medium when young, slow with age.
BEST USE: Specimen lawn tree.
LEAVES: Individual needles an inch or longer in groups of many needles.
LEAF COLOR: Dark green to silver.
FRUIT: Attractive cones up to five inches long and three inches across, standing above foliage like candles.

Indian Cedar cones are interesting and attractive.

Indian Cedar has been grown in the South since before the Civil War, and large plants in old landscapes and parks are common. My father planted several at our home near Lovejoy, Georgia, where I grew up. A handsome specimen standing by the long driveway supplied attractive cones for our Christmas decorations. Unfortunately, it was severely damaged in a zero-degree

freeze on Thanksgiving weekend in 1950, when many large specimens of a wide range of plants in our nursery were damaged or killed. For some reason, however, many Indian Cedar planted about the same time in Atlanta were not damaged significantly and have now reached the wide-spreading stage for which the species is famous.

Indian Cedar is less stark in its youth and early middle age than Atlas Cedar and Lebanon Cedar, making it the best choice for quickly maturing landscapes.

Those of you in the mountains and upper South, use Indian Cedar with caution.

Younger Indian Cedars have a tight pyramid form.

Other Cedars

Japanese Cedar
Cryptomeria japonica

HEIGHT: 50 feet.

HABIT: Tapered to the ground until middle-aged. Develops a crown above bare trunks when very old.

GROWTH RATE: Medium.

BEST USE: In groups as a screen, in avenues, or as specimen lawn trees.

LEAF COLOR: Rich green. May have a bronze cast in cold windy spots.

Above: *A tree-form Japanese Cedar is a beautiful evergreen tree.* Below: *A large old Japanese Cedar*

Japanese Cedar can be used as an attractive screening plant.

Japanese Cedar is often referred to merely as Cryptomeria, its genus name. It is becoming more and more popular as a screening plant in place of the faster-growing and overused Leyland Cypress. To me, it is a much more refined plant with better foliage color and a less stark appearance. In the eyes of some, Japanese Cedar's slower growth rate makes it less desirable, but my view is the opposite. Somewhat slower growth is better when the resulting plant is more graceful and has better character. Look at a screen of huge Leyland Cypress standing like rigid soldiers in close formation, especially after losing individual identity while growing into a solid wall, then look at a planting of Cryptomeria with its grace and charm. Cryptomeria is more tapered and lacks the pillar appearance of Leyland Cypress, a distinct advantage in my opinion.

Cryptomeria branchlets and foliage are looser and show better than Leyland Cypress and other upright arborvitaes, keeping a plant or group of plants from appearing heavily sheared.

Plant Cryptomeria with caution in the upper limits of Zone 7.

Cultivars

There are a number of cultivars listed, some of which are a definite improvement over the species. 'Ben Franklin', 'Taisho Tama', and 'Yoshino' are grown by Southern nurserymen and may be available at your local nursery. Of the three, 'Ben Franklin' and 'Taisho Tama' have richer green foliage.

Red Cedar
Juniperus virginiana

HEIGHT: 40-plus feet.
HABIT: Young seedling-grown trees and those in the wild vary tremendously from columnar to oval. Old trees may be broad-spreading to tightly oval.
GROWTH RATE: Slow to medium.
BEST USE: Specimens and screening.
LEAF COLOR: Variable from rich green to silver-gray.

Red Cedar is as much a part of the South as *Magnolia grandiflora*, but without beauty and grace. Frankly, to me it indicates bad land and abandoned farms rather than well-landscaped and cared-for homes. Yet I have a huge old Red Cedar growing beside my house that I like very much, and we cut small ones on our property for Christmas trees when our boys were young. They make a pretty sight when driving through North Carolina and Virginia, where their rich green foliage relieves a monotonous drive on an interstate highway. It is also the cedar of cedar chests since its wood is long-lasting and its scent repels moths.

I'm not sure I would ever plant one, though some selection is being done to find trees with better forms and color for commercial propagation and sale, so my feelings are subject to change.

If you have a specimen growing, keep and nurture it. If not – that's up to you.

A well-grown Red Cedar is a beautiful evergreen tree.

Cultivars

There are too many new cultivars listed to describe them here, and I don't know how many are readily available in your local nursery. I have seen some silver ones being planted near me, so you may find some where you shop for plants.

Yoshino Cherry in the spring

Cherry
Prunus sp.

Cherries cover a wide range of species in the genus *Prunus*, even when we don't consider those grown for their fruits or such well-known shrubs as 'Otto Luyken' and 'Schipkaensis' Laurel, which are often called Cherry Laurel. However, most Southerners reserve the name Cherry Laurel for our native Carolina Cherry Laurel, *Prunus caroliniana*. The flowering cherries are spectacular in the landscape, but we shouldn't overlook the native Cherry Laurel, which can be trained into a beautiful small evergreen tree. The large-growing Black Cherry, called Wild Cherry by most Southerners, is an interesting native shade tree used for fine furniture as well as a haven for mockingbirds, who delight in its fruits.

The flowering cherries are among the most beautiful spring-flowering trees in the landscape. The cherry planting around the Tidal Basin of our nation's capital is worth a special trip during cherry blossom season. The majority of the planting is Yoshino Cherry, and the rest are Kwanzan Cherry.

In my early days as a nurseryman, I considered Flowering Dogwood, *Cornus florida*, to be the best home landscape flowering tree. Over the years I have reneged a bit after seeing beautiful plantings of Yoshino Cherry in such places as Mountain Brook, a suburb of Birmingham, Alabama. More and more of these beautiful cherry trees are being used throughout the South.

I am particularly impressed with 'Okame', which has red to rose-red flowers, opening earlier than Yoshino and Kwanzan. While taking pictures of dormant trees for this book, I came upon a planting of 'Okame' Cherry that made me stop and use a full roll of film. This planting of 10 or 12 trees on a graded bank was a spectacular sight.

Fruiting cherries can be used as fruit bearing and flowering trees in the landscape, but only when sprayed regularly. Sweet Cherry, *Prunus avium*, does well only in apple country, but Sour Cherry, *Prunus cerasus*, has a much wider range. I have grown a dwarf Sour Cherry cultivar, North Star, which did quite well for a time but eventually passed on during our years overseas. A neighbor has one that is quite beautiful in flower and fruit. Sour Cherry may become overly bushy and should be carefully pruned to make it a landscape tree.

Cherries as Shade Trees

Black Cherry, Wild Cherry
Prunus serotina

HEIGHT: Most are up to 50 feet, though occasionally a large specimen may reach 100 feet.
HABIT: Various from widely spread to upright oval.
GROWTH RATE: Medium to fast when young, medium to slow when older.
BEST USE: Specimen tree.
FLOWER: Long racemes of white flowers in the early spring, which are noticeable but not worth talking about.
FRUIT: Small red cherries turn black when ripe.
LEAF COLOR: Lustrous green above, lighter green underneath.
FALL COLOR: Yellow to wine-red in the fall.

Black Cherry Fruit

Young Black Cherry

Black Cherries are as common in Southern forests and old homeplaces as the mockingbirds that love to sit on their branches and sing to the world. I have one large tree that has survived all sorts of calamities, including a small tornado many years ago. As a result of its enormous reproductive capacity and the ever-present mockingbirds, my tree has sired Black Cherry trees everywhere, which Betsy takes great delight in yanking out of the ground. One of the fun sights of nature is to watch mockingbirds eat the fermented fruit on the ground and get quite tipsy. They flop around and can hardly fly at all, much less in a straight line. Surely there is a powerful lesson here about the dangers of driving while under the influence.

The best advice I can give about Black Cherry is to keep it if you have one but don't plant one. They are messy and subject to a number of pests, even though old ones are often seen doing quite well in forests. The biggest problems with mine are the certainty of leaf diseases, causing early leaf drop in the fall, and its incomparable ability to sire so many young'uns.

In the old days, cherry wood was prized for making furniture. Timber trees were harvested from the many native stands in the wild, since few are ever planted and certainly never for the purpose of making beautiful

Mature Black Cherry

cabinets. The flower is noticeable in the spring but is not in a class with other cherries like Yoshino or Kwanzan. The small fruits start bright red but ripen dark blue and are a mess to clean up when they fall on a walk or drive.

Wild Cherry is another one of our native trees that you keep when you have a good specimen but don't plant for a shade tree in the landscape.

Carolina Cherry Laurel
Prunus caroliniana

HEIGHT: 25–30 feet maximum, 15–25 feet most often.
HABIT: Usually as broad as tall and compact.
GROWTH RATE: Fast when young, slow when the top is maturing.
BEST USE: Excellent small evergreen tree for restricted places.
LEAF COLOR: Glossy evergreen.
FRUIT: Small green cherry, which turns black and hangs on until spring.

Most native Cherry Laurels are planted as shrubs or for tall dense evergreen screens, but when you see one that has escaped the butcher, you will question why it isn't planted and trained more often as a small tree under utility wires and in other restricted places.

Two beautiful specimens grew for many years in the churchyard of St. George's Episcopal Church in Griffin, Georgia. They were better than any playroom for the Sunday school kids who swarmed into their branches as soon as classes were dismissed. Unfortunately time and need for more room did them in, along with the two magnificent Lebanon Cedars that framed the front of the church.

You may not find a tree-form Cherry Laurel in a nursery, but with very little effort you can make one yourself. Choose a large specimen with a single trunk, then remove the lower limbs and plant it like you would a regular tree. As it grows, continue to remove the lower sprouts and limbs until the head develops about 10 feet above the ground. Keep new sprouts pulled or pruned off below the limbs, and in a few years you will have a beautiful evergreen tree which may ultimately reach 25 feet.

The spring flower is more like the Wild Cherry than the fabulous Japanese Flowering Cherries, but I think its evergreen nature more than makes up for the lack of spectacular flowers. Once you have an established Cherry Laurel, you are rewarded with seedlings planted by birds all over the place. I urge you not to complain, but accept these gifts of Nature with thanks. If they are in a bad place, lift them with a trowel or spade and plant them where you need an evergreen shrub or screen.

Carolina Cherry Laurel, Oakland Cemetery, Atlanta, Georgia

Cultivars

BRIGHT 'N TIGHT: a more compact form of Cherry Laurel and a wise choice for a hedge or screen planting, but not for training into a tree. I prefer using inexpensive loose-form seedlings for this purpose.

Asian Flowering Cherries

The list of flowering cherries is long and covers a number of different species. Unfortunately many have insect and disease problems that restrict their use in the South, while others do poorly in the heat of zones 7 and 8. The species and cultivars listed below do well and include some of our finest spring-flowering trees.

Kwanzan Cherry in full bloom

Kwanzan Cherry
Prunus serrulata 'Kwanzan'

Kwanzan Cherry is the most widely grown double-flowering cherry. Flowers start opening after leaves begin expanding, which normally would reduce their effect. In this case, however, the large, heavily double, deep pink flowers obliterate any signs of the leaves until after blossoming. The leaves are bronze when first

emerging but turn a dark green during the summer and bronze to bright yellow in the fall.

Trees are normally about 30 to 40 feet tall and almost as broad with heavy branches arising near the ground. Give it plenty of space in the open for best growth and flowers.

Kwanzan is susceptible to borers and other cherry problems, but I have two 40-year-old specimens growing well despite very little care. They consistently bloom in early April at Sweet Apple.

Mt. Fuji Cherry, Shirotae Cherry
Prunus serrulata 'Shirotae'

Mt. Fuji may have flowers that lack the size and fullness of Kwanzan, but it is nonetheless a tree to consider. Its pink buds open into pure white, fragrant blossoms before the Kwanzan blossoms. It grows to about 25 feet and is almost as broad as tall with graceful, drooping outer limbs.

All cherries may have borer and blight problems, but no more so than any number of other flowering trees, especially flowering peaches. Mt. Fuji is a larger and better tree than Double White Flowering Peach, which is more widely planted in the South.

Okame Flowering Cherry
Prunus x 'Okame'

Okame Flowering Cherry is not new since it was introduced in England soon after World War II, but it has been absent from Southern gardens until recently.

Kwanzan Cherry flowers

Okame Flowering Cherry

What a pity since it is one of the superior flowering trees for the South. Being a devotee of flowering cherries, I feel bereft at wasting so many years without this lovely tree in my landscape.

Okame is an early bloomer, usually opening as the weather begins to moderate and spring is a sure thing. Its carmine-red flowers are cup-shaped and borne in clusters of two or more in such great numbers that limbs are concealed.

For those of us in a hurry, Okame grows rapidly and sets blossoms on young trees, much like Yoshino Cherry. It matures around 30 feet in height and 25 feet across with branches to the ground unless you remove them to see under.

Shirofugen Flowering Cherry
Prunus serrulata 'Shirofugen'

Shirofugen is another excellent double-flowering cherry like Kwanzan and Mt. Fuji (Shirotae). Its habit is spreading and more open with a flatter top than Kwanzan. Pink buds open to a fragrant white flower, which fades to a pink when mature.

There are not too many Shirofugen grown in the Deep South, but it should do well in the upper piedmont where summer heat is not so intense.

Taiwan Cherry
Prunus campanulata

Taiwan Cherry is one of the earliest flowering trees and also one of the best for the lower South. I have heard that Taiwan Cherry does well in Savannah, Georgia, though I have not discovered that on my own. It does very well and is widely grown in Atlanta where it always causes comment when it blooms about the time of Witch Hazel.

There is some doubt if Taiwan Cherry flower buds will survive the cold temperatures of the upper piedmont and mountains. This may be due more to its early nature than to a lack of hardiness, though the risk is the same either way. But be that as it may, Flowering Cherries are extraordinary plants, and finding one like Taiwan for the deep South is a gift for landscapes where other Flowering Cherries don't do well.

The deep rose to red flowers are borne in clusters of two to five in the early spring, or earlier during a warm winter. Bright red cherries up to one-half inch across are attractive against the green leaves.

Weeping Cherry, Weeping Higan Cherry
Prunus subhirtella var. pendula

In my early nursery days, Weeping Cherry was one of the most sought-after plants we listed. Most were grafted on top of a five- or six-foot standard to produce a more upright plant with high arching limbs draping to the ground. When grown well, they were extraordinary plants as their pink flowers opened in mid-spring.

No plants are problem-free, and with time the graft union at the top of the standard was often attacked by borers, decimating the Weeping Cherry part and leaving the seedling understock as the only reminder of a once-fantastic tree. A group of nursery growers began to make grafts near the base of the seedling or to grow

Young Weeping Cherry

Weeping Cherry in bloom

Weeping Cherry from cuttings to overcome the borer problem, or at least make it more manageable.

However, the upward arching tree was not what people wanted or expected, so its popularity declined and more standard types are sold these days. I still believe basal-grafted trees can be just as attractive when carefully pruned to a few heavy limbs that weep upward to about 30 feet and downward almost to the ground.

A neighbor of ours has a standard top-grafted tree that is extraordinary in bloom and a graceful addition to his landscape year-round. In over 30 years, I can't remember when the tree didn't brighten our springtime journeys to and fro, proving a Weeping Cherry on a standard can live many years, if you watch for jelly oozing out of the graft union and treat for borers.

Yoshino Cherry
Prunus x yedoensis

I have already mentioned my great admiration for this tree. Since my first experience with the street plantings in Mountain Brook, Alabama, I have grown in my belief that this is one of the finest and most dependable spring-flowering trees for the South.

Yoshino's fine credentials are also confirmed by the fantastic plantings around the Tidal Basin in Washington, D.C., which also proves its adaptability in the northern range of Yoshino Cherry. The extensive plantings in Macon, Georgia, are the incentive for that town's annual cherry blossom festival, proving how well it grows in the lower South.

Yoshino Cherry grows large and needs plenty of space to show off its rounded structure, which may

Yoshino Cherry blossoms

reach 40 feet high and 20 feet across. Individual specimens may be as broad as tall. Masses of pale pink blossoms cover its branches in mid-spring, generally before dogwood reaches its peak. I have seen Yoshino Cherry growing along with Floribunda Crabapple, making a fantastic display of spring color all at once.

Yoshino grows rapidly and starts blooming at an early age. There is a picture of Chris and me on the back cover of *Month by Month Gardening in the South* planting a young Yoshino Cherry in 1996 in the landscape of our home at Sweet Apple. It has grown well and produces large numbers of flowers each year, despite its trunk having been severely scraped by our neighborhood buck deer during rutting season. Since Betsy first introduced me to the beauty of Yoshino Cherry, and since she also took the picture of Chris and me, it has become Mom's tree and its magnificent flowers are a lasting tribute to her.

Other Yoshino Cherry variations, forms, and cultivars

The outstanding qualities of Yoshino Cherry have led to a number of selections in this country and England. Yoshino Cherry variations include a weeping form, different shades of pink, and a white.

Yoshino Cherry

Old Chinese Chestnut in fruit

Chestnut

Castanea sp.

The American Chestnut, *Castanea dentata*, was one of America's most beautiful trees in forests and landscapes before the chestnut blight destroyed almost all plants in landscapes and in the wild. This insidious blight arrived from Asia at the beginning of the 20th century and spread rapidly, killing American Chestnuts until the only remaining trees are sprouts from old trunks that live for awhile, then also succumb to the deadly disease. In my early horticultural days, the search for a remaining resistant American Chestnut, along with the search for the Lost Gordonia, *Franklinia alatamaha*, provided many interesting hours in the woods, even though neither has ever been found. The American Chestnut is gone, leaving an unfillable hole in our lists of the best trees.

Foreign chestnuts have been introduced from Europe and Asia, but none have the characteristics of our beautiful native. Hybridizing continues with the goal of developing a tree similar to the American Chestnut, but resistant to the disease. Maybe someday scientists will succeed.

American Chestnut
Castanea dentata

Sad as it is to say, do not consider planting this tree even if you find one. Until hybridizers develop blight-resistant crossbreeds, there is no way you can have a majestic American Chestnut that won't succumb to disease.

Chinese Chestnut
Castanea mollissima

HEIGHT: 40 feet or more.
HABIT: Low branching, usually as wide as tall.
GROWTH RATE: Medium to fast when young but slow after 10 years or so.
BEST USE: Tree for large open areas.
LEAF COLOR: Rich green.
FALL COLOR: Yellow, quickly turning brown.

Chinese Chestnuts have been a part of my horticultural life since the late 1930s when I was about 10 years old and accompanied my father on his rounds of nursery growers through the South. One of our early stops each year was a nursery in east Tennessee that produced the chestnuts we planted at our nursery near Lovejoy. I learned a lot from my father about the chestnut blight that was slowly exterminating the American Chestnut.

We grew a number of seedling Chinese Chestnuts at Lovejoy each year for our mail order nursery to help spread the development of commercial nut-growing groves – at least that was my father's idea.

Early instructions were to plant at least three trees since they were self-sterile. Maybe that is true in much the same way that different cultivars are needed to pollinate pecan flowers, but my experience is quite the opposite. One of the first trees my father planted near our home at Lovejoy outlived its companions, but kept producing huge crops of nuts. We had two nice trees when we moved to Sweet Apple, which produced enough chestnuts each year to keep Betsy pulling spines from my boys' feet until they were convinced to keep their shoes on. Chris finally cut one down when it had grown too large for its spot. I was disappointed to think that we would have no more chestnuts. But we now have more than ever, which in my mind was the final proof against the need for more than one tree for pollination.

The tree at Lovejoy was about 60 years old the last time I saw it and must have been 50 feet high and 50 feet across with huge branches arising from three feet above the ground. Our remaining tree at Sweet Apple is about 35 feet tall and much more upright as a result of being too close to adjacent magnolias.

Chinese Chestnut is a tree for a large area and shouldn't be thought of as a lawn tree where the prickly burrs are hard to sweep up and a pain to any children without shoes. Plant it away from the house where it can spread all it wants to, provide delicious nuts for home use, and attract a variety of furry creatures like deer and squirrels. It grows under a variety of soil conditions, making its establishment quite easy.

Chinese Chestnut used as a lawn tree

Sticky burrs of Chinese Chestnut

Cultivars and Hybrids

I remember nurserymen listing several "varieties" (the old nursery term for cultivars) but we only grew seedlings. Work continues on crossing American Chestnut with Chinese Chestnut in hopes of finding a blight-resistant hybrid that has the characteristics of our native species.

Umbrella Chinaberry Tree

Chinaberry
Melia azederach

There is little reason to grow chinaberry, which was introduced from Asia in the early days of our country. It has become so well-established and naturalized that it is a weed tree of the worst sort, growing rampant on the edges of fields and ditch banks.

However, many of us native Southerners remember the Umbrella Chinaberry listed below, which was widely grown in the rural South and, like old chimneys, is a sad reminder of long-gone farm homes.

Texas Umbrella Chinaberry
Melia azederach 'Umbraculiformis'

HEIGHT: Usually about 20 feet.

HABIT: It looks like an open umbrella, but one with several stems.

GROWTH RATE: Fast in youth, slow when maturing.

BEST USE: Interesting specimen tree.

LEAF COLOR: Dark green when fertilized.

FALL COLOR: Yellow but not outstanding.

HARDINESS: Zone 7 to Zone 9. May be damaged at zero degrees, certainly unsatisfactory where temperatures below zero degrees are common.

The sight of this tree at once confirms the accuracy of its common name. It looks like an umbrella as it stands in rural yards or sites of long-gone houses. The mature tree that I grew up with stood halfway between our home and the highway, half a mile away. When we were small children, my sister and I were allowed to go only as far toward the highway as the chinaberry tree, a wonderful outpost from which to spy on a passing world. We would climb up its multiple stems and perch among its branches while making up all sorts of games. When the white chinaberries were ripe, we were fussed at by all sorts of angry birds whose feasting was interrupted by us interlopers.

Recently, I ran across two beautiful specimens within a mile of the one of my youth. Their dense form was perfect as the trees stood on a green sweep of lawn. They were as beautiful as any I have ever seen. My nurseryman friend Glenn Dorsey was with me and we started poking under the umbrellas to see why the trees were so dense. The answer: the trees had been severely pruned many years before because of dieback after the severe freezes of the mid-1980s. I'm glad this reminded me that Umbrella Chinaberry trees are not reliably hardy enough to plant in the upper South.

I'm not sure if I would recommend planting an Umbrella Chinaberry tree unless you are either as nostalgic about it as I am or you love to attract birds. In either case, use it as a small specimen tree in the open so it can develop its unique structure as it should.

Japanese Flowering Crabapple, Malus floribunda

Flowering Crabapple
Malus sp.

Flowering crabapples almost define spring in the South. They seem to have a sixth sense about timing their flowers to open after any cold snap that might turn them brown. I am sure there have been years when crabapple blossoms were killed, since nothing in nature is ever absolute except a snow-free Fourth of July in South Alabama. But year in and year out, the most dependable spring-flowering trees in the South are crabapples.

Since not all crabapples do well in the South, the smart gardener uses only those that have proven suitable for us. Occasionally I see local nurseries offering crabapples grown too far north or west that aren't heat- and pest-resistant enough for our conditions. Crabapples in general are subject to a large number of diseases and insects like blight, borer, scab, scale, and mildew, so be careful when selecting crabapples to use in your landscape. Avoid cultivars that are particularly prone to fire blight, a very difficult-to-control bacterial disease that kills new shoots, and leaves a tree looking like it has been scalded with fire or hot water. Plant moderately susceptible cultivars near the edge of wooded areas or in other places where minor leaf spots are of little consequence to the integrity of the landscape.

Our landscape was sprinkled with flowering crabapples when we moved to Sweet Apple many years ago. Dolgo, Hopa, and *Malus floribunda* brightened our springs immeasurably. I planted a Callaway Crabapple soon after moving in since it was discovered not too far away at Callaway Gardens. Much to the consternation of visiting deer, we had to cut down a Dolgo and Hopa that old age had caught up with. The fawns and yearlings had feasted on their small crabapples while their more adventurous mommas came much closer to the house to eat apples and pears off our orchard trees. Even though I have never sprayed any of our crabapples and only pruned off limbs that were broken or mechanically damaged, they are filled with blossoms each year.

Choose the right spot for planting since most crabapples are large and spreading, making them unsuitable for small corners or in narrow areas between driveways and property lines or between sidewalks and streets, where their limbs can be brushed and damaged by cars or trucks.

Crabapples purchased at retail nurseries are slender and upright, even when balled and burlapped, giving no clue to their height and breadth in a few years. Plant a young crabapple carefully with future growth in mind. It may seem lost in the middle of the lawn and a mile from your house today, but it will be large as all outdoors in five or so years.

Michael Dirr describes a zillion cultivars in his extensive text, *Manual of Woody Landscape Plants*, and Arie den Boer lists a half zillion in his older classic, *Flowering Crabapples*. The task is to find ones that blossom heavily and consistently without being ruined by diseases and insects.

I have observed the South's most widely grown crabapples for many, many years. *Malus floribunda* and Callaway Crabapple are the two most reliable I have found. They have also been my best performers at Sweet Apple for over 25 years. Others like Almey, Dolgo, Eleyi, and Hopa are often sold in Southern nurseries, but have moderate to severe disease and insect problems.

I should mention the native Southern Crabapple, *Malus angustifolia*, which blossoms after most Asian crabapples and may be seen around old country homes, abandoned homesites, near forests, and on the edge of abandoned fields. The pink-to-white flowers are very fragrant. Another native, Sweet Crabapple, *Malus coronaria*, is also very fragrant, but it is only native in the upper South.

Neither of these natives is widely cultivated because of rust disease, which attacks their leaves, though I am constantly amazed at how many Southern Crabapples I spot from time to time when they are in bloom.

The taxonomy of crabapples is not easy to follow since most cultivated ones have come from seedlings with unknown or unsure parentage. Therefore, in some cases you will not find a species listed after the genus name, *Malus*, but only a cultivar name like *Malus* 'Callaway.' In this case, you will note that a single quote mark brackets the cultivar name. This isn't a shortcut or sloppy taxonomy but the way crabapples are correctly listed.

Callaway Crabapple
Malus 'Callaway'

FLOWERS: Pink buds open into single white flowers over an inch in diameter.

FRUIT: Bright glossy red crabapples can exceed the size of a quarter and usually remain on the tree until after the leaves drop in the fall.

HEIGHT: 15 to 25 feet.

HABIT: Large round head. Not suitable for restricted areas of a landscape.

INSECTS AND DISEASES: No crabapple is immune to all insects and diseases, but year in and year out, Callaway is the cleanest one I have seen growing in the South.

Callaway Crabapple is a superb flowering crabapple for the South because of its massive number of blossoms each spring, disease resistance, and bright red fruit in the fall. Pink buds open into large pure white flowers, which appear in early to mid-April in the piedmont, a bit later than many commonly grown crabapples. My Callaway Crabapple is within 20 feet of a *Floribunda* Crabapple and consistently reaches its peak of bloom after the *Floribunda*'s petals start falling. Its growth is clean and disease-resistant, allowing the tree to remain heavily laden with dark green leaves until fall. The large quarter-size crabapples are bright, glossy red, and hang on the tree until most of their leaves have fallen, making autumn one of its showy times. The fruits make excellent crabapple jelly.

Callaway Crabapple is a magnificent small specimen tree in the landscape during the entire growing season, comparing favorably with the Flowering Dogwoods and Yoshino Cherry.

Callaway Crabapple was discovered at Callaway Gardens near Pine Mountain, Georgia, by the well-known horticulturist Fred Galle.

Callaway Crabapple fruit in the fall

Floribunda Crabapple, Japanese Flowering Crabapple
Malus floribunda

HEIGHT: 15–25 feet.
HABIT: Broad oval, often nearly as wide as tall.
GROWTH RATE: Medium.
BEST USE: Specimen tree in the open or against a tree line.
LEAF COLOR: Deep green.
FALL COLOR: Yellow but not spectacular.
FLOWERS: Bright red buds open into pale pink, then white 1¹/₂ inch flowers.
FRUIT: Small and yellow, though some strains are said to have red fruits.

Floribunda Crabapple is the standard against which all other crabapples have been compared since its introduction from Japan in the 1860s. It has remained the leader in the face of hundreds of new cultivars and selections over the years. Two features keep it on top: the tremendous mass of flowers even on young plants, and its resistance to insects and diseases.

I have grown many Floribunda Crabapples in my life and have never had one fail me. The one growing at Sweet Apple when we moved in has never caused a moment's problem, despite being in more shade than is recommended and never having grown as large as it would have in the open. Each year it is filled with masses of pink flowers turning white before the Callaway Crabapple nearby or the dogwood next to it have fully opened blossoms.

I remember a Floribunda Crabapple we planted for a neighbor of one of our garden centers back in the days when we owned the company. The son of our neighbor wanted to give his mother a Floribunda Crabapple along with a Red Maple, which she had longed for. We agreed to plant them but immediately ran into problems over spacing in the small front yard. We compromised between our distances and hers, but the crabapple still grew enough to hinder the front entrance, and the Red Maple reached the roof in five or so years. "I can't believe how big they have grown," she told us one day.

The perfect landscape of my dreams would have three mature, free-standing, flowering trees: Floribunda Crabapple, Yoshino Cherry, and Cloud 9 Dogwood.

Japanese Flowering Crabapple, Malus floribunda

Almey Flowering Crabapple

Hopa Flowering Crabapple

Common crabapple cultivars found in retail nurseries

Almey: Deep maroon red flowers. Very susceptible to scab disease.
Dolgo: Pink buds, white flowers. Large red fruit the size of a quarter. Dolgo is not seriously affected by disease.
Eleyi: Red buds opening to maroon flowers. Very susceptible to scab disease.
Hopa: Dark red buds opening to a rose pink (a bilous pink to me) with a white star at the base of the petals. Susceptible to diseases.

NOTE: With the exception of Dolgo, the above frequently planted cultivars are listed as prone to disease. However, there are many older specimens still growing quite well in the South. I have seen mass plantings on freeways that are free of disease some years and denuded in others, yet they continue to grow and bloom well each year.

I have reviewed a number of publications that list crabapple cultivars and find that most are northern introductions. This is to be expected, since crabapples are the mainstay of spring-flowering trees where flower buds of dogwood and cherry may be damaged by cold. Unfortunately, many of these introductions do not do well in the heat and humidity of the South, except perhaps in mountain cities like Asheville, North Carolina. For the rest of us, it is better to stick to Southern introductions like Callaway and those proved in the South, like Floribunda.

Natchez Crape Myrtle, Charleston, South Carolina

Crape Myrtle
Lagerstroemia indica

HEIGHT: Depends on how it is trained, but the tallest I have seen was about 35 feet.

HABIT: Usually grown as a single or multistem tree with the mass of foliage above head high to expose the fantastic smooth, flaking bark.

GROWTH RATE: Fast.

BEST USE: Specimen flowering tree in the landscape or street tree.

LEAF COLOR: Dark green.

FALL COLOR: Yellow to orange and red.

INSECTS AND DISEASES: Aphids, powdery mildew, and sooty fungus are the worst, though occasionally others appear.

Crape Myrtle is so widely grown in the South that we tend to assume that it is a native, but actually it came from China. I have observed it along with related species growing in all the foreign places I have had vegetable projects, including Egypt, the Philippines, and Malaysia, as well as most of the surrounding countries that I visited. Nowhere have I seen them grow any better than they do here – it is our most spectacular summer-flowering plant.

Until 1970, Crape Myrtles were almost always grown as large flowering shrubs, the more compact cultivars being preferred to the larger-growing ones. Since the '70s, though, they have been grown more often as small flowering trees, which I think is their best use.

I prefer to see them pruned like flowering trees, rather than pruned back each year to a few stubs protruding out of several tall trunks, as is the current rage among some landscape maintenance people. The beauty of a tree-form Crape Myrtle is the wonderful bark complimenting the deep green leaves and stunning flowers. The trunks of most cultivars are a delightful tan with plates of flaking bark revealing a lighter color. However, red bark Crape Myrtles are far more showy.

I was awed, to say the least, the first time I saw the red-bark 'Natchez' Crape Myrtle in downtown Charleston, South Carolina. To me, these were perfect Crape Myrtles, with their extraordinary trunks, rich

Smooth gray-brown Crape Myrtle bark

green foliage, and large white flowers. Since then, I see more and more 'Natchez' growing all over the South. It is one flowering tree that has been extensively planted, yet doesn't seem vastly overplanted like Bradford Pear. The Atlanta Botanical Garden contains a beautiful avenue of 'Natchez' Crape Myrtle that shows the plant at its best.

Since Crape Myrtle has a number of cultivars with different bark coloration and flower colors, it is easy to choose one to fit the color needs of any landscape.

The worst insect and disease problems are aphids, mildew, and sooty fungus. The most unsightly, sooty fungus, makes the leaves look like they have a coating of black soot. I am deluged with questions about this condition, which is caused by aphids attacking the leaves and leaving a honeydew on which the sooty fungus grows. Correct the problem by spraying with a good insecticide to kill the aphids. Wait a week, then wash the tree with a strong water spray to remove the fungus.

White Crape Myrtle

Tree-form Red Crape Myrtle

Peeling red bark of Natchez Crape Myrtle

Cultivars

There are dozens and dozens of Crape Myrtle cultivars, ranging from the dwarfs to the taller tree forms. When choosing which to grow as trees, first decide on the height you want for the location in your landscape, then the flower and bark color that suit your situation. The best cultivars for trees grow 15 feet or higher.

My two favorite cultivars are 'Natchez', as I've mentioned above, and 'Near East', which has very pale pink flowers and tan to gray bark.

The Bald Cypress is beautiful in an urban setting.

Cypress
Cupressus sp. and *Taxodium sp.*

Cypress is the common name given to a number of different plants ranging from small vines to huge trees. The two common tree cypress grown in Southern landscapes are the great Bald Cypress and Leyland Cypress, though in past years the often-used Arborvitae or False Cypress, which are still used as evergreen shrubs, grew into trees when left unattended. I have seen them growing in Europe where they reach 50 or more feet.

Bald Cypress
Taxodium distichum

HEIGHT: 70 feet or more with age.
HABIT: Pyramidal when young and middle age but may develop spreading limbs when old.
GROWTH RATE: Medium.
BEST USE: Specimen lawn tree.
LEAF COLOR: Rich green in summer and a golden brown in the fall. Bare in winter.
SPECIAL INTEREST: Handsome gray to reddish brown bark.

Stately is the best description for this magnificent tree. Drive by a coastal plains swamp to see these trees rising high and mighty above the soggy ground or shallow water's edge with their knees arching upward and back down again to take in needed air to compensate for the roots being under water.

Centennial Bald Cypress are common, and there may be some that sprouted before the Crusades. I thought Bald Cypress were confined to swamps when I was learning about trees in the 1950s, so it was a shock to look up and see two huge specimens as I drove down a street in southwest Atlanta one day. The most incredible part of the sight was how they could grow between the sidewalk and the street. Cities are tough on trees, especially street trees, yet time and again I have made the journey to this part of town while saying a little prayer that these two magnificent specimens had not fallen prey to a chain saw. I am happy to say that they made it into the third millennium.

Their slender pyramidal shape makes Bald Cypress a great landscape tree, a fact that's being recognized more and more by landscapers. I see them with increasing frequency in landscapes, indicating that they are being taken seriously as a general landscape tree rather than just a special-location tree for poorly drained wet areas.

Their longevity belies their growth rate, which is medium to fast, usually an attribute of shorter-lived trees. A Bald Cypress planted in the early 1970s in front of a church near where I live is now a beautiful pyramidal tree well over 35 feet tall.

Bald Cypress is deciduous, which might be a drawback to someone looking for an evergreen, but for those who merely seek a beautiful, stately tree in their landscape, it is a good choice.

Cultivars

Several cultivars are on the market and more should follow, making it possible to find the right tree to fit your location. Use narrow cultivars for more restricted spaces and broad cultivars for specimen lawn trees.

Leyland Cypress
xCupressocyparis leylandii

HEIGHT: 75 feet or more.
HABIT: Columnar to slightly pyramidal during its life in the landscape.
GROWTH RATE: Very fast.
BEST USE: Tall screens.
LEAF COLOR: Rich evergreen.
SPECIAL NOTES: Leyland Cypress is the tall screen of choice by landscapers.

Amazingly, a huge Bald Cypress growing between a sidewalk and street.

I firmly believe that interesting and unique plants are the keys to good landscaping, and I cringe when every subdivision, lot, and commercial property has identical plantings. I would feel the same way if every driveway held a red Chevrolet or blue Mercedes Benz.

Leyland Cypress has good attributes, which I must note. It grows fast, has good texture, and screens well. Happily, it grows so fast that its cost is not prohibitive for the average homeowner who needs a quick screen but doesn't want to pay a fortune for 10-foot-high balled-and-burlapped trees.

Unfortunately Leyland Cypress plantings, like most screening plants, are set too close together and develop problems as they meld with age. I have observed too many lines of Leyland Cypress planted four or five feet apart, in which a plant or two will die and leave holes in the screen. If this happens early on, the surrounding plants spread into the holes, but many times it occurs when the roots of adjacent plants become crowded and drought causes the weaker to die. In these cases, the adjacent plants have lost growth in between, and filling the spaces with new growth happens slowly or not at all. If you use Leyland Cypress for a screen, set them twice as far apart as usually recommended (four feet) so each plant has a chance to perform at its best. Otherwise, remove every other plant when they begin to touch.

Several years ago I had the opportunity to visit the Royal Botanical Gardens at Kew near London, England, where trees have been growing for centuries and Leyland Cypress for almost a century. It was amazing to see the tall pillar plants of the South's landscapes growing as huge trees with limbs starting 30 feet or more above the ground – and a wake-up call to what will happen to Leyland Cypress a number of years down the road.

A further difficulty has developed in the sudden occurrence of fungal diseases that may restrict the use of Leyland Cypress, especially in close plantings.

Leyland Cypress can look like a squad of marching soldiers.

Leyland Cypress grown as a screen

Interplanting in a Leyland Cypress screen is a bad idea.

Cultivars

Many named cultivars are on the market. Be sure to match the qualities of the cultivar with your own specific needs before making a purchase.

Dawn Redwood

Dawn Redwood
Metasequoia gliptostroboides

HEIGHT: 35–50 feet in 25 years, ultimate height exceeds 100 feet.

HABIT: Upright pyramidal form from narrow to broad.

GROWTH RATE: Fast.

BEST USE: Specimen tree where there is plenty of room.

LEAF COLOR: Rich green in the summer, golden brown in the fall.

This beautiful tree was first described in 1941 from a Pliocene Age fossil found in Japan. Living trees growing in Szechwan Province in China came to the attention of botanists at about the same time, and their seeds were brought to the United States in late 1940. I recently read that reexamination of some western United States fossils originally identified as Sequoia are actually *Metasequoia*, which means they were once natives in our country as well as in Asia. No wonder they like us so well.

Since *Metasequoia* was introduced into the United States in the late 1940s, it has been widely grown and is now seen throughout the South. The first large tree I saw was at Auburn University. Its beauty and clean structure convinced me that it had a place in the landscape but only where it had plenty of room to grow. Time would show that the small trees being sold were too often planted in restricted areas.

We planted one in 1955 at the Hastings' Cheshire Bridge Garden Center in Atlanta, and it had grown into a huge tree by the time we sold the company in 1976. About the same time, the City of Atlanta planted two trees at what is now the Atlanta Botanical Garden, and they are more impressive every year.

Metasequoia grows fast. Since none can be older than 50 or so years, the huge ones growing now are really adolescents in the world of trees. I am sure the two at the Atlanta Botanical Garden are at least 50 feet high.

Dawn Redwood looks like it should be an evergreen but it isn't, which should not be an important consideration since its red bark and bare limbs are attractive. Its feathery texture complements other deciduous trees in the landscape, and it stands out as either a specimen lawn tree or in groups where space accommodates its size. From its early stages until maturity, it maintains its pyramidal shape.

I have read how it needs moist soil since, as a native in China, it was found growing beside rice paddies. As a result of the common recommendations, we planted the Dawn Redwood at our garden center where moisture was plentiful near the bottom of a stone wall. However, the ones at the Atlanta Botanical Garden were planted on a man-made rise back of the Blind Garden in a generally dry area. I personally believe they accept a wide range of conditions.

I have grown many Dawn Redwoods from seeds collected from mature trees where my wife Betsy worked for a number of years. I collect the seeds as soon as the cones expel them in the fall, then plant as soon as possible in cell packs in the greenhouse, using a peat-light mixture that I keep damp but not wet. Germination occurs over the winter. Commercial growers use cold stratification, which helps germination percentage, but I don't bother since I get ample germination for planting on my place without the bother. Dawn Redwood is one of the few newer trees that don't seem to be overplanted, though many can be seen in landscapes.

White Flowering Dogwood in the spring

Dogwood
Cornus sp.

When Southerners talk about dogwoods, they refer to Flowering Dogwood, *Cornus florida*, but many other dogwood species are used as ornamentals in the snow belt. Most have brightly colored stems that can be very attractive in the winter emerging from snow-covered landscapes. But none have flowers that can begin to compare with our native Flowering Dogwood.

Chinese Dogwood, *Cornus kousa var. chinensis*, is quite popular in the South as a late spring-flowering tree, even though its flowers never achieve the spectacular appearance of our native because the flowers come after the leaves, muting their show.

During my days at Cornell University in upstate New York, I missed many things about being home in Georgia, but most of all I missed seeing the dogwoods in bloom during the spring, especially after one of Ithaca's hideously cold winters. Things may have changed a bit as new bud-hardy cultivars are being developed, but in the old days, it was a pain learning about Bloodtwig and Red Osier Dogwood and all the other bush species rather than what I knew was the most beautiful flowering tree of all.

Flowering Dogwood has long been our standard landscape flowering tree as well as a spectacular breath of spring in woods and forests. As fad trees come and go, Flowering Dogwood remains our premier flowering tree each spring.

The origin of the name "dogwood" is interesting. In his extensive work, *The Standard Cyclopedia of Horticulture*, L. H. Bailey says the term arose because "a decoction of the bark of *C. sanguinea* was used in England to wash mangy dogs." *Cornus sanguinea* is the botanical name for Bloodtwig Dogwood, one of the bush types mentioned above. Bailey's theory must have come along after 1737 because one of my favorite old books, *The Complete Family-Piece: And Country Gentlemen, and Farmer's Best Guide*, published in London in 1737, gives a gross remedy for mange that I dare not repeat.

White Flowering Dogwood
Cornus florida

Please note that the following information is for the species and not the many cultivars, which may vary in some aspects.

HEIGHT: Generally 30–40 feet but variable according to the growing conditions.

HABIT: From a low-branched rounded tree to a more upright tree with a layered, spreading top.

GROWTH RATE: May be very slow until established, then medium until mature.

BEST USE: Specimen tree.

LEAF COLOR: Rich green.

FALL COLOR: Red to purple.

FLOWERS: White flower on the species, white, pink, or red flowers on varieties and cultivars. Four two-inch-long bracts arise from a small yellow flower. Bracts may have space between them or touch each other.

FRUIT: A cluster of three or four smooth, bright red, very showy flesh-covered seeds that are attractive to a large number of birds.

One of my early jobs in the nursery business was to travel through much of the South visiting a select list of nurseries that produced plants for our mail order department. Three stops were particularly enjoyable and enlightening: Chase Nursery Company near Huntsville, Alabama; Commercial Nursery Company at Decherd, Tennessee; and Tennessee Valley Nursery at Winchester, Tennessee. All three owners, Henry Chase, Hubert Nicholson, and Hoskins Shadow, were devotees of dogwoods. Their love and enthusiasm for this plant helped develop my strong feelings about Flowering Dogwood and its preeminent place as a landscape tree.

More importantly, they taught me the best ways to use the tree in the landscape as well as to maintain its vitality under home conditions.

Since they are native from Washington, D.C. to Upper Florida, dogwoods grow well throughout the South and are used in many different landscape situations. It is one of the three most popular spring-flowering trees; crabapples and flowering cherries are the other two, but they are more difficult to grow in the lower South.

William Bartram wrote this great description of dogwoods he saw in northwestern Butler County, Alabama, during his travels through the South in 1776:

> We now enter a very remarkable grove of Dog wood trees, *Cornus Florida*, which continued nine or ten miles, except here and there a towering Magnolia grandiflora; . . . these trees were about twelve feet high, spreading horizontally; their limbs meeting and interlocking with each other, formed one vast, shady, cool grove, so dense and humid as to exclude the sun-beams

Dogwoods are the South's finest flowering tree.

Dogwood berries are a brilliant red in the fall.

and prevent intrusion by almost every other vegetable, affording us a most desirable shelter from the fervid sunbeams at noon-day.

Dogwoods may grow large after many years, but seldom to the size of either cherries or crabapples. The largest listed are 33 feet high by 42 feet wide and 31 feet high by 48 feet wide. The largest I have ever seen was in the small front yard of a home in an old subdivision in Atlanta. It reared over the one-story house and filled up half the front yard. This tree crashed down during a storm before it could be crowned as the state champion dogwood.

Plant dogwoods in rich, well-drained soil suitable for azaleas and other broadleaf acid-loving plants. Semishady spots are perfect, though the best specimen in our area is in full sun, proving that good soil is more important than exposure. Dogwoods should never be planted too deeply. Soil on top of the ball of earth is dangerous and soil piled against the base of the tree can be disastrous. However, too shallow planting can also be bad. I have seen many plantings of slowly dying dogwoods with three or four inches of the ball above ground level. Heavy mulching against the lower trunk provides a moist environment for borers to develop in the trunk. Wrapping the trunk with tree tape does the same thing.

Dogwoods are prone to a number of problems in urban areas, not the best environment for any plant. Fungus attacks on flowers and leaves are frequent but not an annual occurrence. I have a native tree on a bank that we enjoy from our kitchen. It has bad leaf

Dogwoods have spectacular maroon-red fall color.

spots about every third year, which we never worry about or bother treating.

Borers can decimate dogwoods, especially trees under stress in urban areas. Mechanical damage on the lower trunk is a special invitation to borers. Power equipment, children whopping the trunks with anything handy, and nicks from automobiles account for a majority of dogwood borer problems, but poorly growing trees provide the opportunity.

Keep cars, lawn mowers, power trimmers, and children's toys away, and don't plant dogwoods near driveways or streets. Fertilize trees when they are not growing well to keep them healthy and stress-free. Always keep an open space between the mulch and the trunk. Since dogwoods are acid-loving plants, it is better not to apply lime in the area under their branches.

This advice is not unique to dogwoods but also applies to crabapples, flowering cherries, and most other flowering trees in the landscape.

I must add that the term "flower" is botanically incorrect when describing a dogwood blossom. The showy parts we admire are bracts and not a part of the small yellow flower in the center, in the same way that the magnificent red parts of a Poinsettia "flower" are showy bracts. Bracts are modified leaves arising from near the true flower.

But since few people are familiar with the term "bract," I'll continue to use the commonly accepted language.

Cultivars and Botanical Varieties

Cloud 9 Dogwood
Cornus florida 'Cloud 9'

I feel like Cloud 9 Dogwood is a part of me since Henry Chase introduced it to my father and me as a well-marked isolated tree growing in a field at Chase Nursery near Huntsville, Alabama. They had dubbed it "Cap's Special" in honor of one of their senior staff members who spotted it blooming among a group of large plants. Another of Cap's findings had already been chosen by Wayside Gardens for introduction. Henry convinced my father that Cap's Special was superior in bloom and had a more desirable spreading growth habit than Wayside's choice. Since it was late August, we didn't see the blossoms, but we were impressed by the number of flower buds already showing. The next spring we

Cloud 9 Dogwood

Cherokee Chief Dogwood
Cornus florida 'Cherokee Chief'

Cherokee Chief has the best red-colored flowers of any dogwood I have ever seen. Michael Dirr attributes its introduction to Ike Hawkersmith of Winchester, Tennessee, which may be true, but to me, Hoskins Shadow of Tennessee Valley Nursery was its greatest admirer and most ardent grower. Hoskins could spend an evening telling about the great attributes of Cherokee Chief, all of which I heartily agreed with.

The flowers are numerous and a deep red, set on an upright clean-growing tree. The best color is found on trees that are growing well.

Cherokee Chief Dogwood

visited the field when "Cap's Special" was in bloom and immediately agreed to list it in our catalog.

My father and Henry debated long and hard over a suitable name in place of the mundane "Cap's Special," which failed to emphasize the fantastic qualities of the tree in bloom. Later at a nurserymen's meeting, Henry and I were visiting with Mrs. James I. George, the premier producer of Clematis plants. When we mentioned our problem, Mrs. George said without batting an eye, "Name it Cloud 9." That settled the matter, and Cloud 9 was the name we used in introducing this fabulous dogwood to our customers.

Hoskins Shadow was growing Cherokee Princess White Dogwood as a companion to his red-flowering Cherokee Chief, and there was a great deal of friendly debate between him and Henry Chase over which was better. I thought then, and still think, that Cloud 9 is superior to any cultivar of Flowering Dogwood that I have ever seen. The bracts overlap rather than having a space in between, giving the impression that the huge numbers of flowers form a white cloud over the bare branches. Another extraordinary quality of Cloud 9 is the huge numbers of flower buds set when the tree is young. Our small-size mail order offerings always had a few flower buds, and I have seen three-year-old trees in Henry's fields with 50 or more flowers. Because of its more open habit and heavy bloom, I can always spot a Cloud 9 growing in a landscape.

Pink Flowering Dogwood
Cornus florida rubra

Pink Flowering Dogwood has lighter pink flowers than the new red cultivars, but may be less stark in a landscape and thus more desirable. Much attention has been paid to bud-hardiness of this variety, which seems to lose buds to cold in more northerly climates. If you are in the higher elevations of the Appalachian Mountains, I recommend caution when choosing this tree.

Pink Flowering Dogwood

Other Dogwood Cultivars and Introductions

You may see dogwoods in nurseries tagged *Cornus florida 'Plena'*, which refers to double flowering forms. There is a nice specimen of *'Plena'* planted at our post office in Roswell, Georgia, near several beautiful White Flowering Dogwoods that also may be cultivars. Unfortunately this *'Plena'*, as well as most others I have seen, blossoms later than white forms and their flowers are not only muted by expanding leaves but also emerge downward from under twigs rather than upward on top.

Nursery growers are active in the selection of dogwood cultivars with unusual qualities. The current list is lengthy, but I have not heard of any that are significantly better than the two above. If your area has particular disease problems that are not general to the South, I suggest discussing with your local nurseryman which cultivars are most resistant.

Chinese Dogwood
Cornus kousa var. chinensis

HEIGHT: 20–30 feet in height and an equal breadth when mature.

HABIT: Oval to upright when mature. Young trees may be oval to rounded. Limbs are layered which gives them an interesting appearance, especially in the winter when they are bare.

GROWTH RATE: Slow.

BEST USE: Specimen tree. Good in restricted places.

LEAF COLOR: Dark green.

FALL COLOR: Red and purple.

FRUIT: Half-inch to one-inch orange to red balls (drupes), which look something like a hard reddish-orange blackberry.

Chinese Dogwood has been around since the late 1800s, yet it has never gained anything like the popularity of our native dogwood, *Cornus florida*. Its widely used selling point is an extension of the dogwood season, since it blossoms in mid-May in the mid-South, a month after our native dogwood.

The blossoms open after the leaves are fully unfurled, muting their effect. Though a pleasing sight, it's a far cry from our White Flowering Dogwood.

However, if we don't compare Chinese Dogwood with our native dogwood in our minds, it can be an effective

specimen tree in its own right. The large white blossoms are beautiful lying on the green leaves, and the orange-red fruit balls make a great show when they are ripening in the fall. The tree is more formal, but with its layered limbs, it is still graceful.

An interesting anomaly occurred in the fall of 2000 when three trees in plantings near Longstreet Press, my publisher in Atlanta, blossomed heavily in late September and October. In addition, the flowers remained for several weeks longer than they usually do when blossoming on time. Another planting in an older area of Atlanta bore

Blossoms of Chinese Dogwood

fruits more heavily than I had ever seen before. They were so stunning hanging from four-foot-tall trees that I had a hard time figuring out what plants I was looking at until I realized that these were stunted Chinese Dogwoods.

Choose *Cornus kousa var. chinensis* instead of the species, *Cornus kousa*, since its flowers are larger and are borne more profusely.

Cultivars

I am amazed at the number of selections and hybrid crosses of Chinese Dogwood that have been introduced, though only a few are ever found in retail nurseries. There seem to be more cultivars than of our native, *Cornus florida*. Gardeners and landscapers are apparently searching for cultivars of Chinese Dogwood with pink blossoms, though I don't think this would be an improvement.

Pink cultivar of Chinese Dogwood

Chinese Dogwood blossoms appear after leaves.

Unusual showy fruit of Chinese Dogwood

Ulmus parvifolia, True Chinese Elm, a good tree

Elm

Ulmus sp.

The ruler of the elm world has long been the great American Elm, which has stood mightily in some of the nation's finest estates, parks, botanical gardens, and ordinary homes. Unfortunately, the Dutch Elm disease and innumerable other bacterial and fungal diseases have made the planting of this heritage tree unthinkable. One of my sadder moments was returning to the Cornell campus many years after graduation and finding that most, if not all, of the great American Elms that had stood so magnificently on the main quadrangle were now gone as a result of fatal disease attacks. Occasionally, you will look up and see a huge shade tree that looks like an American Elm, and, indeed, it is one that somehow has survived.

In my early nursery days, the so-called Chinese Elm, *Ulmus pumila*, was the rage and widely planted, more often as a super fast-growing tree than a replacement for the American Elm. Somehow, nurserymen were growing the Siberian Elm instead of the true Chinese Elm, *Ulmus parvifolia*, a far superior tree.

The true Chinese Elm is a much better tree, but in my opinion still inferior to many other available trees. Unfortunately, they are being planted as street trees at a rate exceeded only by Bradford Pear.

Zelkova serrata is often used in the same situations as true Chinese Elm. I will discuss it later on.

American Elm
Ulmus americana

Enjoy this tree in poetry and verse but forget about planting it. The risks of Dutch Elm disease are too great to take a chance. If you have one growing in your landscape, nurture it as long as possible, but stash away a fund to pay for removing it when its last days arrive.

Chinese Elm
Ulmus parvifolia

HEIGHT: 50 feet.
HABIT: Rounded.
GROWTH RATE: Fast.
BEST USE: Makes a suitable street tree, but is better in an open landscape.
LEAF COLOR: Dark green.
FALL COLOR: Variable from yellow to burgundy.

True Chinese Elm with its showy seeds

A struggling American Elm

The true Chinese Elm, *Ulmus parvifolia*, should not be confused with Siberian Elm, *Ulmus pumila*, which is a useless tree at best. Always check the tag on a Chinese Elm you might buy to be sure you've got the right botanical name. Otherwise you're likely to be disappointed.

I see many Chinese Elms being planted as street trees and I really don't understand why. In my mind, its only use is in a landscape filled with other trees where a small-leaf tree offers a pleasing contrast to maples, oaks, and other more desirable and interesting trees.

Cultivars

I am amazed at the number of Chinese Elm cultivars being introduced and grown. I ran across one in the parking lot of an antebellum home that had deep red seed formations and a touch of red in its summer leaves. I have no idea which cultivar it was, but found it quite attractive. It was a perfect tree for a particular spot, proving that there are always exceptions to my rules and opinions.

Siberian Elm
Ulmus pumila

Nelson Crist, my early tree mentor in the nursery business, used to say that there was nothing wrong with a Siberian Elm (like most nurserymen, he called it a Chinese Elm) that pruning at the ground with a good sharp ax wouldn't cure.

I saw a young planting of Siberian Elm in a small park that I pass occasionally. Curiosity made me stop and inspect the trees, and sure enough they looked pitiful. Their leaves were decimated by Elm Leaf Beetles and the summer wasn't half over.

There are a number of large, older Siberian Elms still around. Most have encountered considerable breakage in wind storms and have barely survived Elm Leaf Beetle and mildew attacks. What remains is an unsightly testament to a bad choice of a shade tree.

Fast growth is the highlight in Chinese Elm's resume. My question is fast growth into what? Do you really want a quick tree that can't keep its leaves on when you need shade?

Siberian Elm, formerly called Chinese Elm, is a worthless tree.

Empress Tree

Empress Tree
Paulownia tomentosa

Empress Tree is attractive only when in bloom.

Empress Tree is unattractive and trashy most of the year.

HEIGHT: 40–50 feet.
HABIT: Rounded, much like Catalpa.
GROWTH RATE: Fast.
BEST USE: Where it isn't seen when not in bloom.
FOLIAGE TEXTURE: Coarse.

LEAF COLOR: Medium green.
FALL COLOR: Zilch.
HARDINESS: May be damaged or killed by cold in higher
  elevations.

The only redeeming feature of Empress Tree is the
lavender blue flowers that cover it in late spring and
early summer. Otherwise, it's another tree that can best
be handled by pruning at ground level. After the flowers,
the messy fruits ripen and explode, sending enormous
numbers of floating seed all over everything. The empty
pods turn brown and remain unsightly until they finally
fall off the next year.

I have seen these trees used in landscapes, but for
the life of me I don't know why. Besides the seed problems, its wood is brittle and weak, breaking easily in
high wind or under the weight of ice or snow.

My best advice is to leave this tree in the wild where
you can see its beauty for a short time each year, then
forget it until the next year when you can ask once
again, "What is it?"

Champion Fraser Fir, High Hampton Inn, Cashiers, North Carolina

Fir

Abies sp.

A good reason to live in the Southern highlands is to be able to grow fir trees.

I think no other evergreen conifer matches its beauty and grace. Most of us have grown up decorating Balsam Fir Christmas trees with their rich green foliage and pleasant, woodsy fragrance. Firs were so plentiful in Ithaca, New York, where I went to college that they were hardly worth mentioning, but I have tried and tried to grow Balsam Firs here in the Georgia foothills with such poor success that my memories are all I have left of these gorgeous trees.

One tree that stands out in memory is a huge Fraser Fir, sometimes called Southern Balsam or Double Balsam, on the grounds of High Hampton Inn near Cashiers, North Carolina, where my mother and father frequently vacationed many years ago. I remember the tree but admit that during those high school and college days, it was just another beautiful tree that my father said we could not grow at Lovejoy, Georgia, where we lived. Recently I found out that this tree at High Hampton Inn is a national champion tree, which is like suddenly realizing that I once knew an Olympic gold medalist.

If you live in the South where firs grow, I recommend the Fraser Fir over the Balsam Fir. The form is fantastic and its thickly packed needles make it a far better choice.

Balsam Fir
Abies balsamea

HEIGHT: 50 feet or more.
HABIT: Pyramidal when younger, irregular when older.
GROWTH RATE: Slow.
BEST USE: Specimen in open areas.
LEAF COLOR: Dark green. Leaves are very aromatic.
RANGE: Mountains of the South.

Most of us know Balsam Fir from its use as a cut Christmas tree whose rich green needles and balsam fragrance are a traditional part of the holiday season. Few trees rival Balsam Fir when it is growing well in the open. Unfortunately, few of us Southerners are able to grow it successfully since heat and drought are its greatest enemies. Balsam Fir can be grown in the southern Appalachians where temperatures are more suitable. Lucky are you who live in the higher elevations.

Do you know how to tell the difference between a Balsam Fir and a spruce, which is sometimes used as a Christmas tree and often as a landscape plant? Find a young bare branch and rub a finger up and down. If it is smooth, it is a Balsam. If it is rough and a bit prickly, it is a spruce. That is a bit of horticultural information to impress your family and friends.

Fraser Fir
Abies fraseri

HEIGHT: 40 feet.
BREADTH: 25 feet.
HABIT: Pyramidal.
GROWTH RATE: Slow.
BEST USE: Specimen tree in the open.
LEAF COLOR: Rich, deep green. Very aromatic.
RANGE: Upper elevations, though it can be grown with success in a cool moist spot in the lower elevations of the upper piedmont.

Fraser Fir is tighter, thicker, more aromatic, and a better tree in all respects than a Balsam Fir for us Southerners who live in the upper elevations. There are a few that struggle in Atlanta, but I have seen nice specimens growing 100 miles north.

Fraser Fir has replaced Balsam Fir as the preferred cut Christmas tree due to the efforts of tree growers in the Southern foothills. Since they are cut closer to the hol-idays, they are fresher and more able to withstand the dry heat indoors that's so deadly to decorative greens.

Fraser Fir is best described as a noble tree. Consider yourself among the fortunate elite if you can grow it well.

China Fir, Monkey Tree, Cunninghamia
Cunninghamia lanceolata

HEIGHT: 50 feet.
BREADTH: 20 Feet.
HABIT: Narrow pyramid.
GROWTH RATE: Medium-fast when young, medium when older.
BEST USE: Specimen tree away from often-used areas.
LEAVES: Compound. Needles are arranged flat or spiraled from the leaf stem. Leaves remain on the tree for several years, then die and hang or shed onto other branches.
LEAF COLOR: Bright green.
RANGE: Hardy and well-adapted as far south as Florida.

China Fir

Prickly needles of China Fir

China Fir is seldom seen in landscapes these days. It was once a popular evergreen tree but now is only a curiosity. Before her death, our wonderful neighbor and well-known author Celestine Sibley wrote a column about seeing one and asked her readers what it was. Our learned local horticulturist Roy Wyatt and I immediately recognized her description. Roy had an advantage over me because he had one growing back of his house, while I had only memories of the one in our backyard at Lovejoy. The incident revived my interest, and I was surprised to discover many growing in older areas of Southern cities as well as out in the country.

A stately pair grew back of a pool in my mother's rock garden, a perfect place since China Fir does best in acid, moist, but well-drained soil. They stood like tall sentinels guarding the area. My mother called them Monkey Trees, a common name used in the South because their needles were so sticky that monkeys wouldn't dare climb them.

I vaguely remember their being planted when I was very young, but clearly remember how tall they were in the 1950s when my interest in Southern trees had grown. The last time I visited the old home place, they still stood as huge 60-foot-tall guardians back of the abandoned garden.

China Fir was never my favorite tree, an attitude originating when I was young. Their dropped leaves lay on the ground like rapiers waiting to pierce unsuspecting boys' bare feet. As they say in the country, "Man, did it smart."

Age makes me more objective. China Fir is a beautiful tree and would be classified as magnificent if the dead leaves didn't hang among the outer limbs, resulting in a rather trashy appearance much of the time.

I have read plantsmen's complaints about bronze leaves in cold winters, but that is certainly no reason to reject this stately tree. In the right place away from barefoot boys' feet and where they can spire upward toward the sky, China Fir can be a great addition to a landscape.

Cultivars

Much work is being done on selecting better cultivars of China Fir, something all lovers of trees should applaud. My choice would be quicker leaf shedding, deeper green color, and less rigid leaves.

Ginkgo biloba is one of our best shade trees.

Ginkgo, Maidenhair Tree
Ginkgo biloba

HEIGHT: Mature trees are over 70 feet with a spread of 30 feet or more.

HABIT: Pyramidal to vase-shaped when young, but broad and spreading when older.

GROWTH RATE: Slow to medium.

BEST USE: Specimen shade tree.

LEAF COLOR: Rich green.

FALL COLOR: Bright yellow.

PROBLEMS: No diseases or insects, but fruit has a foul odor.

Ginkgo is truly unique – as valuable a tree in the landscape as the hype that surrounds it would suggest. In my opinion it is one of the top four or five trees grown today; if pressed, I would insist it be placed near or at the top of that list.

Ginkgo is the sole survivor of a family of plants which existed during the Jurassic Period along with dinosaurs and flying reptiles. It was found growing in Guizhou and Zheijiang, China, where a tree estimated to be 3,000 years old is over 300 feet tall and still growing. Trees of the genus were common in North America during the Jurassic Period but none has survived on our continent like Ginkgo biloba has in China.

Ginkgo is a gymnosperm, like the conifers, but it has broad fan-shaped leaves rather than needles. There are some beautiful specimens growing in the South, one of which is on the north side of the Woodruff Arts Center in Atlanta.

Ginkgo should be considered a medium- to slow-growing tree, though good deep soil and plenty of fertilizer will speed up its growth considerably. We planted two at Lovejoy in the early 1950s, one of which grew extraordinarily fast while the other sat and waited for the millennium. The faster-growing one was in the lawn, where it received high-nitrogen fertilizer, while the other was planted in the bed of an old driveway. Over the years, we tried several methods of fertilizing to make the smaller one grow, but nothing worked, which proved to me that fertilizer alone was not the answer. Ginkgo grows best where the roots can penetrate deeply.

The leaves turn a bright yellow in the late fall and, after delighting passersby for a week or so, suddenly drop almost overnight, to the joy of all of us who have to rake leaves. Ginkgo has no leaves hanging on until spring, as oaks are prone to do.

Ginkgo has no pests to worry about, and for those in metro centers, it is resistant to pollution and makes a long-lasting street tree – if no power-line trimmers cut them apart.

But nothing is perfect, not even the Ginkgo. The Ginkgo's fruit is foul-smelling and messy after it falls from the tree. Fortunately, the different sexes are on separate trees and fertilization is restricted to plants rather close together. When you buy a seedling Ginkgo at a nursery, you have a 50/50 chance of getting a male or a female tree. If you plant only one tree, it will not be pollinated even if your tree is female. If it is a male tree, it has no fruit to worry about. Nursery growers are propagating a number of male cultivars, which guarantees that there won't be any fruit, so always buy a male cultivar whenever you can.

Too much acclaim often makes me suspicious about a new tree since I can count on one hand the number of great "new" trees that I have seen in my lifetime. In case Ginkgo is a new tree to you, don't be concerned that it might be a new rage tree because it isn't new at all. Ginkgo has been around for so many millennia that newness is out, but hopefully rage is in.

Ginkgo biloba was introduced into the United States in the late 1700s soon after we gained our independence. Of more recent interest to us senior citizens is the news that an extract from Ginkgo biloba fruits helps improve memory – if we can remember to take it regularly.

Cultivars

The list of Ginkgo cultivars is growing like a weed. Most are propagated for their unique form or fall color and for being a male plant, eliminating the possibility of foul-smelling fruit.

Summer-flowering Golden-rain Tree

Golden-rain Tree
Koelreuteria paniculata

HEIGHT: 30–45 feet.

HABIT: Dense and slightly spreading when young. Broad as tall when mature.

GROWTH RATE: Fast.

BEST USE: Large ornamental flowering tree.

FLOWER: Large panicles of bright yellow flowers cover the tree in early summer.

FRUIT: Papery capsule which reminds you of a Japanese lantern. Turns from green to yellow, then brown.

LEAF COLOR: Rich green.

FALL COLOR: Usually yellow but may have some orange under some growing conditions.

Showy seed pods of Golden-rain Tree

I wish writers and landscapers would stop comparing this tree with Laburnum, whose flowers are far more magnificent, but which unfortunately does not grow well in most of the South. I don't mean to suggest that Golden-rain Tree isn't one of our better summer-flowering trees, because it definitely is. But the comparison gives the wrong impression about its beauty and use, which is quite different from that of Laburnum.

I was talking about the tree with Glenn Dorsey at his nursery south of Atlanta when he took me to his home nearby. The sight of a huge Golden-rain Tree in bloom above the house was thrilling. Since plant dictionaries list it at a maximum height of 30 to 40 feet, this tree was certainly at the upper end of the scale.

We planted a Golden-rain Tree at our garden center in the early 1950s, and it caused considerable comment when in bloom – and afterwards as its interesting seed pods developed. Since we sold the company in 1976, I missed a large part of our Golden-rain Tree's growing up, but it was certainly beautiful when a mere adolescent at 20 years old. The bulldozers ended its life in the late 1990s, and I hate driving by the flattened site where it, along with other such specimens, have been replaced by tacky stores.

The Golden-rain Tree has beautiful yellow flowers in the early summer.

Golden-rain Tree rapidly develops into a wonderful tree. For those who don't stick around in one spot very long, it is a good choice for an excellent summer-flowering tree that becomes attractive in only a few years.

The showy yellow flowers are borne in large panicles that cover the tree's canopy. The seed capsules, which remind you of small Japanese lanterns, start out green, then turn yellow, and finally brown. The seeds scatter and often come up in odd places. They can be easily transplanted to other spots or given to admirers.

Hackberry

Celtis sp.

The Hackberries listed below are native to the South, and both are excellent trees where a large shade tree is called for. Their smooth gray bark and strong upright growth make them noteworthy in a landscape.

I am indebted to Henry Chase, a wonderful nurseryman from Huntsville, Alabama, for introducing me to the more southerly of the two species. Henry was looking for a faster-growing shade tree and began propagating Mississippi Hackberry, sometimes called Sugarberry. I was thrilled to start listing it in our catalog.

Both Hackberries are more upright when young but spread like an American Elm when older. Their rapid growth makes them ideal for slash-and-grade developments where houses are built sitting in the broiling sun and shade is imperative.

Mississippi Hackberry, Sugar Hackberry
Celtis laevigata

HEIGHT: 70 feet.
HABIT: Rounded to open.
GROWTH RATE: Fast when young, medium with age.
BEST USE: Shade tree or lawn specimen.

LEAF COLOR: Dark green.
FALL COLOR: Not outstanding.
BARK: Smooth, silver-gray, and a definite asset in the landscape.

Mississippi Hackberry is preferred for most of the South since it can be grown in the coastal plains as a large, faster-growing shade tree than Live Oak and other lower South natives. It also does well in the upper South where it is faster-growing and almost as beautiful as American Beech.

The small berries are attractive to a number of song birds, which adds life and interest to any garden.

Common Hackberry
Celtis occidentalis

Common Hackberry can be grown in the southern piedmont and mountains, but has no better characteristics than our Southern species. I recommend planting Mississippi Hackberry instead. If Mississippi Hackberry is unavailable in your part of the upper South, Common Hackberry is a good substitute.

Halesia, Silverbell

Halesia sp.

The native Silverbells listed below are not often planted in landscapes. But at one time it must have been a popular plant with landscapers since my father grew it at our nursery near Lovejoy, Georgia. We sold them as large balled-and-burlapped plants in our retail nurseries, but we never sold smaller plants in the catalog since they don't transplant easily as bare-root plants. Their popularity faded and we weren't growing any when I finished college in 1950. I found a large ten- to twelve-foot plant left growing in part of an old nursery field, which at the time was the largest I had ever seen. My son Chris has found some in the wild that are more normal in size, and I was happy to see them planted in groups along River Walk in Augusta, Georgia. I am convinced that Silverbell is one of those native plants that have fallen through the cracks in the landscaping world and hope it will be rediscovered by growers and landscapers, to the delight of us all. Container-grown plants transplant much better than those that are dug, balled, and burlapped.

Carolina Silverbell
Halesia tetraptera

HEIGHT: 25 feet or more.
HABIT: Low branched with a rounded to spreading head. May be multistemmed.
GROWTH RATE: Medium.
BEST USE: Small specimen tree in cool shaded areas.
FLOWERS: White, bell-shaped. Flowering is in mid-spring before its leaves appear, a definite plus since they stand against bare stems rather than being muted by a background of leaves.
LEAF COLOR: Dark green to yellow green in mid-summer.
FALL COLOR: Not significant.

Carolina Silverbell should be more than a collector's item. It is a beautiful small native tree easily grown in part shade under conditions similar to native azaleas. It does poorly in dry soil and where the soil pH is above 6.0, which is true for most azaleas and camellias.

In moist, low pH situations, Silverbell adds a great deal to a landscape and invites enthusiastic comments. For best results, plant only container-grown trees.

Two-winged Silverbell
Halesia diptera

Two-winged Silverbell is a close cousin to Carolina Silverbell but not as widely propagated and grown in nurseries. Its flowers are more showy than Carolina Silverbell and come a week or so later, extending the spring-flowering tree season. Grow the Two-winged Silverbell in the same types of conditions as the Carolina Silverbell.

Either of the Silverbells are worthy in a landscape, so choose whichever your nurseryman has growing in containers.

Canadian Hemlock

Hemlock
Tsuga sp.

Hemlocks make me feel like I am in the mountains even when I'm not. They grow best at higher elevations and seem to be a part of every mountain village in the South. Actually, their habitat is much broader than the mountains, since they do well in most of the piedmont.

Hemlocks develop into handsome pendulous trees or can be used as evergreen hedges. My wife's family in Danville, Virginia, had a beautiful Hemlock hedge screening their backyard from the neighbors. Visit older parts of Birmingham, Atlanta, Charlotte, and Richmond where trees and hedges are common, and you will certainly find hemlock specimens and hedges growing well.

Hemlocks are much less stark when planted as a screen and don't grow as fast as the greatly overused Leyland Cypress . Now that Leyland Cypress are seen dying as they become older, I hope hemlocks will return to plant lists.

Many years ago, I planted two Canadian Hemlocks to block an old trail near our gravel road. They had been growing for a number of years when my wife Betsy caught someone with axe in hand ready to cut one for a Christmas tree. The resulting conversation blew leaves off trees and surely convinced the thief that cutting someone else's tree – even far from the owner's house – was not a good idea. The remaining tree has done reasonably well despite little attention, heavy shade, and competition with other trees and shrubs.

I much prefer a naturally growing Hemlock over a heavily sheared one. Its feathery appearance is more graceful than thicker-growing plants like Nellie R. Stevens Holly and Leyland Cypress. Soldiers marching across my property line are not my cup of tea.

Hemlocks are not for the lower South, but do well in the upper piedmont and mountains from Alabama to Virginia.

Canadian Hemlock
Tsuga canadensis

Height: 60 feet.
Habit: Upright pyramidal. Finely textured.
Growth Rate: Medium.
Best Use: Screen plantings or a lawn specimen.
Leaf Color: Light green new growth followed by dark green during the summer.

I am partial to hemlocks, especially the Canadian Hemlock, which has a more graceful appearance than the Carolina Hemlock and does just as well in the Southern piedmont and mountains. Canadian Hemlock is easily distinguished by its needles, which lie almost flat along a branchlet, giving a layered effect. Its tall pyramidal shape makes a beautiful specimen tree, which is my favorite way to see it grown, though a well-grown hemlock hedge can be very attractive.

Excessive heat and drought are its greatest enemies, so planting too far south may be unwise. I have seen several reports about its adverse reactions to city conditions, but I have also seen fine mature specimens in older sections of Atlanta, which has become a city with high pollution rates.

Carolina Hemlock
Tsuga caroliniana

Height: 50–60 feet.
Habit: Pyramidal, without the graceful appearance of Canadian Hemlock.
Growth Rate: Slow to medium.
Best Use: Lawn specimens, screens, and tall hedges.
Leaf Color: Dark green.

The distinguishing characteristic of Carolina Hemlock is its needles, which wrap around a branchlet like a bottle brush rather than lying flat like Canadian Hemlock. The result is less airy and graceful. Older Carolina Hemlock specimens found in the upper piedmont and mountains can be beautiful. It grows slower and generally not as tall as Canadian Hemlock.

I'm probably splitting hairs when I suggest that Carolina Hemlock should give way to Canadian Hemlock in Southern plantings. Either is preferable to any number of overused evergreens.

Above: *Canadian Hemlock can be a beautiful hedge or screen.*
Right: *Carolina Hemlock has a looser form than Canadian Hemlock.*

Shagbark Hickory

Hickory
Carya sp.

Several *Carya* species grow in the South, where they are found in forests . . . and maybe on your property. They have colorful names like Bitternut, Swamp Hickory, Pignut, and Shagbark Hickory. Pecan is in the same group but is treated separately later on.

Few nurserymen grow any of this group, with the exception of pecan, because their deep tap roots make nursery production, transplanting, and sale difficult. I list hickory because you may find it already growing on your property. Encourage a good hickory to grow whenever you are fortunate enough to have one, but don't consider it a tree to plant.

Hickories, bitternuts, and pecans grow throughout the South in great abundance. They are handsome trees and a prize in the landscape but frankly a bit difficult to identify precisely, since they cross-pollinate and many variations occur. I list Shagbark Hickory as a good example of what might be lurking in your woods or in old parks in many cities of the South.

Shagbark Hickory
Carya ovata

HEIGHT: Older specimens in the wild may be 80 feet or higher.

HABIT: Upright.

GROWTH RATE: Slow.

BEST USE: Near wooded areas, though it is quite attractive as a lawn specimen.

LEAF COLOR: Variable from deep green to a yellow green in the summer, turning to a golden yellow to brown in the fall.

Shagbark Hickory in the early fall

Hickory nuts in the husks

Savannah Holly in full berry

Holly

Ilex sp.

Many species of hollies are grown as shrubs, but there are also a number that grow into trees. Tree-form hollies can be imposing in the landscape, especially during the winter when their red berries lie on a bed of evergreen leaves. Add some snow and you have a perfect Christmas-card scene. I suspect that many of the finest holly trees seen in landscapes started out as background shrubs and were allowed to assume their natural tree form as they grew large. That's what happened to us. When we moved into our country home, a fine American holly grew near a small *Magnolia grandiflora* in the back of the house. They both grew upward, forming a great relationship; the magnolia with branches to the ground shielding us from our country road and the spire-shaped American Holly doing its bit to ensure our privacy.

Betsy has been the *de facto* shaper of this holly tree. For 30 years she has been clipping off branches hindering her path to the mailbox, and the result is a beautiful sentinel to guard and protect us from the world outside our property lines.

American Holly is only one of many hollies that can take tree form. Yaupon Holly, *Ilex vomitoria*, is a fantastic small tree with both upright and weeping forms. Landscapers are now using Foster Holly, *Ilex x attenuata 'Fosteri'*, as an attractive small tree. Also, a number of natural crosses have been found growing in many parts of the South. I have experience growing a few and have watched many others being developed into lovely trees for various situations in the landscape. Recently, I saw a 15-foot-tall Burford Holly, *Ilex cornuta 'Burfordii'*, tree, which reminded me of a crazy but rather successful tree I once made out of an overgrown and very unsightly Chinese Holly, *Ilex cornuta*, growing in a dead corner in the front of my house. It is an overstatement to say that all holly trees are the result of saving overgrown shrub hollies by pruning them into trees, but many come about in that way.

New holly cultivars are being introduced all the time and should be considered when you or your landscaper has direct knowledge of their characteristics. Some have proven unsuited to their original purpose. Nellie R. Stevens, *Ilex x 'Nellie R. Stevens'*, was touted as a fine foundation plant when it was first being propagated by wholesale nursery growers. However, its natural shape, growth habit, and ultimate size make it a huge burden on a foundation planting and its ultimate removal necessary. Nellie R. Stevens Holly is a clear example of how a bit of investigation into a plant's true character will give rich rewards rather than great disappointment.

If you have a large overgrown holly in a suitable place, consider pruning it high into a multistem tree rather than butchering it back severely, and often unsuccessfully, to retain its shrub form.

A magnificent American Holly tree in the winter

Heavily pruned Weeping Yaupon Holly tree

Tree-form Burford Holly

Winter berries of American Holly

Hollies have been the subject of extensive hybridizing both by scientists and by nature. The results are enough introductions with excellent characteristics to choke an elephant. Most of these are considered shrubs, but there are a few true tree forms, and many that can go either way.

Holly berries are a prize part of winter landscapes and the larger and more numerous, the better they show. Some hollies are said to have alternate-year, heavy berry production, because the berries often remain on the plants until after flowering, which reduces their ability to set fruit. But the hollies in my rural landscape don't have this problem because birds feast on the fruit most of the winter. Cedar waxwings often come through in the early winter and gorge themselves on their way south, then stop again on the way north in the spring, leaving precious few berries to hinder fruit set for the coming year.

Hollies usually have male and female flowers on separate plants; thus only female plants produce berries and then only if a male holly plant is near enough for pollination. Fortunately for most homeowners, holly flowers are wind- and insect-pollinated, allowing pollen to come from quite some distances. Some species of holly have a few male flowers (about one in ten) along with the females, and can pollinate themselves. The name for this condition is *polygamodioecious.* Can you believe such a name, much less pronounce it?

Over the years I have been contacted by disappointed gardeners who bemoan their hollies' lack of berries. The answer seems simple – plant a male holly nearby. But nothing is ever that simple, since only better and more specialized nurseries carry male hollies. If you want berries, keep searching for a male plant.

Holly pollination is more of a problem in large subdivisions where almost all naturally growing plants have been bulldozed away. Without mature wooded areas close to your home, wind and insects have no place to pick up pollen and bring it to your holly plant's flowers.

American Holly
Ilex opaca

HEIGHT: 40 feet or more.
HABIT: Tightly pyramidal and occasionally conical with a width about 1/3 of the height.
GROWTH RATE: Listed as slow, but I have seen plants growing at a medium rate.
BEST USE: Lawn specimen.
LEAVES: Dark green and leathery with needlelike spines.
BERRIES: Bright red and very noticeable.
INSECTS AND DISEASES: Holly leaf miner and leaf spots may be present but seldom to the point that spraying a large tree is necessary.

The native American Holly grows well throughout the South from upper Virginia to Florida. Once established, it grows easily with little care and, despite its rather slow growth, soon becomes an outstanding plant in the landscape. American Holly is primarily

An American Holly tree used in a small area

either a male or female plant. Avoid buying a seedling plant or digging one from your woods, unless you have seen enough berries to prove it is a female plant. Also male plants are seldom as attractive as female plants. Sounds like the human race, doesn't it?

An old mature American Holly is a magnificent tree as it stands tall like an inverted cone with bright red berries nestled against its dark green leaves. I have such a tree growing near my house and am always delighted at the compliments it receives. We particularly enjoy it when brightly colored birds are feasting on its berries during the winter.

Though mine is in a perfect spot according to our landscape design, it sure is the devil in disguise when we try to work the flower beds underneath and near by. Fallen American Holly leaves are rigid and tough enough to elicit a hideous cry of pain when you grab them up by mistake barehanded. Plant one where your design calls for a beautiful evergreen tree with bright red berries, but always wear thick gloves when working underneath.

Cultivars

Hundreds of American Holly cultivars have been introduced, though few are widely sold. I strongly recommend using a female cultivar that will set large numbers of berries. My beautiful tree is *Ilex opaca 'Croonenburg'*, which not only has excellent form but is polygamodioecious (there's that word again) and sets berries well.

Foster Holly
Ilex x attenuata 'Fosteri'

HEIGHT: 15 to 25 feet.
HABIT: Inverted narrow cone-shape.
GROWTH RATE: Medium.
BEST USE: Small specimen tree in restricted places.
LEAVES: Small, dark green with spines.
PLANTING RANGE: Throughout the South.

Foster Holly makes an extremely attractive small tree, ideal for restricted places where few other trees will grow without butchering. Its gray bark is a beautiful contrast to its tight head of dark green leaves, especially when filled with red berries.

I have observed more and more Foster Holly being

Tree-form Foster Holly

trained into a tree, though you may not find it in nurseries specializing in smaller plants. You can train it yourself, though. Just purchase a small one with a single trunk, then remove all the lower limbs. Continue removing its lower limbs until it reaches the height you want the head to begin, usually above your own head, which allows easy working in flower beds or borders underneath.

Savannah Holly
Ilex x attenuata 'Savannah'

HEIGHT: 30 feet.
HABIT: Loose pyramid.
GROWTH RATE: Medium to fast.
BEST USE: Tall screens as a large shrub or tall tree over lower-growing shrubs.
LEAF COLOR: May be light green in the summer if not well-fertilized.
BERRIES: Large for a holly, very bright red.
RANGE: Grows well in the Deep South. It can take below zero temperatures in the upper South.

I have been particularly fond of Savannah Holly ever since I planted a row soon after they were widely grown

Savannah Holly produces many beautiful berries even when young.

by nurserymen. Their purpose was to screen my vegetable garden from the house, which doesn't speak too well of how attractive I keep my vegetable garden. Fortunately, I planted them 10 feet apart rather than the 6 feet recommended at the time, allowing them to grow ultimately into beautiful berry-filled trees.

After they were growing for a year, I noticed that one was an East Palatka Holly rather than a Savannah Holly. East Palatka was the more highly touted of the two, so I left it alone. Over the years, I have become more and more convinced that Savannah Holly is far superior to East Palatka, with its looser, less refined form. Horticulturists and landscape designers have argued the point, but I have now seen too many East Palatka Holly plantings to be swayed from my original opinion.

Their argument is that East Palatka Holly has darker green foliage and therefore is more attractive. Mine is that good foliage on a sprangly plant hardly justifies planting it, especially when a little fertilizer will keep a much better plant almost as green.

Yaupon Holly
Ilex vomitoria

HEIGHT: 15 feet or more.
HABIT: Loose when young, more regular when older. Makes excellent single or multitrunk trees.
GROWTH RATE: Fast.
BEST USE: Small specimen tree or grouping.
BARK: Extremely attractive silvery-gray, very striking when grown as a tree.
LEAVES: Small, dark green with no spines, somewhat similar to boxleaf holly, *Ilex crenata*.
FRUIT: Translucent red berries, some of the most attractive of all hollies.

Yaupon Holly is well-known for its many low-growing cultivars, and is becoming better known as a tree. A quick view of a group of older Yaupon Holly trees in the churchyard of All Saints' Episcopal Church in downtown Atlanta will convince you of its beauty and make you want it in your landscape.

Nurseries may have tree-form Yaupon Hollies on occasion, but if you can't find one, choose an upright container-grown plant with a dominant trunk and make your own the same way as described above in the section on Foster Holly.

Be sure to choose only upright-growing forms, since the more common shrub types cannot be successfully trained as trees.

Cultivars

There are a number of excellent cultivars of Yaupon Holly that make excellent trees. Most are noted for berries that may be larger and more plentiful than the species. There are also weeping forms that make delightful trees with branches weeping to the ground. These are generally smaller-growing than the species but can have a definite weeping-tree effect.

Natural form of Weeping Yaupon Holly

Again I caution you not to buy a cultivar like Schillings, which is a dwarf mound plant.

I was very pleasantly surprised to find an upright-growing cultivar named 'Hoskins Shadow'. When I saw its name and found out that it was discovered by my late friend Hoskins Shadow, I knew it must be good. Hoskins Shadow introduced Cherokee Chief Dogwood, the finest of the red dogwood cultivars, and many other exceptional plants.

Hoskins Shadow Holly has exceptionally dark green leaves, red berries, and a thick form that's great for developing into a tree.

A monster Horse Chestnut at Kilfane House, County Kilkenny, Ireland shows how large and beautiful a 250-year-old tree can be.

Horse Chestnut and Buckeye
Aesculus sp.

Several Aesculus species are native in the South, but they are a far cry from the magnificent European Horse Chestnut, *Aesculus hippocastanum*, and the Ohio Buckeye, *Aesculus glabra*, both of which do poorly in all but the upper South. What a pity, since they are some of the showiest shade trees during their blossoming time in the late spring.

Our native Buckeyes, *Aesculus parviflora* and *Aesculus pavia*, inhabit wooded areas all over the South, but few nurserymen offer them for sale, which restricts their landscape use. I have native colonies of *Aesculus pavia* in my woods at Sweet Apple and have easily started new plants from its buckeyes. Its blossoms are not as large nor as full as those of the European Horse Chestnut, but they are a delightful sight dotting Southern forests in the spring.

Bottlebrush Buckeye, *Aesculus parviflora*, grows as a large shrub rather than a tree and thus belongs in a different discussion from this one.

Common Horse Chestnut, European Horse Chestnut

Aesculus hippocastanum

HEIGHT: 50-plus feet.

HABIT: Broad rounded head, often as wide as tall.

GROWTH RATE: Medium.

BEST USE: In large lawns and other open areas. Not suitable except possibly in northern Virginia, West Virginia, and Kentucky.

LEAF COLOR: Light green opening but dark green when fully expanded.

FALL COLOR: Insignificant.

FLOWERS: Tight panicles of many creamy-white flowers with blotches of color. Each panicle stands upright.

European Horse Chestnuts are not widely adapted to the heat and weather of most of the South, except in Kentucky, West Virginia, and upper Virginia. My first introduction to this magnificent tree was when I was a student many years ago at Cornell University, where huge specimens grew with ease. I miss seeing them blooming here at Sweet Apple and have tried and tried to grow one into a large tree, but with no success.

The largest European Horse Chestnut I have ever seen is at Kilfane House, County Kilkenny, Ireland, which was noted in *Ripley's Believe It or Not* in the 1930s. It is over 150 feet wide and more than 200 years old, which means it was a large tree when Andrew Jackson beat the English at the Battle of New Orleans and may have sprouted about the time our Constitution was written. I was given several horse chestnuts, called conkers in Ireland, from the tree, one of which germinated and is limping along at Sweet Apple, looking pretty sad and homesick in our heat and humidity. I keep hoping that age and cooler summers will bring happiness and prosperity to my little Irish friend.

If you are in London at the end of May, stroll through Hyde Park, especially the part along Kensington Road near the Albert Memorial, where rows of Horse Chestnuts are in bloom, including the red form. It is a sight you will always remember, and if you become too envious, remember you seldom see huge *Magnolia grandiflora* specimens like we have here in the South. I believe Nature gives and takes away, so in most of the South we must be satisfied with our own magnificent native trees.

Horse Chestnut flowers

Still, I do envy those Southerners who live in the upper elevations like in Asheville and the Shenandoah Valley of Virginia, where Horse Chestnuts may grow. In the meantime, those of us in the piedmont and coastal plains have to be content with our native Buckeyes, the diminutive relatives of the Horse Chestnuts of Ireland, England, and the northern United States.

Related Species

Red Horse Chestnut
Aesculus x carnea

One of my first experiences in the nursery business was when Nelson Crist introduced me to a Red Horse Chestnut in Atlanta's Piedmont Park. Nelson had watched it being planted when he worked for the city parks department as a landscape architect in the 1920s. The tree bore little resemblance to the ones I had seen in the northeast when I was in college. It was much smaller and not nearly as broad, and acted as unhappy with Southern heat as I was with northern cold. But its blooms were as beautiful as any I had ever seen, though of course not as plentiful as those in happier circumstances. Unfortunately, during times of neglect by the city parks department, it died. The largest and most beautiful I have ever seen were in London growing along with the European Horse Chestnuts mentioned above.

After that trip to London when Betsy and I spent happy hours strolling through Hyde Park, I was determined to plant one and succeed as well as Nelson's tree in Piedmont Park. I spotted one at my

Red Horse Chestnut flowers

friend Glenn Dorsey's nursery, which I grabbed hold of and planted at Sweet Apple. The best I can say is that it is living, expanding slightly in breadth, and inching upward each year. It had five nice blossoms during the spring of 2000 and several conkers, which the squirrels beat me to.

Red Horse Chestnut is not for every homeowner since it is such a challenge to grow well. But if you try and are rewarded with blossoms, it's worth the effort.

Ohio Buckeye
Aesculus glabra

I mention Ohio Buckeye only because it is so well known and can often be seen in areas of the South near the Ohio River. My Ohio relatives praised them as if there was no tree so fine. I wasn't convinced, though I did appreciate the real honest-to-goodness buckeyes they brought when visiting us. I am glad I didn't know that the National Champion is said to be in Liberty, Kentucky, because I might have been unable to resist sharing that piece of information.

Ohio Buckeye is not nearly as impressive a tree as the European Horse Chestnut, so you lucky gardeners in the upper South who can grow Horse Chestnuts should use the faraway import rather than the one from nearby.

Red Buckeye
Aesculus pavia

HEIGHT: 25 feet or more.
HABIT: Round-headed, often with multiple trunks.
GROWTH RATE: Medium.
BEST USE: Specimens in open woods, shaded gardens, and other lightly shaded, moist areas.
LEAF COLOR: Dark green.
FALL COLOR: Yellow but not significant.
FLOWERS: Most often light red open clusters, though occasionally native colonies may have plants with yellow flowers.
FRUIT: Contains two buckeyes.

Our woods at Sweet Apple as well as many others in the area have colonies of Red Buckeye, some of which have been here since before we arrived over 30 years ago. Others have sprouted from fallen buckeyes and are now reaching the size of our original ones. Their May blos-

Red Buckeye is seen in wooded areas throughout the South.

A Red Buckeye rescued from a bulldozer now growing well in a garden

soms come after our colonies of native azaleas have finished. Most of our Red Buckeye flowers are more rose-colored than bright red but still quite showy. We also have one colony with yellow flowers. Only a few of our trees have grown more than 12 feet tall, most being slightly above head-high. Since all are in heavily wooded areas, their form is quite open, bordering on sprangly.

One of the more beautiful specimens I know was rescued from bulldozers working on a highway project by my friend Judge James Hancock in Mountain

Brook, Alabama. He planted the doomed orphan by his drive, where it has grown for a number of years until it has become a fixture in his landscape, especially when the tighter-than-normal, head-high tree produces large numbers of flowers each spring.

To appreciate Red Buckeye, you have to forget about the Red Horse Chestnuts, or you will be terribly disappointed. Consider it as a wonderful native plant that adds late spring color to woods and shady places in the landscape.

Red Buckeye flowers

Mature fastigiate form of European Hornbeam

Hornbeam, Ironwood

Carpinus sp.

Hornbeams are not well-known trees of the landscape even though the American Hornbeam, *Carpinus caroliniana*, is often found in Southern forests. My son Chris discovered the Georgia State Champion American Hornbeam in a native plant area in Alpharetta, Georgia, raising my interest in the plant. I doubt that it will become a standard in Southern landscapes because of its slow growth, but it is a great tree for estates, parks, and edges of open areas.

The European Hornbeam, *Carpinus betulus*, especially the cultivar 'Fastigiata' is widely grown as a street tree and for screening. Betsy called my attention to a specimen that she saw at an upscale business development in Atlanta and urged me to see it. It is more upright and less spreading than widely planted street trees like Chinese Elm and Japanese Zelkova, which develop much larger heads.

The fastigiate form of European Hornbeam makes an excellent street tree.

Upright Hornbeam
Carpinus betulus 'Fastigiata'

HEIGHT: 30 feet.

HABIT: Tight vase-shaped when young, more upright-oval when older.

GROWTH RATE: Slow.

BEST USE: Formal locations; also good as a street tree but not directly under utility wires.

LEAF COLOR: Dark rich green.

FALL COLOR: Yellow, rather late.

Carpinus betulus 'Fastigiata' is a tight-pyramid form of the European Hornbeam, which is used as a sentinel tree in the landscape or as a street tree. Its upright form keeps limbs out of power lines and prevents regular, and sometimes disastrous, pruning by large trucks knocking the stew out of lower branches.

The smooth gray bark is far more attractive on or near a street than the lacy bark of Chinese Elm. To me, it looks clean and never trashy, which is important in many places in the landscape. Older gray trunks have the look of rippled muscles while keeping their smooth, clean appearance.

Its leaves are richer green than those of Chinese Elm and Japanese Zelkova and about the same size.

Katsura Tree is a newer tree being grown in the South.

Katsura Tree
Cercidiphyllum japonicum

Fall color of Katsura Tree

HEIGHT: 60 feet.

HABIT: Usually pyramid to upright oval, but sometimes broad.

GROWTH RATE: Fast.

BEST USE: Where quick shade is needed or as an outstanding lawn specimen.

LEAF COLOR: Bluish green.

FALL COLOR: Yellow with shades of pink, becoming lightly fragrant as they change color.

My son Chris introduced me to Katsura Tree when he was at Cornell University getting his Masters degree in horticulture. He got some seed from a nursery up there and started growing them here at our place. I must have seen Katsura Tree somewhere, sometime, but paid no attention to it until I saw Chris's young seedlings. I scolded myself for not being more observant when I saw a large one growing on a campus in Virginia. It is, as Chris told me, a magnificent tree that doesn't take forever to become beautiful. When you read that the leaves smell like cotton candy when they begin to color in the fall, don't be skeptical. They do.

Chris was kind enough to add his impressions of Katsura Tree:

"The Katsura Tree is nothing short of magnificent. I first came to know this Asian hardwood shade tree during my years at Cornell. An inspired campus grounds manager had planted about 10 of them 50 years ago in prominent positions around the campus.

What a sight they are! It was always a treat to leave the campus library and gaze up through the gothic arches of stout branches and fluttering blue-green leaves. As an added treat, the leaves change to a yellow/apricot color in the fall and emit the delightful scent of cotton candy. I would often pause on a sidewalk here or there to inhale deeply while the economics students bustled by in oblivion.

The Katsura Tree grows to be a tree 60 to 80 feet tall with a broad oval crown.

Its leaves are situated opposite one another on branches and twigs and are heart-shaped, much like a small version of a redbud leaf. They are a light blue-green and cast a delightful dappled shade. In old age, the bark begins to peel, almost like a Shagbark Hickory, and the trunk becomes a giant mass of thick upward-arching branches.

If the sheer beauty of the Katsura is not enough, consider the fact that it is an extremely adaptable tree. If grown unimpeded in a large grassy area, a Katsura Tree may reach 75 feet tall and 60 feet wide. I have also seen Katsura Trees planted 10 feet from buildings and then conform magically to the contours of walls without growing into them. They will also grow in full sun or part shade exposures.

The Katsura Tree is diocieous, meaning some trees are male and some are female. It has been reported that the different sexes grow in different manners. But I have observed no such difference and have discussed the matter with a Japanese horticulturist who has researched the subject in the forests of Hokkaido, Japan (where they grow wild). His research shows male and female trees grow similarly.

Katsura Trees are relatively new to the South. There are nice specimens growing in wide and varied situations, though, and I can confidently say that the tree is proven in our climate. I have grown numerous Katsura Trees and have found them fully capable of withstanding our harsh summer temperatures in full sun exposures. The key to success is water. Katsura Trees are extremely tough but their root systems are fibrous and susceptible to a Southern drought until their roots grow well into the surrounding soil.

A Katsura Tree should be nursed with consistent irrigation for a year or two after planting. After that, they will be fine. Trees planted in partial shade are not as susceptible to drought in their early years."

A Katsura Tree at the Atlanta Botanical Garden

Fall leaves of Katsura Tree smell like cotton candy.

Little Leaf Linden is beautiful when given ample room to develop.

Linden

Tilia sp.

Two Lindens are found in Southern landscapes. American Linden or Basswood is native to the South and frequently seen in our forests. European Linden is referred to as Little Leaf Linden or Lime Tree and is often used in landscapes where a large tree can be grown.

American Linden grows well but is seldom planted because of its large growth and coarse texture. However, if you are fortunate enough to have one, keep it for sure. The creamy to yellowish flowers have a delightful fragrance and its growth and habit are attractive, though less so than its European kinsman.

A number of new cultivars have been introduced, but I would still recommend the European Linden, *Tilia cordata*, instead.

Linden, Little Leaf Linden, Lime Tree
Tilia cordata

HEIGHT: 60-plus feet.
HABIT: Upright oval.
GROWTH RATE: Medium.
BEST USE: Lawn specimen with plenty of space.
LEAF COLOR: Rich green in the summer.
FALL COLOR: Yellow.
FLOWERS: In June and very fragrant.

My fascination with Little Leaf Linden goes back many years and has waxed and waned ever since. Huge specimens stand in Piedmont Park in Atlanta near where I lived in the 1950s, and they still perfume the whole area each June. I visit these trees on occasion when I need a bit of the past to lift my spirits. Time, storms, and neglect have taken their toll, but the surviving trees are still magnificent. The Piedmont Park Conservancy, now with the responsibility for the park, has planted a number of Little Leaf Linden to continue the heritage. Many of them have now reached 10 feet in height and are developing into beautiful trees.

Pleasant reminders of Nature's regenerative powers can be seen by poking around in the residential areas near these large trees. Every now and then you will see or smell a Little Leaf Linden seedling that has taken on the task of keeping the species alive and well.

I visited a large estate in Ireland that had two rows of Little Leaf Linden flanking a grassy lane. The hundred or so years of pruning kept me from having any idea what they were. I was told they were Lime Trees, a name I was unfamiliar with, but on closer inspection I recognized them as European Lindens. The confusing part was the way the enormous numbers of basal suckers were kept pruned into an interesting green skirt around the base of each tree.

Lindens do sucker rather constantly, something that needs tending in order to prevent a messy-looking tree in your landscape – unless you happen to want a green skirt after a couple of hundred years.

Seedlings as well as cultivars are medium to fast-growing, which makes it a good tree for homes where you don't want to wait until you die to enjoy some results. But the many cultivars on the market should be more trustworthy in uniformity and noteworthy characteristics than seedling trees.

The flowers of Little Leaf Linden are very fragrant.

Black Locust

Robinia pseudoacacia

I mention Black Locust not to recommend it for planting, but to warn you if you find one growing on your property. Over the years, the one I have has become a large, unattractive, messy tree that seeds its ugly little offspring in part of my lawn as well as other hard-to-get-to spots. I should have listened to Betsy, who kept telling me to cut it down. I am not alone in my procrastination, however, because you see them growing in cities, towns, villages, and anywhere else there is a bit of soil.

The only good points I have ever discovered about Black Locust are that its wood makes fabulous long-lasting fence posts, and bees make great honey from its blossoms.

Thornless Honey Locust

Gleditsia triacanthos var. inermis

I list Thornless Honey Locust only to let you know that it isn't a tree for the South and to urge you to run the other way when you see one in a nursery. The nicest way to describe this tree is to say that it is extremely trouble-prone.

The first of the Thornless Honey Locust cultivars, 'Moraine', came on the scene when Mimosa trees started dying from the blight. Many of us hoped that its light airy foliage was a perfect replacement for all the sick and dying mimosas. Its fast growth and similar effect seemed almost too good to be true. As it turned out, it was.

With high hopes we planted a row of Moraine Locust at Lovejoy to give shade to one side of a new garden, then a row of Shademaster Locust on the other. Both grew rapidly for about five years, but as soon as they were tall enough to start providing shade, Spider Mites attacked in droves, denuding both cultivars.

I had long conversations with a grower who insisted that they were fabulous trees, notwithstanding my tales of woe. "Just spray them with a good miticide," was his remedy. Instead, we cut them down.

Unfortunately, our tales of woe were being recited by gardeners all over the South, and our nursery dropped them like a hot potato from our offerings.

The list of insects and diseases on Thornless Honey Locust looks like a small town's telephone book. I can't recall ever seeing as many. I think the chance of finding a blight-resistant Mimosa is far better than finding an insect- and disease-free Thornless Honey Locust.

Magnolia
Magnolia sp.

Our native Magnolia *grandiflora* epitomizes the perfect evergreen tree and is treasured wherever it is grown, yet it is only one of the many fabulous trees found in this genus. All magnolias have interesting blooms, but the oriental magnolias have extraordinary spring flowers on bare branches, while our native magnolias are more noteworthy as shade and specimen trees in the landscape.

I list the oriental and native magnolias separately to prevent confusion over which to grow as a shade tree and which as a flowering tree. I hope the taxonomists, horticulturists, and landscape purists won't fuss too much.

Native Magnolias

For simplicity, I will separate our native magnolias into those with smaller leaves, which are evergreen or semi-evergreen, and those with larger leaves, which are deciduous.

The most noteworthy of all magnolias is Southern Magnolia or Bull Bay, *Magnolia grandiflora*. This evergreen tree has no peer when used properly in the landscape. Its glossy green leaves and large, delightfully fragrant white flowers combine perfectly to provide the definition of a Southern landscape tree.

The Virginia Magnolia has smaller leaves with gray to white backing and much smaller white flowers. Though evergreen in the lower South, Virginia Magnolia sheds most of its leaves in the colder winters of the piedmont, foothills, and mountains. It doesn't have the noble appearance of Southern Magnolia, but should be considered because it offers a different effect than its larger-leaved cousin.

Large-leaved magnolias are found more often in parks, estates, and botanical gardens than in home landscapes. They are "What are those?" trees when seen for the first time. All have attractive blossoms, which unfortunately are muted because they appear after the foliage comes out.

Large-leaved magnolias are seldom found in mass market nurseries or in nursery catalogs even though they are interesting plants. Homeowners are fortunate when they find one growing on their property or stumble across one at a nursery that specializes in rare and unusual plants.

A few outstanding landscape architects use large-leaved native magnolias to create special interest in their clients' gardens. Edward Daugherty of Atlanta has used Bigleaf Magnolia, *Magnolia macrophylla*, very effectively in the restricted confines of the churchyard at All Saints' Episcopal Church in Atlanta.

Evergreen and Semi-Evergreen Native Magnolias

Southern Magnolia, Bull Bay
Magnolia grandiflora

HEIGHT: 50 feet in home landscapes, may grow much larger with ample space.
HABIT: Densely pyramidal with limbs touching the ground. Younger trees are taller than wide but old ones may be almost as wide as tall.
GROWTH RATE: Slow to medium when unattended, but medium fast with fertilizer and water.
BEST USE: Specimen tree in open areas.
LEAF COLOR: Dark green with a lighter underside. Some may have brown undersides.
FLOWER: White and large, approaching 12 inches; very fragrant.

No tree of any kind or class defines a Southern garden better than the Southern Magnolia. The eight-inch-long evergreen leaves are rich glossy green above and vary from rusty brown to light brown on the underside. When properly grown, it has outstanding density, making it appear as a huge impenetrable mound of green. The pure white, delightfully fragrant flowers, which to me smell like lemonade tastes, are eight to 12 inches across and quite noticeable while nestled against the green foliage. A definite plus is the sight of the fall fruit cones as they expel bright red seeds on a tiny silk thread to the delight of birds, especially pileated woodpeckers, which are always a sight to behold when they swoop into a huge magnolia while squawking like mad.

A Southern Magnolia at All Saints' Episcopal Church in Atlanta survives well on a busy street.

Left: *Blossom of Southern Magnolia.* Right: *The fruits of Southern Magnolia attract a wide variety of birds.*

Southern Magnolia is a large-growing tree and should never be planted in confined spaces, where they will grow poorly and awkwardly. Planting too close to a structure is dangerous because their roots can undermine foundations. I have seen plants so close to buildings that their trunks caused damage by expanding against the bricks and mortar.

The most beautiful specimens have limbs to the ground. Some homeowners, who want to mow their lawns up to the trunk, prune off the lower ones. The short-term result is a strange-looking tree, and, long-term, the effort is futile. Head-height limbs eventually grow outward and downward until they fulfill Southern Magnolia's mission of having limbs sweeping the ground – and, in the process, of becoming the most beautiful tree in a Southern landscape.

Southern Magnolia does not shed leaves on a strict schedule, so what do you do about their dead leaves? My solution is to leave them alone as long as they are under the tree and hidden by the outer limbs touching the ground, where they eventually decompose. Rake up and remove only the ones that escape into lawns, flower beds, and shrub plantings.

Before a magnolia starts fulfilling its mission, it may look a bit awkward and sparse. Keep it fertilized and watered until it becomes your best specimen plant. The most beautiful Southern Magnolia specimens are those left alone to grow naturally – and to be envied by all parts of the world where they don't survive.

Southern Magnolia needs acid, porous, and well-drained soil. It does poorly in dry, humus-deficient places where it becomes sparse, bearing little resemblance to the stately tree you want. Southern Magnolia is surface-rooted and should never be planted too deeply. Planting too shallowly is just as bad. Transplanted trees with soil over the top of the ball of earth or three or four inches of the ball of earth above the ground may take years to adjust and start growing well, if they survive at all.

There are all sorts of theories about the best time to plant a Southern Magnolia. I have always felt that early spring planting was best. A good rule is to plant when forsythia blooms. Winter planting results in severe leaf drop, while late planting can be just as bad for container-grown or poorly dug balled-and-burlapped plants. However, large balled-and-burlapped or wire-bound basket plants that have large root systems can be planted later in the spring, if they are set with no more than an inch of the ball above the ground and kept thoroughly watered.

Cultivars

Seedling-grown magnolias may vary tremendously, even when seeds are harvested from isolated trees. As a result, nurserymen have done a great job in developing cloning methods for propagating the most outstanding specimens. Cultivars are now plentiful, allowing you to choose the form best suited to your landscape. Many cultivars are available, at least in grower lists. You can find dwarfs, columnar types, brown-back leaves, small-flowered types, and many others if your local nursery carries them. I have found the two listed below in most nurseries I have visited. However, if you run across a cultivar in your local nursery, be sure you know its characteristics before buying it. A dwarf-growing or tall columnar type may look strange where you want to plant a magnolia.

Column-forming cultivar of Magnolia grandiflora

Bracken's Brown Beauty Magnolia

Bracken's Brown Beauty is one of the best cultivars of Southern Magnolia.

A tight-growing cultivar with smaller leaves and flowers than the species. Leaves are dark green with brown backs, averaging six inches long. The flowers are also smaller than those found on the species, but are dependably produced. I have seen numerous flowers in the late summer, a time when they are sparse on seedling-grown trees.

Bracken's Brown Beauty is a perfect choice for smaller landscapes as well as for screening. One of the most beautiful plantings I have seen was a small formal garden protected on three sides by Bracken's Brown Beauty.

Its eventual height is less than normal seedling-grown trees, probably between 25 and 35 feet, depending on growing conditions. It is said to be more cold-hardy and thus good for the southern highlands.

Little Gem Magnolia

Little Gem is a dwarf cultivar – almost more of a shrub than a tree, even though after many years it may reach 15 or 20 feet in height and about half that in width.

The flowers are small but prolific, blooming well late in the season. A Little Gem is in the center of a small planting at the edge of the parking lot of my photo processor in Atlanta, so I observed it all one summer and fall. Its last flowers were killed by a mid-October frost in 2000.

Little Gem is a far cry from my ideal, a Southern Magnolia standing tall and stately in a large sweep of green lawn. But in the real world, most home lawns are too small to accommodate my ideal. Little Gem is a way to enjoy the beauty of a Southern Magnolia without the space required for the stately ones.

Sweet Bay, Virginia Magnolia
Magnolia virginiana

HEIGHT: 50 feet or more in the wild, but usually less in a landscape.
HABIT: Upright pyramid. May have multiple trunks.
GROWTH RATE: Medium.
BEST USE: Background tree.
LEAF COLOR: Dark green above, silver-gray underneath.
FLOWERS: Creamy white, three inches across. Largest numbers are in the spring, but usually has a few all summer.

Sweet Bay, *Magnolia virginiana*, is a wonderful garden tree when you don't try to compare it with a Southern Magnolia, *Magnolia grandiflora*. Everything about Sweet Bay is diminutive in comparison: it is smaller growing, looser in habit, and has smaller leaves and flowers, yet it is a distinctive tree and can be useful where something different is needed.

The creamy white flowers are about four inches across and quite attractive, though not always numer-

Sweet Bay Magnolia grows well in damp shady places.

The gray back of Sweet Bay leaves is a distinctive feature.

ous, especially in younger trees. They are reported to have a lemony fragrance, but my nose must be bad since I have often been around them and never noticed it.

The leaves are eight inches long when it's growing well in the lower South, but generally somewhat smaller farther north. Still, I have seen them near the coast of North Carolina and Virginia as large as those in the low country of South Carolina and Georgia. The undersides of the leaves are silvery and a delightful sight as they flicker in the wind.

Sweet Bay is described in technical books as semi-evergreen but that depends upon where in the South you live. I have seen no evidence of leaf loss in the lower South, but farther north, the trees are pretty bare in most winters. As far as I am concerned, it is a small matter. A Sweet Bay in the back of a garden is a great plant.

We planted a Sweet Bay along with a Bald Cypress on a stream at our nursery in Atlanta in the 1950s. Both grew fantastically since their feet found plenty of moisture. The Sweet Bay grew at least 25 feet in 20 years, which is above the average growth rate, and about half its ultimate height in a good location. I have seen Virginia Magnolias growing in the wild that were at least 50 feet tall, with leaves at least eight inches long.

Large-Leaf Native Deciduous Magnolias

Bigleaf Magnolia
Magnolia macrophylla

HEIGHT: 30–50 feet, depending on soil conditions.
HABIT: Round in the open, looser in shade.

GROWTH RATE: Medium when young, slower when older.
BEST USE: Specimen tree in large open areas or next to woods.
LEAVES: Extremely large, ranging from 15 inches on trees in poor conditions to 32 inches when trees are growing well.
LEAF COLOR: Bright green above, silver-gray beneath.
FALL COLOR: Yellow but quickly turning tan.

Bigleaf Magnolia, *Magnolia macrophylla*, is reputed to have the largest leaf of any tree in North America. Credit for its identification goes to Andre Michaux, who assigned the name *Magnolia macrophylla*. William Bartram described a similar tree, but most critics believe the tree he saw was the smaller-leaved Fraser Magnolia described below.

I think I shall pass into the next life still mad as a hornet at Georgia Tech for allowing one of the largest and most beautiful specimen Bigleaf Magnolias in Georgia to be killed during grading for their nuclear lab. The tree dwarfed a one-story house on State Street adjacent to the school's campus, and the owner told me

Bigleaf Magnolia

Bigleaf Magnolia leaves may grow 36 inches long.

the tree was a regular stop for arborists and horticulturists who were amazed at discovering a magnificent specimen in such an odd place. The vision still imprinted in my mind is of the rare specimen sitting on a tall pillar of soil with its roots dangling down the side surrounded by bulldozers, those horrible instruments of tree destruction. The companion house was gone, leaving the tree alone and dying.

What that school needs is a good course in botany, so as to temper their technical proficiency with some old-fashion feeling for living things.

Even lesser specimens of *Magnolia macrophylla* are a sight to behold, with their 30-plus-inch leaves adorning rather plain-looking trees. Besides for their size, the leaves are interesting for the two earlike lobes at their base. The mildly fragrant creamy white flowers have unusual purple blotches at the base of each petal. The flowers are larger than those of *Magnolia grandiflora* but less conspicuous, being nestled among the leaves and opening over a shorter period of time.

Bigleaf Magnolia leaves turn a delightful tan in the fall as they fold upward into an interesting boat shape before falling. The dried leaves are prized by flower arrangers, especially for long-lasting dried arrangements.

While trout fishing in North Georgia many years ago, I frequently sighted specimens of Bigleaf Magnolia growing along the Toccoa River and Cooper Creek in Fannin County, as well as near Woody Gap on Georgia State Route 60. The area we now live in, north of Atlanta, is home to a number of fine native colonies of Bigleaf Magnolia. I found two small plants on my property, which undoubtedly sprouted from seeds dropped by the pileated woodpeckers who gorge themselves on the fruit in the fall, then fly away, depositing seeds as they go.

Many years ago a well-known Atlanta attorney, Granger Hansell, lived in Mimosa Hall, a beautiful antebellum house in Roswell, Georgia. He took great interest in preserving a particularly fine colony of Bigleaf Magnolia beside U.S. Route 19 near where it crossed the Chattahoochee River. He labored hard to prevent the widening of the highway, which would decimate the colony. His death and a booming interest in the area removed opposition to the highway's expansion. All that remain are a few scraggly trees. Fortunately, other

Left: *The basal ears of Bigleaf Magnolia.* Middle: *Note the unusual purple blotches at the base of the flower petals.* Right: *Fall color of Bigleaf Magnolia.*

colonies can still be found along a number of creeks in the area.

Most specimens seen in landscapes don't reach the size of the magnificent tree at Georgia Tech. More often they are smaller and more upright with a less-defined head.

Use Bigleaf Magnolia as a specimen tree in open areas or against a tree line. The best specimens result from planting in well-drained soil, high in humus to hold the right amount of moisture, and with a low pH.

Fraser Magnolia
Magnolia fraseri

HEIGHT: Old, solitary, well-grown specimens may reach 50 feet or taller, but most you see will be in the 30-foot-high range.
HABIT: Single trunk plants usually develop a loosely rounded head. Multitrunk clumps are common and have a much looser form.
GROWTH RATE: Slow to medium. Faster when growing well under ideal conditions.
BEST USE: Near wooded areas or as specimen trees for just the right spot to accommodate such an unusual tree.
LEAVES: Usually 18 to 24 inches long, though I have seen them larger on trees growing under ideal conditions.
LEAF COLOR: Bright green above, lighter green underneath.
FALL COLOR: Yellow to tan.
FLOWERS: White, up to 10 inches across, without the purple blotches at the base found on Bigleaf Magnolia blossoms.

Fraser Magnolia is in many respects a smaller version of *Magnolia macrophylla*, with leaves a maximum of only 24 inches long, but with the same interesting lobes at the base. My own personal observation is that Fraser Magnolia is more likely to form a clump than the Bigleaf Magnolia. At least the native Fraser Magnolia colonies back of my boyhood home at Lovejoy did and many I have observed since then. The flowers appear with the leaves and are a bit smaller than those of Bigleaf Magnolia and without the purple blotches at the base of each petal. One report I saw stated that the flowers had a bad odor, something I've never noticed even though I have sniffed the air under a zillion of them. Maybe my nose is thinking about the unusual tree above, rather than a bad odor. It certainly doesn't

have the really obnoxious aroma of the Skunk Magnolia, *Magnolia tripetala*.

Fraser Magnolia's tendency to form a clump gives it extra appeal for spots in the landscape that need something different.

Other Native Deciduous Magnolias

There are a number of other native magnolias that you might run across in woods, parks, or botanical gardens, but seldom in home landscapes. The two described below are quite common in forests of the mid- and upper South and may be growing on your own property.

Cucumber Magnolia or Cucumber Tree
Magnolia acuminata

HEIGHT: 50 feet or taller.
HABIT: Pyramidal when young, round and broad when older.
GROWTH RATE: Rather fast growing when well-tended.
BEST USE: Specimen tree in large open areas where its form can be fully appreciated.
LEAVES: Up to a foot long but usually closer to 10 inches.
LEAF COLOR: Dark green above, light green underneath.
FALL COLOR: Seldom of any interest.

Cucumber Magnolia is an excellent tree for large open areas where you want something different to invite interest and comment from visitors. The leaves are smaller than on Bigleaf, Fraser, and Umbrella Magnolia, as are the flowers. The interesting feature of Cucumber Magnolia is its size, form, and large lateral branches.

Umbrella Magnolia, Skunk Magnolia
Magnolia tripetala

HEIGHT: Most often 20 feet or under, though 30- and 40-foot trees are not uncommon.
HABIT: Upright and loosely branched with whorls of leaves at the top and ends of branches giving an umbrella effect.
GROWTH RATE: Slow to medium.
BEST USE: Background (because of the bad-smelling flowers), but where the unusual umbrella appearance can be duly noted.
LEAVES: Anywhere from 12 to 24 inches long.

LEAF COLOR: Bright green.
FALL COLOR: Unimpressive.
FLOWERS: Creamy white and foul-smelling. Blossoms earlier than *Magnolia macrophylla*.

I have always known this tree as Skunk Magnolia because the flowers have a foul smell that's quite evident when you stand underneath a tree in blossom. The more genteel people I know call it Swamp Magnolia. Though it grows well in rich, moist uplands, the edges of swamps and streams are its more frequent habitats. Strangely, many tree books don't mention the foul smell, which should restrict its use to spots away from human traffic. However, the whorls of large leaves at the top and at the ends of the outer branches make it such an interesting umbrella-like tree that the once-a-year unpleasant aroma seems unimportant.

Magnolia tripetala

Oriental Magnolias

White Bark Magnolia
Magnolia hypoleuca

HEIGHT: 50 feet.
HABIT: Open and loose.
GROWTH RATE: Fast when young.
BEST USE: Edge of wooded areas which are rich with humus, moist and well-drained.
LEAF COLOR: Bright green above, gray-white beneath.
FALL COLOR: Not impressive.

I had only read about *Magnolia hypoleuca* before it caught Chris's eye. He was impressed enough to get some seeds and start a group of young plants at Sweet Apple. The more they develop, the better they look, though we haven't seen any blossoms. I pass on to Chris, our family's *Magnolia hypoleuca* expert, the pleasure of describing it:

White Bark Magnolia is a big-leaved deciduous magnolia native to Japan. It is similar to our native Bigleaf Magnolia and Swamp Magnolia. White Bark Magnolia leaves grow to 12 to 18 inches, and the flowers arrive afterwards. The creamy-white flowers are six to eight inches across and are illuminated by a mass of red stamens in the center. The tree is named for its white/gray bark, which is quite noticeable but not as striking as the common name implies.

I have grown White Bark Magnolias for several years in the South and have found them to do well in our climate. They are fast growers and may add two to three feet a year in partial shade. While they are said to reach 100 feet tall in the forests of Japan, we can reasonably expect a tree to mature at 40 to 50 feet in the South. A White Bark Magnolia's ideal location is at the edge of a lawn with its roots in rich, moist, well-drained soil. The large leaves flutter magnificently in an autumn breeze as they flash their white undersides against a dark green backdrop. The flowers are quite showy.

One word of warning. Watch out for borers when the trees are young.

Oriental Flowering Magnolias

Oriental Magnolias include the beautiful spring-flowering Star Magnolia, Saucer Magnolia, and Lily Magnolia, along with their hybrids and cultivars. All except Star Magnolia are often called Tulip Trees, which should not be confused with Tulip Poplar, *Liriodendron tulipifera*, which is also called Tulip Tree. The general group, Oriental Magnolia, contains a huge number of magnificent cultivars and hybrids seen in landscapes throughout the South. Star Magnolia and its cultivars are mainly tree form while Saucer Magnolia and Lily Magnolia are large shrubby plants that may grow 15 feet or higher and can be trained as trees.

In general, the main problem with early-flowering Oriental Magnolias is the tendency for flower buds to show color and be damaged during February and March in areas of the South prone to springlike warm spells occurring between severe cold waves.

I describe the following species, without mentioning Yulan Magnolia, *Magnolia denudata*, Kobus Magnolia, *Magnolia kobus*, and Loebner Magnolia, *Magnolia x loebneri*, which I hope purists and specialist growers won't fault me for. The omission doesn't mean they should be rejected outright if found in a nursery. However, ask a lot of questions before you plant one in your landscape.

Lily Magnolia
Magnolia liliflora 'Nigra'

Lily Magnolia is more of a shrub than a tree and is more correctly reserved for books on flowering shrubs. However, in South Georgia I have seen old plants of the cultivar 'Nigra' that had assumed a more or less tree form with a head of limbs above an eight- or ten-foot trunk. The result was an attractive spring-flowering tree with large flowers made up of almost purple outer petals with a lighter purple inside.

Magnolia liliflora 'Nigra'

Though Lily Magnolia has many cultivars, 'Nigra' is the one most often grown in the mid-South because its blossoms have the best chance of escaping frost damage. Earlier-flowering Lily Magnolias pop open during late-winter warm periods, then are damaged when an "Arctic Express" roars through. Good specimens are more often found in the lower South where early-flowering cultivars escape the cold-damage problem.

We had a rather large shrub-type 'Nigra' at Lovejoy that was quite a sight when its flowers weren't damaged. No one in my family had much use for purple and purple-pink flowers, but somehow 'Nigra' survived my mother's usual antipathy for its color.

Saucer Magnolia
Magnolia x soulangeana

There are dozens of Saucer Magnolia cultivars on the market. Most must be purchased from specialty nurseries, since few reach mass market and local nurseries in

Flower of Magnolia Liliflora 'Nigra'

Magnolia x soulangeana 'Alexandrina'

the South. We grew the cultivar 'Alexandrina' at Lovejoy, and it is quite common in the mid-South. Its blossoms appear earlier than 'Nigra' and were frequently damaged by frost at Lovejoy, south of Atlanta. However, I pass a magnificent specimen – and a less-frequently damaged plant – on my route out of the Sweet Apple area, north of Atlanta. The blossoms of 'Alexandrina' are more pink-purple than purple, less intense than 'Nigra' and much more to my taste.

Saucer Magnolia, like Lily Magnolia, is more often grown as a large shrub than a tree, though it is handsome as a 15- to 20-foot tree with a rounded head. In flower, it is a spectacular sight. The one I frequently pass has a beautiful tree form.

Star Magnolia
Magnolia stellata

Hurrying across the main quadrangle one spring day during my freshman year at Cornell, I stopped dead in my tracks at the sight of several large white-flowering trees, which I assumed were dogwoods. Since I hadn't started any woody plant material courses, I didn't know any better. They were *Magnolia stellata*, not dogwood, which seldom lives, much less blooms, in the frigid climate of upstate New York. Once I was underneath the trees and saw that they were not dogwoods, I adopted them as a beautiful substitute for my beloved trees at home.

A well-grown Star Magnolia is one of the most beautiful of all spring-flowering trees. Masses of white, lightly fragrant, multipetal (correctly called tepal) flowers cover the branches each spring. Unfortunately, Star Magnolia is a very early bloomer and its flowers are lucky to finish before a hard frost or freeze turns them brown. But the tree is so beautiful that it's worth the wait for another mild year. It may be more of a shrub when small, but it is easily pruned up to make a fine tree, which is my favorite way of seeing it growing.

Those of you in the lower South should have far better success than those of us in the mid-South, where alternating warm-ups and freezes are our nemesis.

Flowers of Star Magnolia

The beautiful Star Magnolia

Cultivars

Star Magnolia has a large number of cultivars, ranging from large white flowers with more flower petals to various shades of pink. The main advantage of planting a cultivar is that their forms are more consistent than from seedling or cutting-grown trees. However, if you live in the mid-South, be sure any cultivar you buy is late-blossoming.

A 40-year-old Acer rubrum, Red Maple, which I planted at Sweet Apple.

Maple
Acer sp.

When people ask "Which is the best shade tree?" or "What is your favorite shade tree?", they're surprised that my response is a blank stare. But how can I answer such a question? Southern Magnolia is a favorite, but so are Ginkgo and Sugar Maple. Dawn Redwood is fantastic, but I also like Bald Cypress. Of course, the only possible answer – "It depends" – is no more helpful than the blank stare.

Trees are my friends, so how can I favor one over another, which would be like taking sides when close friends argue? My best boyhood friend was a Sweet Gum tree, but I'm not sure I would recommend it to a lot of people. It took many years to get over a really severe scolding when I knocked the top out of our young Southern Magnolia. I was devastated when the Sugar Maple we planted and nurtured for 25 years died. Trees have that effect on most gardeners. They last longer and build more memories than almost any other plants in the landscape.

If I had to answer the question on pain of death, I would not choose a single species, but the genus containing maples. I know of no other trees that thrill me as much as they do. Among them you find everything from small-growing Japanese cutleaf red cultivars barely reaching eye level to huge Sugar Maples, *Acer saccharum*, growing 80 feet or more. In between the small and the large maples are other extremely important trees for the Southern landscape. A number of these, like Paperbark Maple, *Acer griseum*, and Trident Maple, *Acer buergerianum*, are not well-known or readily available in nurseries but are worth using whenever you can find them.

Maples provide excellent shade for a home with their heavy leaf populations and compact shape. Like many deciduous trees, they are a blessing, blocking hot sun in the summer and allowing warm sun through their bare limbs in the winter. Even in these days of efficient furnaces and excellent central air conditioning, a well-placed maple will increase the comfort level of a home significantly.

My appreciation for maples comes from personal experience at our country home where we have lived for over 30 years. The previous owners planted Sugar Maple and Red Maple saplings some years before we arrived, and they were both growing well when we moved in. The Red Maple was extraordinary, with its branches weeping to the ground, until it crashed to the ground during the ice storm of January 2000. The Sugar Maple remains a beautiful upright tree.

When we first moved to Sweet Apple, in the days before central air, our western exposure rooms were almost unbearable in the summer, even with individual room units running full speed. I planted three 10-foot-tall maples, one Sugar Maple and two Red Maples, hoping they would grow up and block the afternoon sun. The two Red Maples – now magnificent trees reaching over 40 feet in height and almost the same breadth – have served us well. It took only a few years before our living room was pleasant all year round.

The Sugar Maple died during a severe drought that followed a very wet summer the year before, but the two Red Maples keep getting more beautiful every year.

In areas where a large tree is not warranted, two medium-sized maples, Trident and Paperbark, are excellent through much of the South. Japanese Maples are great in areas that call for trees under 15 feet. Rapid leaf drop in the fall is one of those characteristics that aren't discussed much, but it's important to anyone who rakes his own leaves. Maple leaves drop quickly, an advantage they have over oaks, for example, which seem to drop their leaves from late fall until spring.

Not all maples do well in the South. The fast-growing Silver Maple, *Acer saccharinum*, is prone to so many problems that it is best left standing in the nurseries. The Norway Maples, *Acer platanoides*, are also best left alone, even though you might see 'Crimson King' Norway Maple being sold. Box Elder, *Acer negundo*, native to much of the South, is a trashy tree that seems to pop up in strange places on my property. Box Elder does have some interesting leaf color forms, which

seems to be the reason it is offered for sale, but the tree has so few good qualities that it is best avoided unless you are a plant collector whose curiosity overcomes his better judgment.

A good recommendation is to choose a maple, or for that matter any shade tree, that you have seen do well. The maples listed below, except those I list and then "bad mouth," are tried and proven throughout most of the South.

Japanese Maple
Acer palmatum

HEIGHT: 20–30 feet.
HABIT: Single or multiple trunks, rounded to layered head.
GROWTH RATE: Slow.
BEST USE: Specimen.
LEAF COLOR: Green.
FALL COLOR: Red.

A very old Japanese Maple

Lower branches of the above Japanese Maple

Japan has given us many fine plants, including flowering cherries, camellias, and azaleas, but none finer than Japanese Maples. Within this group are many forms in many sizes, from chest-high dwarfs with finely cut leaves to much larger 30- to 40-foot trees whose leaves have larger lobes. The term *palmate* describes their leaves perfectly. Open your hand and spread your fingers. Most but not all Japanese Maples have three large fingers or lobes in the center and two smaller ones on the sides, just like humans. The species has fingers like a football tackle – big and fat. But many cultivars have fingers like a lady's – small and dainty.

Cultivars

Most Japanese Maples you find in nurseries are cultivars, so decide the form, leaf color, and leaf dissection you want before buying a plant. Remember that the more colored the leaves and the more widely they are dissected, the slower and smaller they grow. Each type has a place in the landscape, and you don't want to end up with a bushy plant when you had a small tree in mind.

Bloodgood Japanese Maple

There are hundreds of cultivars being grown, so it is impossible to list them all or for you to find many of them in a retail nursery. Larger-growing, green-leaved cultivars also have a great place in the landscape, though nowadays they seem to be scarce as hen's teeth. Most you find are red-leaved and deeply dissected.

Following is a broad sample of the different types you may find:

Non-Dissected Leaf Types (more like the fingers of a football player than a lady)

Burgundy Lace Japanese Maple

'Bloodgood': I have known this cultivar for many years and am always impressed with its growth and rich red-purple leaf color. An excellent choice for the upper South and the mountains since it is cold-hardy. It matures at 15 to 20 feet with a rounded head in light shade but is more layered and has less color in deeper shade.

'Burgundy Lace': This is another well-known cultivar that has been around for a long time. It is smaller-growing than 'Bloodgood', seldom reaching 12 feet and usually smaller than that. The lobes are finer and cut closer to the leaf stem (petiole) than with 'Bloodgood'. It doesn't hold its rich summer color as well as 'Bloodgood', but people choose it for its finer leaf structure. It should color better in the upper South and the mountains, which are not so hot during the summer.

Cut Leaf Japanese Maple

Dissected Types (deeply cut narrow lobes – more like a lady's fingers, though there may be seven or nine)

Note: Be careful when choosing a dissected leaf Japanese Maple. Some are extremely dwarf (less than head high), and some are yellow or bronze yellow in the summer, turning red in the fall. Others may be taller-growing (never as tall as the species) and red during the summer.

Cut Leaf Japanese Maple

Acer palmatum dissectum atropurpureum may grow 12 feet in height and almost as broad over many years, but count on eight feet in most locations. Dark purple foliage in the summer, turning more orange in the fall.

Here I leave you to your own devices. Every time I find a cultivar I like, no one seems to have it. Instead there is always a better one, or so the salesman says.

Yellow Cut Leaf Japanese Maple

A typical plant of the species has green leaves and grows as wide as tall, while selected cultivars may have red leaves and grow smaller. Other cultivars vary in size, leaf color, and leaf dissection. I have seen large, beautiful Japanese Maples at Callaway Gardens in Pine Mountain, Georgia, with green leaves and single trunks. I found a very large tree, which was wider than tall, in the Ansley Park area of mid-town Atlanta. Its huge limbs arose from its trunk near to the ground. Its size and the age of the house next to it suggest that it may have been growing since the 1920s when the area was developed. For many years, I have observed a beautiful dissected-leaf form at a well-landscaped funeral home not far away. It represents the other end of the size spectrum, never reaching head-height.

Trying to define Japanese Maples is like defining snow flakes – all have common characteristics but every one is a bit different. This is a good news, bad news story. The good news is that you can plant the same species for many different effects in the landscape. The bad news is the difficulty in identifying and purchasing the best one. Within the species, *Acer palmatum*, are botanical varieties, like *Acer palmatum atropurpureum* and *Acer palmatum dissectum*, plus hundreds of cultivars. Choose the best Japanese Maple to plant by asking your nurseryman or landscaper many questions, then decide which to buy from those available.

Plant Japanese Maples in the late winter or early spring before the leaves expand. You can plant balled-and-burlapped and container-grown plants later, but growth the first several summers may be less than if you had planted earlier. You can plant later only if you promise faithfully to water until the plant is well-established.

Carefully choose the location for your Japanese Maple. They do best in light to moderate shade, especially those with red or purple leaves that usually turn green in heavy shade. They will take full sun if growing where their roots can reach moist soil during the heat of summer. In the upper South, they do better when protected from cold wind in the spring as their leaves start putting out.

Japanese Maple does best in high humus soil, which you will probably have to provide when you plant them, since so much of the South has humus-deficient soil. Once a tree is growing well, it seems to thrive on its own, though fertilizer and water keep them growing well when it is dry.

Norway Maple
Acer platanoides

HEIGHT: 40-plus feet.
HABIT: Rounded head two-thirds as wide as tall.
GROWTH RATE: Medium.
BEST USE: Specimen plant in cool locations. Best used in the upper South and cool mountain areas.
LEAF COLOR: Dark green during the summer.
FALL COLOR: Bright yellow.

Norway Maple, including its cultivars, is not for the South. It does poorly in our hot summers and long growing seasons. I have seen nice specimens in the mountains, but close by were even better specimens of Sugar Maple.

The main reason for mentioning Norway Maple in a discussion of Southern trees is the cultivar 'Crimson King', which you may see and wonder about. Crimson King Maple seems to pop up in nurseries where it is sold, especially in full leaf, as a fabulous specimen tree. It is, if you live above Washington, D.C.

Crimson King Maple struggles in the mid- and lower South.

Leaves of Crimson King Maple

At the insistence of a tree grower with an offer of a free tree, we planted one at our nursery in Atlanta in the early 1950s in an area near a Red Maple. By the time we sold the company in 1976, the Red Maple was huge and the Crimson King Maple was still struggling along at less than a third the Red Maple's size. The Crimson King Maple did have beautiful foliage when the leaves first reached full-size in the spring, but by mid-summer, they were dull and ratty-looking. There were two camps on our staff: those who wanted to get rid of it and those who wanted to keep it as an example of how poorly it grew, since we had so many inquiries from customers who read about its fine qualities in northern publications. We kept it, at least until 1977, when I was no longer involved in the company.

The saga of Crimson King continues in the mid-South. I discovered several at the edge of a parking lot in front of a small business compound near where I live. Even though the other trees in the same planting were outgrowing them, they had remarkably nice foliage all during the summer of 2000.

But I haven't changed my opinion: plant some other tree unless you live in really cool areas in the South, and enjoy Crimson King Maple as well as other Norway Maples when driving above Washington, D.C.

Paperbark Maple
Acer griseum

HEIGHT: 20-plus feet.
HABIT: Rounded.
GROWTH RATE: Slow.
BEST USE: Where an outstanding small tree is needed.

Paperbark Maple, a beautiful under-used tree

Paperbark Maple's distinctive peeling bark

LEAVES: Trifoliate with three coarsely toothed leaflets.
LEAF COLOR: Rich green all summer.
FALL COLOR: Red.
BARK: Its exfoliating bark reveals red areas. Young twigs are generally a rich red.

Paperbark Maple has been around since the early 1900s when it was brought from China. I think it must have been placed in a closet, at least as far as the South

Left: Red Maple gives some of the first colors of spring. Middle: Red Maple gives excellent shade. Right: Red Maple changing color.

is concerned, since it was almost unknown here when I wrote the tree section of *Gardening in the South: Trees, Shrubs, and Lawns* in 1985. I opened my eyes when Chris began to sing its praises. When giving a talk at a symposium held at the Georgia Botanical Garden in Athens, Georgia, I spotted a beautiful specimen that made me want to shut up and go sit under it. I hope those at the symposium didn't feel the same way – at least they seemed attentive.

Acer griseum is like Natchez Crape Myrtle when you first see one; your eye goes immediately to the red areas of its trunk, overlooking the other fine characteristics of the tree. It is such an interesting and distinctive tree that, since being introduced to it, I look at landscapes of all sizes and shapes and think how beautiful an *Acer griseum* would be in this or that spot.

Like Japanese Maple, it may grow slowly, but makes up for it by being a lovely tree at whatever age.

Red Maple
Acer rubrum

HEIGHT: 60-plus feet.
HABIT: Rounded.
GROWTH RATE: Medium.
BEST USE: Where a large shade tree is needed.
LEAF COLOR: Rich green on top and lighter gray-green underneath with a red petiole (leaf stem).
FALL COLOR: Variable from yellow to red, depending on the individual seedling or the cultivar.
INSECTS AND DISEASES: Nothing major that seems to damage the tree or make it unsightly. Leaf spots may appear in some years, but don't worry about them — they are virtually harmless and seldom detract from the looks or from Red Maple's vigor.

Red Maple Cultivars

October Glory Red Maple

Nurserymen have been active in choosing dozens of new cultivars of *Acer rubrum*. I haven't seen them all, but I've been extremely impressed with October Glory and Red Sunset, especially October Glory. I have seen them successfully grown in several mall and shopping center parking lots where most trees suffer greatly. I would certainly choose October Glory or even Red Sunset if I were planting a Red Maple in front of my house now instead of 30 years ago.

October Glory Maple
Acer rubrum 'October Glory'

HEIGHT: 40-plus feet.
HABIT: Rounded, two-thirds as wide as tall.
GROWTH RATE: Medium.
FALL COLOR: Orange-red to red.

Red Sunset Maple
Acer rubrum 'Red Sunset'

HEIGHT: 40-plus feet.
HABIT: Rounded, two-thirds as wide as tall.
GROWTH RATE: Medium.
FALL COLOR: Orange-red.

October Glory Red Maple

I am very partial to this native Southern tree. It may not grow as rapidly as a Silver Maple, Catalpa, or Tree of Heaven, but it grows fast enough to perform its role quickly as an excellent shade tree. Its head is dense, providing excellent shade as well as good sun blockage. Since Red Maples grow large, when you are setting out young nursery-grown trees, plant them farther from a structure than you think you should (I suggest at least 30 feet). Even then you may eventually have to remove some limbs that might grow over your house.

Red Maple is especially attractive when its red blossoms come out in late winter or early spring, giving a preview of the bright flowers soon to come on other spring-flowering trees.

Silver Maple
Acer saccharinum

HEIGHT: 50-plus feet.
HABIT: Oval to round, two-thirds as wide as tall.
GROWTH RATE: Fast.
LEAF COLOR: Medium green with a pale gray underside.
FALL COLOR: Not much color in most of the South, but what there is is a dull yellow.

PROBLEMS: Weak wood, resulting from its rapid growth and inability to perform well in our heat, along with susceptibility to insects and diseases.

Silver Maple, a tree to be avoided

Michael Dirr, in his excellent book *Manual of Woody Landscape Plants,* lists an enormous number of pest problems for this tree. My own experience is the prevalence of leaf spots by mid-summer and the appearance of Maple phenacoccus, which hang on the undersides of the foliage, being hideously unsightly while dripping a sticky material on everything underneath. Cottony Maple Scale is also a serious problem, especially when Silver Maples are used in parking lots and hot commercial areas.

As far as I am concerned, Silver Maples in the South have no redeeming value. I have seen a few in the mountains that might be passable, but I always think, why bother? There are too many other maples – and other hardwood trees – that are much better. I have never heard any argument on its behalf except that it grows fast. But its rapid growth produces weak wood and a less appealing and useful form.

Sugar Maple
Acer saccharum

HEIGHT: 60-plus feet.

HABIT: Oval to round, two-thirds as wide as tall.

GROWTH RATE: Slow.

BEST USE: Lawns and open areas where it grows unhindered.

LEAF COLOR: Rich green.

FALL COLOR: Flame orange-red.

DISEASES: Several leaf spot diseases occasionally show up but never seem to be serious enough to effect the beauty of the tree or for you to worry about.

OTHER PROBLEMS: Sugar Maple is not as drought tolerant as Red Maple and should not be planted in poor soil, dry spots, or where the drainage is bad.

I am convinced that this tree rivals the American Chestnut, which has been almost completely destroyed by blight, as the most magnificent of all hardwood trees in the Eastern United States. My early memories of spreading Chestnut trees, enhanced by the poem I learned as a tenth grader, and my love for huge Live Oaks along the Southern coast are both powerful, but a magnificent Sugar Maple, especially when it is a blaze of color in the fall, is what dwells in my mind when I think of a perfect shade tree.

Sugar Maple is best used in the Southern piedmont

Sugar Maple is a magnificent tree.

Cultivars

Writing about Sugar Maple cultivars is like opening a bag of marbles at the wrong end and watching them come rolling out. You see one new Sugar Maple cultivar listed, then another, and another until the bag is finally empty.

Most cultivars are from northern nurserymen, which makes them suspect until proven in the South. However, an *Acer saccharum 'Legacy'* has grown into a beautiful tree in a cavernlike part of downtown Atlanta, thanks to the efforts of "Trees Atlanta," a fabulous organization helping to reforest Atlanta's ever-declining tree population. A large planting at a high school near me has all the characteristics of Legacy Maple, but none of the staff can verify it. The beauty of these young trees is their tight oval heads, rich dark-green leaves all summer, and orange-red fall color. After they survived less-than-ideal planting methods for a couple of years, they finally started growing well and have survived and expanded during our extremely dry summers of 1998, 1999, and 2000.

Legacy Sugar Maple

or Appalachians and not the sandy soils of the coastal plains, though I have seen good specimens below Macon, Georgia. When you plant a Sugar Maple, give it plenty of room to show off its magnificent rounded head filled with rich green foliage. It doesn't do as well in dry, red clay soil, so plant where it can get plenty of moisture but where it is never sticky or soggy.

I could wax eloquent for pages about this wonderful tree and still not praise it enough, but I will close by saying that it should be the first tree you consider planting in a Southern landscape, except in the coastal plains.

Trident Maple
Acer buergerianum

HEIGHT: 30-plus feet.
HABIT: Oval to round.
GROWTH RATE: Slow.
BEST USE: Specimen tree or for shade where a small tree is required.

LEAF COLOR: Spring foliage may be bronze to purple while summer color is deep green.
FALL COLOR: From yellow to red or purple.

I am constantly looking for new trees for special locations, so I was thrilled at the sight of a Trident Maple growing in a planting area at the entrance to an apartment complex in Atlanta. What a relief from the ubiquitous Bradford Pears.

This is a relatively new tree to me, though a large tree I had been told many years ago was a Sycamore Maple seems to be a very large Trident Maple. Most of us tend to use a shade tree that grows far too large for its alloted place in the landscape. But the relatively small Trident Maple is a good choice for restricted spaces, and its roots aren't likely to push up driveways or undermine the foundation of homes.

The bark on older trees flakes gray to orange, making it an attractive sight especially in the winter. The only possible negative is that trees that produce large numbers of seed may turn light green while the seed mature.

Mimosa
Albizia julibrissin

HEIGHT: 30 feet.

HABIT: Broad, sometimes flattened, head. Limbs arch upward and outward without looking like a vase.

GROWTH RATE: Fast.

BEST USE: Avoid planting until blight-resistant cultivars are found.

LEAF COLOR: Light green.

FALL COLOR: Insignificant.

FLOWERS: A delightful pink powder puff.

ORIGIN: From China to the Middle-East.

Mimosa causes much comment and many questions when it blooms each year. The powder-puff pink flowers are great to tickle childrens' noses with, something all of us over sixty used to do. Its upward and outward arching form is perfect for shading a garden. The fine one in our garden when I was growing up performed this task very well, until the wilt slowly killed the tree.

You seldom see one in a garden any longer, but they are plentiful along highways, which is a tribute to their tenacity and staying power. The vascular wilt disease first struck this native of northern India and Nepal in the fifties and eventually kills almost every tree. Not to be done in by this arch enemy, younger trees still produce enormous numbers of seed and dying trees sucker at the bottom. These two strategies perpetuate the colonies and keep our roadsides and natural areas filled with their delightful flowers during the summer.

The best we can hope for is a breakthrough in science or the discovery of a truly immune tree from which trees for the garden can be propagated. In the meantime, don't consider planting a Mimosa until blight-resistant cultivars are found. If you have one, cherish it and keep your fingers crossed. Maybe it will survive as long as you live there.

Mimosa flowers

White Mulberry trees at Colonial Williamsburg

Mulberry

Morus sp.

I have often been asked about purchasing mulberry trees to plant in the landscape. I suspect that most of the interest comes when a child reads an American history text about bringing mulberries and silk worms from China to the Southern colonies for producing silk – a plan that obviously failed. When you visit Colonial Williamsburg, you will see ancient, living relics of those unsuccessful efforts.

The project failed but the imported mulberries thrived, liked us, and are widespread and quite common throughout much of the South. One seems to like a bank on my property and has survived my determined effort to get rid of it by cutting it down over and over. If nothing else, they are persistent. Better specimens are found in Europe than here.

On the other hand, the native American Mulberry is a handsome tree with dark green foliage. I seldom see one in a nursery because few people know it well enough to want it in their landscape.

White Mulberry, Common Mulberry
Morus alba

HEIGHT: 40 feet or more.
HABIT: Tight, rounded head that may become messy looking.
GROWTH RATE: Fast.
BEST USE: Plant collections; otherwise forget it.
LEAF COLOR: Light green.
FALL COLOR: Yellow, but more often they just turn brown.

The only people who should be interested in this historical tree are historians, plant collectors, and bird lovers. Otherwise, leave it alone. It has no redeeming value except for its place as an oddity of early American agriculture. The fact that birds delight in its unusual-looking fruit might keep a bird lover from cutting it down. But as for me, I prefer to cut it off at the ground, then plant a better tree that birds also like . . . or put up a bird feeder.

Red Mulberry
Morus rubra

HEIGHT: 35 feet or more.
HABIT: Open head that may spread as wide as the tree is tall. I have often seen trees irregularly upright.
GROWTH RATE: Medium.
BEST USE: Specimen tree.
LEAF COLOR: Dark green.
FALL COLOR: Yellow.
FRUIT: One-inch-long fruits are first red, then turn dark purple.

Red Mulberry is a far cry from the imported White Mulberry, which is more of a weed than a desirable tree. Red Mulberry is a handsome tree with dark green foliage and good upright form, but it's seldom used in the landscape and therefore is hard to find in a retail nursery. It has dark green leaves, yellow fall color and grows to a medium height of about 35 or 40 feet with a nice wide head. Larger specimens to 70 feet are mentioned in literature, but the largest I have seen are about half that.

Its main attraction is the red to purple inch-long fruits that always provoke comments when they are ripe. They are said to be edible, but I haven't ever tried them since they were gathered for hog food when I was young – not a very good selling point, as far as I am concerned.

Birds do like Red Mulberry fruits and gather in droves to enjoy them, a definite plus unless the limbs are over a driveway or walk.

Most are found in the wild where it is moist but well-drained, though I have seen them growing quite well in some drier and more impossible places.

The native Red Mulberry

Red Mulberry fruits

This Live Oak known as the Middleton Oak is growing at Middleton Place, Charleston, South Carolina, and is estimated to be between 800 and 900 years old. Be sure to visit it when you are in the area. It is magnificent! Picture courtesy of Middleton Place.

Oak

Quercus sp.

The word *oak* evokes adjectives like mighty or majestic. Since many survive for centuries with dignity and grace, a centennial oak fills us with the hope that we can be as strong and useful as they are when age creeps up on us.

The South is filled with many different kinds of oaks. Some are fantastic, some are good, and some are useless. "Mighty" and "majestic" are perfect descriptions of a 300-year-old White Oak. Live Oaks are almost the definition of the coastal South from New Orleans to Charleston, where these trees envelop streets with their limbs like a mother holds a baby. Some oaks like Willow Oak and Water Oak are vastly overused because they grow faster than the longer-lived and stronger White Oak, Red Oak, and Live Oak. Keep an old mature Water Oak or Willow Oak if you already have one (and chances are that you do if you live in an older neighborhood), but why choose to plant one when there are many far better types?

"Scrubby" more aptly fits a few oaks in the South, like Black Jack Oak and Scrub Oak. They pop up in fields, lightly shaded woods, fence lines, and other strange and undesirable places. "Ah," you say, "a nice young oak. I think I'll let it grow." Then you wait and wait and wait for something good to happen. Nothing ever does. Born a Scrub Oak, it dies a scrubby oak.

There are practical considerations when choosing which oak to plant. If you hate to rake leaves, remember oak leaves hang on much of the winter and need raking over and over again. This isn't a big problem when the leaves are large, but when they are small, like those on Water and Willow Oak, it is a real pain. Acorns can also be a problem to remove. Like leaves, the larger they are, the easier the job is. But the small ones – also from

Water Oak and Willow Oak – are almost impossible to get rid of. The result is little oak trees sprouting everywhere, especially in ground covers like English Ivy and Liriope.

The best advice I can give about oaks is to keep the large ones even if it means raking leaves and removing acorns. Natural White Oaks, Red Oaks, and Chestnut Oaks should be protected, nurtured, and cherished no matter what the cost or problems. Keep and enjoy mature Water Oaks and Willow Oaks, even if their limitations irritate you. If you happen to have a large Live Oak gracing your property, realize that you are living in the presence of something more than a mere tree, something that must be preserved at all costs. Realize also that all us uplanders are jealous.

If you have moved into a house in a treeless development, choose an oak wisely. Developers love to saturate lots and line streets with faster-growing oaks that may not be the best for your property. In fact, you may be better off replacing them after a year or two than putting up with them over the long haul.

Reading a list of Southern oaks is like seeing the bunny in TV ads keep going and going and going. You

Betsy Hastings is dwarfed by the Middleton Oak.

spot names you recognize, then you see many more you never heard of. Oaks have naturally hybridized over the centuries, resulting in species that may or may not be good for you or for growers to propagate. The list below contains very good oaks and is a good cross-section of those with useful and interesting forms for planting in a home landscape. If you see one in a nursery that's not on the list below, ask your nurseryman hard questions, like where is it a native and is it really good for the South?

Live Oaks almost define a shade tree for the lower South.

Chestnut Oak
Quercus prinus

HEIGHT: 50-plus feet.

HABIT: Oval to rounded.

GROWTH RATE: Medium. May grow at least a foot per year in good soil.

BEST USE: Large specimen.

LEAF COLOR: Dark green.

FALL COLOR: Yellow (some may be orange), but usually not spectacular.

Nelson Crist introduced me to two large Chestnut Oaks in Atlanta's Piedmont Park over 50 years ago. A half century and hundreds of thousands of stomping feet later, they are even more beautiful than the day I first saw them. The Chestnut Oak is a tough tree. It grows and develops best in moist but well-drained soil, but even in poor and rocky soil it will become a beautiful tree.

Sweet Apple, where we have lived for over 30 years, was once typical North Georgia farmland, consisting of bottom land, rolling hills, and steep drops with rock outcroppings near a small river. I have discovered many native colonies of fine Chestnut Oaks on steep hillsides as well as on more level and fertile land.

If I were told that I could have only one oak to plant, Chestnut Oak would probably be my choice. Chestnut Oak is not always available at local retail nurseries, which only handle fast-turnover material. However, it is worth the search because it will become a much better tree than more widely sold oaks.

Chinese Evergreen Oak
Quercus myrsinifolia

HEIGHT: 25-plus feet.

HABIT: Loose in poor soil, rounded in rich, moist locations.

GROWTH RATE: Slow to medium.

BEST USE: In restricted places where a handsome evergreen tree is perfect.

BARK: Smooth, gray.

LEAF COLOR: Dark green in good soil, yellow green in nitrogen-deficient soil.

Small-growing evergreen trees are in great demand for 1/4- to 1/2-acre lots. They don't overpower the landscape and are perfect for restricted areas like between the drive and a property line or in an L-shaped corner of a house. Earlier, I mentioned a number of smaller-growing hollies, like Yaupon and Foster, that can be developed into small trees for restricted spots. Chinese Evergreen Oak may be even better because it grows naturally into a small tree.

I planted two Chinese Evergreen Oaks many years ago as a trial to find out what this tree was all about, since it was little-known and seldom produced by nurs-

Left: *Very old Chestnut Oak.* Middle: *Well-defined Chestnut Oak.* Right: *Chestnut Oak has a defined structure when planted in the open.*

An Old Chinese Evergreen Oak at Oakland Cemetery in Atlanta, Georgia

ery growers. My friend James Patterson of Patterson Nursery at Putney, Georgia, introduced me to it. James felt it was an ignored tree, but one that would do well in Southern landscapes.

Over the years, there has been confusion in the nursery world between Japanese Evergreen Oak, *Quercus acuta*, and Chinese Evergreen Oak, *Quercus myrsinifolia*. The characteristics are similar, but important differences eventually emerge. Chinese Evergreen Oak grows larger, has better form, and is more cold-hardy than the Japanese Evergreen Oak. Mine at Sweet Apple was undamaged by minus 10-degree temperatures in 1985. Chinese Evergreen Oak is definitely superior in all of the South, doing well from Savannah, Georgia, to Washington, D.C. Ask questions and read the tag on any Evergreen Oak in the nursery so you can be sure you are buying Chinese Evergreen Oak, *Quercus myrsinifolia*, the much better tree.

Live Oak
Quercus virginiana

HEIGHT: 50-plus feet.
HABIT: Broad and spreading with huge laterally grow-ing limbs. Massive appearance.

GROWTH RATE: Medium when young, very slow when older. Fertilizer helps young trees to grow faster.
BEST USE: Large specimen tree for huge expanses of lawn area.
LEAF COLOR: Dark lustrous green.
FALL COLOR: Evergreen, retaining its deep rich color all winter.
RANGE: The lower Southern coastal plains from Louisiana to North Carolina.

Glorious, magnificent, massive, and beautiful are among the superlatives that don't quite do justice to an old Live Oak filled with Spanish Moss. To those of you who live where Live Oak thrives, appreciate the fact that you live where one of the most beautiful trees in America grows. The rest of us poor souls must drive hundreds of miles to ride down a street lined with Live Oaks whose limbs arch over and dwarf a measly car.

Perhaps the best example of Live Oak is the famous Middleton Oak on the grounds of Middleton Gardens near Charleston, South Carolina. This tree is estimated to be 800 to 900 years old, which means it sprouted about the time Europeans left for the Crusades. Standing

Live Oak is the most beautiful oak on the lower southern coasts.

A street lined with Live Oaks is a beautiful sight.

under the limbs of Middleton Oak, Betsy and I were almost dumbstruck at its beauty.

Beautiful Live Oaks are found in all the large coastal cities from New Orleans to Charleston. But they are also plentiful in Southern cities like Thomasville and Albany, Georgia. One large specimen on a Georgia plantation I visited had a huge branch that grew parallel to the ground for over 50 feet.

Young Live Oaks are very attractive in the landscape. Their beauty is much different, since they are much more compact when young. But take my word for it, you don't have to wait until a Live Oak is old to enjoy its appearance.

Live Oak grows well in a number of different soils, from sandy to moderate clay. For those of you close to the sea, Live Oak is said to be salt-tolerant. It grows best when you fertilize young trees up to the time their branches begin to arch outward. After that, they will grow and grow on their own until several centuries pass.

Pin Oak
Quercus palustris

HEIGHT: 60-plus feet.

HABIT: Strong pyramid shape until quite old, when it becomes more rounded.

GROWTH RATE: Medium-fast (one of the fastest-growing oaks).

BEST USE: Lawn tree, street tree, parking areas, and widely used in commercial plantings around buildings.

Pin Oak has red fall color.

LEAF COLOR: Dark green all summer.

FALL COLOR: Red.

LIMITATIONS: Should not be used in high pH soils where it develops severe chlorosis.

This tree should not be confused with Willow Oak, which is often called Pin Oak in the lower South. The true Pin Oak is a far better tree, though I wonder if it isn't being overplanted. You see them everywhere! A good way to spot a Pin Oak is to look for a young 5- to 10-year-old tree with typically oak leaves whose head is a distinct pyramid. After 25 years or so, Pin Oak develops a less severe, more oval head than when younger, but even so, it lacks the easygoing grace of a maple.

If your landscape design calls for a more formal tree, Pin Oak is a good choice. I would choose one in a minute before planting a Willow Oak or Water Oak.

Red Oaks

Red oaks are massive, handsome trees often found in woods and forests, but less often planted in the landscape. Most red oaks found in the landscape were left standing by better builders during their grading for houses. If you have red oaks on your property, keep them, since they can be handsome complements to your home and landscape.

Northern Red Oak is more likely to be found growing on your property in the upper South, while Scarlet Oak and Southern Red Oak are native to the whole South. No matter which you find, try to save a red oak since all are worthwhile trees.

All three Red Oaks listed below may be found in specialty tree nurseries, though Northern Red Oak is

Left: *An older Pin Oak with an oval canopy.* Right: *A younger Pin Oak is pyramid-shaped.*

more common since its root development is better for transplanting. That made it the choice even in my nursery days, even though it seldom develops as well in our heat. However, good specimens may be seen all over the mid-South.

All three are large-growing trees, often reaching 50 feet in height with an equal or wider breadth. Old trees may be over 100 feet tall.

Northern Red Oak
Quercus rubra

Northern Red Oak grows rather slowly, but with time develops into a beautiful tree. Fall color is only fair, but in some years can be a rather muted red.

Scarlet Oak
Quercus coccinea

Scarlet Oak is the fastest-growing of the red oaks but should be used in landscapes with well-drained soil. The fall color is scarlet in most years.

More nurserymen are growing Scarlet Oak now, so it might be the red oak you find in your local retail outlet.

Southern Red Oak
Quercus falcata

Southern Red Oak is the least likely to be found in a retail nursery since it doesn't transplant as well as Northern Red Oak or Scarlet Oak.

I have a naturally growing 50-year-old Red Oak in my pasture that's as nice a tree as you could want. Its main drawback is its lack of fall color, something I am willing to forego because of the beauty of the tree all summer.

Sawtooth Oak
Quercus acutissima

HEIGHT: 40-plus feet.
HABIT: Upright, mildly pyramidal when young. Oval to rounded when older.
GROWTH RATE: Medium fast (fast for an oak).
BEST USE: Specimen lawn tree, shade tree, and street tree.
LEAF COLOR: Light green, almost yellow when emerging in the spring, but quickly darkens to a rich green.
FALL COLOR: Yellow.

Southern Red Oak

The interesting leaves of Sawtooth Oak

Sawtooth Oak is one of my favorite smaller-growing oaks and ranks high on my list of better trees for the South. Even though it came from the Far East in the mid-1800s, it wasn't used much in the South until the last 20 or so years. I know I would have planted one in my landscape if they had been readily available during my nursery days when I was planting trees at Sweet Apple. After I returned

Left: Sawtooth Oak is great as a street tree. *Middle:* Sawtooth Oak is also a good lawn tree. *Right:* Young Sawtooth Oak

from one of my stints overseas, I saw a number of Sawtooth Oaks used as street trees. I was so confused at the sudden appearance of a new tree (at least what I thought was new to me) that I pointed out a planting to Chris and asked him about it. "Where have you been? Those are Sawtooth Oaks," he replied. I really felt like a dummy. Actually, I had seen older Sawtooth Oaks, but failed to recognize the younger form.

Sawtooth Oak is easy to recognize up close. Its six- to seven-inch-long and three-inch-wide leaves have bristly teeth from top to bottom. Its acorns are rather large and very abundant. The cup has a fringe of scales and covers almost 2/3 of the acorn. When you pick up an acorn still in its cup, it looks like a buggy with a fringe on top. The ground beneath a row near a small shopping strip I go by is almost covered when they are plentiful.

Consider planting a Sawtooth Oak instead of a Pin Oak, Willow Oak, or Water Oak. As an Egyptian potato chip maker advertised, "Try it and you will adopt it."

Water Oak
Quercus nigra

HEIGHT: 50–60 feet.
HABIT: Broadly oval to round.
GROWTH RATE: Fast.
BEST USE: Where it has plenty of room to grow.
LEAVES: Small, a mess to rake up.
ACORNS: Small and too plentiful.
LEAF COLOR: Dark green.

FALL COLOR: Not significant.
STRENGTH: Rather twiggy when young and weak-wooded when old.

Water Oak

Water Oaks are fast-growing and brittle, breaking easily.

Having been brought up "correctly," I try to follow the admonition, "If you can't say something nice, don't say anything at all." Therefore I will say this about Water Oak: "It is a tree." I can't think of anything nicer.

Water Oak is native to the South and grows almost everywhere, usually where you don't want it to. Its fast growth is sometimes offered as an inducement to plant it, but many other fine trees grow almost as fast and aren't trashy, weak-wooded, messy trees. Yes, there are some large attractive specimen trees found on abandoned farms and near lonely chimneys, the only remaining indication of long-gone houses. There are a few on one of my routes through the country that look fairly respectable, but I think, "At what price, with broken limbs, pierced roofs, and their progeny sprouting in every nook and corner?"

Before you bemoan not cutting one down on your property many years ago, welcome to the crowd of us who didn't cut ours down either. I was going to cut down a small one many years ago, as well as Black Locust nearby. I never cut down either and both have

grown too large, remaining as unpleasant reminders of things I should have done a long time ago.

If you have a large Water Oak growing in your landscape, you have discovered that it's impossible to grow grass underneath and keep all its seedlings out of Liriope, Vinca minor, and Ivy. You are fortunate if the tree is away from your house. If it isn't, be sure your insurance covers tree damage.

If you don't have one growing in your landscape, please don't plant one.

That's probably more than a polite Southern gentleman should say.

White Oak
Quercus alba

HEIGHT: 60-plus feet.
HABIT: Upright broad-oval when younger, develops large spreading limbs with age.
GROWTH RATE: Slow.
BEST USE: Large specimen tree.
LEAF COLOR: Rich green.
FALL COLOR: Red to wine colored.

White Oak is to the upper South what Live Oak is to the lower South, a fantastically beautiful tree. Unfortunately, it doesn't transplant well and is sensitive to almost all the

250-year-old White Oak

Left and Right: *Willow Oaks*

environmental problems modern living brings. It does best in acid, high-humus, and loose forest soil.

Changes in grade and grading compaction are deadly to White Oaks. We had a magnificent one growing on our Cheshire Bridge Road Nursery property when we began developing it into a garden center. Despite all our efforts and too much money spent, we lost the tree. I have seen the same situation many, many times.

If you are a collector of native trees, buy a small one growing in a container. Find an area that has well-drained woodsy soil, then plant it carefully, using peat moss when mixing the backfill. Someday you will have a beautiful tree.

Willow Oak
Quercus phellos

HEIGHT: 60-plus feet.
HABIT: Pyramidal when young, upright oval with age.
GROWTH RATE: Medium.

BEST USE: Large specimens.
LEAF COLOR: Dark green.
FALL COLOR: Usually yellow with some red in the mountains.
LEAF SIZE: Too dadgum small, if you have to rake them by yourself.
ACORN: Small, prolific, and a pest.

Some people like Willow Oak; others don't. I got tired of all the ones planted when I was a nurseryman 30 years ago, and hate to see so many being used once again. Sure, it makes a beautiful allee along a mile-long drive, but how many of us have a mile-long drive? A well-planted entrance to a subdivision near us used them and they are pretty trees while still young. But I have seen similar entrances with Pin Oak that looked a lot better.

I have also lived long enough to see those planted in several older areas of Atlanta in the early 1920s have the same sort of breakage problems that plague Water Oak. I just think there are far better trees than Willow Oak.

Flowering Peach

Prunus persica

HEIGHT: 12–15 feet.

HABIT: Broad oval.

GROWTH RATE: Fast.

BEST USE: Specimen flowering tree.

LEAF COLOR: Medium green.

FALL COLOR: Insignificant.

PROBLEMS: Subject to a number of insects and diseases common to edible peach trees. The most serious and life-threatening is the peach borer.

Many years ago, my sons Don and Chris planted an apple and a peach to grow up with them. After one of our extended stints overseas, a small dispute arose over whose was the apple and whose was the peach. Frankly, nobody could really remember which belonged to whom. The apple had grown quite well and had a smattering of nice fruit while the peach was in pitiful condition with only a limb or two. Now the apple produces a bunch of delicious fruits each year and the peach is only a memory. The experience teaches a pretty good gardening lesson: peaches are more prone to insects and diseases than apples, which is the reason there are far more flowering crabapples in the landscape then flowering peaches.

In the days when dual-purpose trees were often planted, fruiting cultivars were used quite effectively as ornamental trees, but life is more hectic these days. Not many homeowners are prepared to spray every week or so all spring and summer to control everything from scale to leaf and fruit diseases. From an ornamental standpoint, the worst problem is peach borers, which riddle a tree and can ultimately destroy it unless properly treated.

A double-flowering peach planted alone in a landscape can be beautiful, though a bit stark. The flowers are magnificent and make up for its lack of graceful character and its demands for extra care. I have seen some 20- to 30-year-old trees that remain attractive.

Cultivars

The double-flowering peach cultivars you'll find in a nursery – probably with fancy names like 'Peppermint Stick' or 'Alba Plena' – have likely been chosen for better and more uniform blooms. However, all cultivars I have seen or read about have the same problems of the species.

The three double forms that have been planted in the South for many years are: Double Pink Flowering Peach, Double Red Flowering Peach, and Double White Flowering Peach.

A huge old Pecan tree

Pecan

Carya illinoinensis

HEIGHT: 75 feet or more.

HABIT: Upright spreading.

GROWTH RATE: Fast when finally established and growing (two or three years) but slower when older.

BEST USE: Specimen tree.

LEAF COLOR: Medium green.

FALL COLOR: Insignificant.

INSECTS AND DISEASES: Pecans are subject to a number of insects and diseases, most of which are not worth worrying about when using it in the landscape.

Pecans are a gift of Nature to all of us in the South. The American Indians prized their delicious nuts, which are far more tasty than those of its first cousin, hickory. Pecan trees are the largest-growing member of the hickory family and make much better specimens in the landscape.

The pecan is normally thought of as a commercial crop tree, though it can be a handsome tree in the landscape despite its problems with leaf and nut diseases. Huge 75- to 100-foot trees still grow around old homes and guard abandoned home sites throughout the Southern piedmont and coastal plains.

Ancient pecan trees are extraordinary and should be preserved and enjoyed. I ran across one in an older part of Atlanta on the deep lot of a house being restored. Most of the old landscape plants were overgrown and useless, and I know I sounded discouraging to the property owner who had visions of plant restoration along with home restoration. As we wandered to the back of his lot, he asked what a particular tree was. At first I was stumped by the sight of a monster lower limb I couldn't reach around, which grew straight out from the trunk for 20 or 30 feet parallel to the ground. But then I realized with some excitement that we were looking at a magnificent pecan planted when the house was built in the early 1900s.

Pecans are difficult to transplant because of their long tap roots, which make digging their holes a major project. Some horticulturists play down their use in the landscape because of leaf diseases that may cause some early shedding and their lack of fall color. Others are not happy about the falling nuts, which can cause problems when you're mowing the lawn. I think their leaves are less trouble to rake and their nuts better to have than the smaller leaves and acorns of a Water Oak or Willow Oak, two trees that are much overused.

Pecans can reach 150 feet with an upright oval head that is more compact than an oak's. The recommended spacing for trees in a grove is 40 to 60 feet, which gives an indication as to their ultimate size and a warning not to plant them too close to a house or street. Since they grow rather slowly, many growers plant them 20 to 30 feet apart, then remove every other tree after they produce good crops but become crowded.

Driving through the country, I often spot small groves that were planted near home sites and are no longer tended. The huge trees are too crowded for either good landscape design or pecan nut production. Most suburban lots are too small for more than one or

A Pecan in a large lawn

A Pecan in a corner works well.

two trees of any kind, so don't overplant with a bunch of pecan trees.

If you are planting pecans for their nuts, be sure to use a combination of cultivars for proper pollination.

Persimmon

Diospyros sp.

It's been years since I saw a 'possum in a 'simmon tree or gave a persimmon fruit to a girl before frost so she would take a bite and "pucker up real good." We have many opossums around us, and their nocturnal wanderings have driven a succession of Golden Retrievers into states of hysteria, and there are many persimmons on which they and other animals feast. In our small world at Sweet Apple, the 'possums are doing better than the persimmons. Developers seem to disparage persimmon trees. Two beautiful specimens stood by the paved road since before we arrived more than 30 years ago, but when a developer bought the old farm to which they belonged, the grading machines took care of these local landmarks in one afternoon.

I like the looks of a well-grown native persimmon, especially when it is filled with ripe fruit in the fall, and I rue the day when we first moved to Sweet Apple that I mistakenly cut down a small one back of my vegetable garden.

Persimmon tree with fruit

Persimmons are best planted at the edge of a wooded area.

The native persimmon has silver-dollar–size orange fruit that are ready to eat after frost but are showy from late September on. Grown-ups used to warn us boys that eating too many persimmons would make us feel like our insides were going to explode. I never did, so I can't attest to the truth of their warnings, though Michael Dirr also mentions this caveat in his book, *Manual of Woody Landscape Plants.*

The Japanese Persimmon has larger and tastier fruit, but is a less hardy tree than our native. It should be grown with caution in the upper piedmont and avoided in the mountains.

Common Persimmon
Diospyros virginiana

HEIGHT: 35 to 60 feet.
HABIT: Upright oval to broad oval.
GROWTH RATE: Slow to medium.
BEST USE: As an interesting specimen tree.

Wait until after a hard frost to eat native persimmons.

LEAF COLOR: Dark green.
FALL COLOR: Yellow to deep red.
FRUIT: Very showy orange fruit in the fall. Often remain on the tree until after the leaves fall.

Our native persimmon has deep green foliage when grown in good soil, though may look anemic when planted in old worn-out cotton land. The orange fruits vary in size from an inch up to two inches, depending on soil conditions as well as the variable character of the plant, since most are grown from seeds. Few persimmons are planted, though native trees are found everywhere and should be cherished rather than destroyed by mistake like I did mine.

Native persimmons can be seen at more or less mature heights from 35 to 60 feet. More commonly, they reach a mature size of about 45 feet, great for small lots and against pine backgrounds. The upright oval shape is also good since they can give shade and block the sun without spreading too much and ruining a lawn. Fescue grass grew up to the trunks of the now-lamented specimens that stood by our paved road before the developers came.

I doubt if landscapers ever put a persimmon on a plan unless specifically instructed to either for nostalgic reasons or to attract wild animals. I think it has a place on larger lots, if only to develop a more interesting landscape than those rubber-stamp plans with a pair of Willow Oaks and too many Bradford Pears.

The fall color is variable from a deep red to yellow, depending on its genetic inclination as well as growing conditions. Since the fruits hang on after most of the leaves have dropped in the fall, the tree remains interesting until the fruits have fallen or been eaten by wandering two-legged strangers, 'possums, raccoons, or other wild animals.

Japanese Persimmon
Diospyros kaki

HEIGHT: 20-plus feet. Smaller the farther north you go.
HABIT: Low-branching and as wide as tall.
GROWTH RATE: Slow.
BEST USE: Ornamental interesting tree for its fruit.
LEAF COLOR: Dark green.
FALL COLOR: Yellow to orange.
FRUIT: Orange-yellow. At least four inches in diameter.
RANGE: Probably cannot stand zero degrees or below.
  Customers of ours many years ago reported difficulty when temperatures fell into that range.

Once you see and taste the marvelous Japanese Persimmon fruits in the grocery store, you will be

The large fruit of Japanese Persimmon

tempted to plant a tree or two somewhere in your landscape.

It is smaller-growing than the native persimmon, only about 20 feet tall in the best conditions, but it spreads far more than its native kinsman. What a sight it presents in the late fall when the orange fruits are still hanging on a bare tree!

Japanese Persimmon fruit are almost the size of an apple. They can be eaten when soft, without the astringent quality our native persimmons have before frost.

My father planted one at Lovejoy when we listed them in our catalog many years ago. Unfortunately, the zero-degree Thanksgiving weekend freeze in 1950 did it in. Reuben Dorsey of Dorsey Nursery fame planted one about the same time less than a mile away and his still survives, though it has never grown as tall as it should. I have never seen any surviving much north of Atlanta, though there might be some. My guess is that they will do quite well below a line from Jackson, Mississippi, through Birmingham, Atlanta, Charlotte, and ending in Norfolk, which encompasses the coastal plain and the lower piedmont plateau.

Japanese Persimmon seems to be free of insects and diseases, making it a great fruit tree for the homeowner since it won't need the strict and frequent spray schedules of peaches and plums.

Pine

Pinus sp.

Pines grow all over the South from the coastal plains to the tallest mountains. They are planted for pulp, grown to extract resin, and are a major source of lumber. Millions are planted each year as an economic crop. However, the homeowner's most likely question is whether to cut one down, not whether to plant one.

I am partial to large old pines, having spent the early part of my life sleeping with one right beside my window. The sound of wind blowing through a pine is like angels singing. But as with most plants, too many pines can be worse than none at all. Pine islands instead of lawns are cherished by all who are in charge of mowing, and they can be extremely attractive when filled with azaleas and camellias, plants which, in turn, think they are in heaven. But an island of spindly pines is neither a heaven for azaleas and camellias nor for larger pines overhead. Pines need room to develop and perform, and they become spindly and unattractive when too many are crowded together. Removing weak and spindly pines in a group allows the remaining trees to develop attractive crowns and plants underneath to thrive.

White Pine grows in the upper piedmont.

A good way to develop a healthy pine island is first to remove all the small weak trees that are in the shadows of the larger trees. Then stand under each remaining tree and look up to see if its crown is in the open. Leave trees that are not competing for light by growing into the crown of another and remove any that are. You will be surprised at how few pines it takes to be attractive and provide an area with good conditions for colorful plantings underneath.

Pines for the landscape are neither created equal nor will they all grow well throughout the South. Fast-growing Slash Pines, *Pinus elliottii*, can be damaged severely by ice storms while White Pines, *Pinus strobus*, may do poorly below the foothills of the piedmont.

Longleaf Pine, *Pinus palustris*, is one of the most beautiful southern pines but unfortunately is seldom seen above the coastal plain.

There are situations where pines outperform other trees and should be considered for the landscape. Slash Pine and Loblolly Pine, *Pinus taeda*, grow faster than any good hardwood tree I know. I have seen them used as tall screening plants back of evergreens, making an effective and impenetrable sight and sound barrier. They can also be used to quickly block the sun from an area that gets too hot.

Though pines are considered fast-growing trees, the oldest living tree in America, a Bristlecone Pine, has been growing in the White Mountains of California for over 4,500 years and stands only about 30 feet tall.

Pines are hard to treat in the same way as other plants I have discussed, since you seldom buy them in retail nurseries to plant in your landscape. Most homeowners are not even interested in the pine specie(s) they have growing on their property – only what to do with them.

Pines for Quick Screens

Loblolly Pine
Pinus taeda

Loblolly Pine is the pine species of choice for quick screens in the upper South. Eventually it reaches over 50 feet, but that takes many years. I have seen small container-grown Loblolly Pines planted 10 feet apart along a back property line quickly reach 12 feet and block unpleasant sights. The owner planted two Burford Hollies in front of each space between the Loblolly Pines. When the pines began to lose their lower limbs, the Burford Hollies were large enough to fill the open space. As the pines grew taller, so did the hollies. After about ten years, the owner had a 25-foot-high screen of Loblolly Pine and Burford Holly. Leyland Cypress, the more common tall screening plant these days, would not have given the desired results so quickly.

Slash Pine
Pinus elliottii

Slash Pine, an important source of pulpwood and timber in the deep South, is more attractive than Loblolly Pine, with longer and more graceful needles. It grows as rapidly and remains graceful longer when used as a screening plant. I have seen it used in reforesting projects along highways with great success. Its major flaw is a higher susceptibility to breaking in winter storms than Loblolly Pine, restricting its use in areas of the mid-South where ice and snow are likely.

Virginia Pine
Pinus virginiana

Virginia Pine has received much attention in recent years as a plantation-grown Christmas tree. Southern Christmas tree growers have planted hundreds of acres with great success in areas where Fraser Fir will not grow. My main complaint is that Virginia Pine tends to lose its rich green color during the winter, requiring it to be sprayed with a green dye to satisfy buyers.

Landscapers are using Virginia Pine with some success as a screening plant, especially on dry banks and other poor soil areas. It isn't one of my preferred plants for such a situation, but I list it here since you may well find it in retail nurseries.

My major complaint is that older Virginia Pines look scrubby, with large numbers of pine cones hanging on the tree for months at a time. Of course, any tree is better than none in situations where everything does poorly, and Virginia Pine may be what you need. But under normal conditions, I'd try something else.

Specimen Pines

Japanese Black Pine
Pinus thunbergii

Japanese Black Pine withstands salt spray and is used with some success along the Southern coast next to the sea. It develops slowly into a dark green specimen with an irregular head. The largest I have seen along the coast was only about 12 feet high, but I have read that with time they will grow taller.

Japanese Black Pine is subject to a number of insects and diseases, limiting its use away from the sea coast.

White Pine
Pinus strobus

White Pine is as beautiful as any evergreen in the landscape. It is far more graceful than firs, spruces, Leyland Cypress, or any other pine and an extraordinary specimen in the areas of the South where it grows well. The five-inch-long, bluish-green needles are soft and flexible and borne in bundles of five. It grows to 50 feet or more in the landscape and 100 feet or more in the wild. It is pyramid shaped when young and loosely pyramidal to upright oval when older. Older trees develop branches that grow more horizontal with some of them pointing downward, giving a graceful appearance.

Virginia Pine screen

Virginia Pine

White Pine is limited to the cooler climates of the South. I have seen beautiful specimens in the higher elevations in Alabama, Georgia, Tennessee, North Carolina, and Virginia. We tried many times without success to grow a White Pine at Lovejoy, 30 miles south of Atlanta, but I have seen a few good specimens in Atlanta. At Sweet Apple, 30 miles north of Atlanta, there are some handsome old trees, but on our main road, some live and thrive while nearby trees suddenly turn brown and die. Some reports state rather categorically that this condition is the result of urban pollution. I believe there is more to it than that. I have observed too many White Pines dying when growing in heavy red clay where drainage is poor. My suggestion is to use them only in the upper piedmont and to plant them in well-drained, high-humus soil.

Left: *Specimen White Pine.* Below: *White Pine screen.*

American Plane Tree

Plane Tree, Sycamore
Platanus sp.

Two sycamore species grow in the South: Eastern Sycamore and the London Plane Tree. Both have good points and can be attractive in the right setting, especially with their white winter bark. But since neither is on a par with so many other excellent trees, I frankly see no real reason to plant either.

American Plane Tree, Eastern Sycamore
Platanus occidentalis

HEIGHT: 75-plus feet.

HABIT: Broad head consisting of a number of large branches.

GROWTH RATE: Medium. Fast under good conditions.

BEST USE: Large specimen tree where its white bark can be seen. It is not a good lawn tree since it is messy.

LEAF COLOR: Medium to light green.

FALL COLOR: Insignificant. Usually turns brown without coloring.

Every Southerner has encountered this interesting tree at one time or another since they are native and so easily recognizable by their flaking bark and white underbark, which stands out in a forest. I have a number of them growing on my place, not by my choice but because they were here when I arrived or because they keep sprouting over the years in strange places.

Once we stayed in a motel on Sea Island, Georgia, that had some very interesting plantings on the grounds, including several American Plane Trees between the entrance lanes as well as others near a small pond. They were beautiful with their white bark set against a well-kept Centipede Grass lawn and a surrounding pine forest. It almost changed my negative opinion of this tree. But I came home and held fast to my rule: If you have a beautiful American Plane Tree, keep it, but if you don't, forget it.

One great characteristic is no reason to plant a tree when, as in this case, there are plenty of reasons not to. The leaves are susceptible to an anthracnose disease that can almost denude a severely infected tree. The sycamore fruits, called sycamore balls, are a mess to clean up, and the trees drop twigs and small limbs so much that they can be a perpetual problem.

My major complaint, though, is their rather light green foliage, which is a far cry from the deep green leaves of oaks and maples. By the way, when in Europe, especially Great Britain, when you ask about sycamore trees, they will show you a maple, *Acer pseudoplatanus*, which they call sycamore but which is a far more beautiful tree.

London Plane Tree
Platanus x acerifolia

HEIGHT: 75 feet.

HABIT: Pyramidal when young. Open and wide when old.

GROWTH RATE: Medium.

BEST USE: Large specimen where it has ample room to develop.

LEAF COLOR: Medium to dark green.

FALL COLOR: Insignificant. Usually turns brown rather than coloring.

This cross between American Plane Tree and Oriental Plane Tree was found in London back in the days when few street trees did well due to the tremendous amounts of sulfur from burning soft coal. After soft coal was banned, better trees were planted and there aren't that many London Plane Trees left. I remember staying at a hotel on one of these London Plane Tree–lined streets in the late 1960s and being impressed by their stamina and good growth. On a later visit, I found other trees showing up in their place.

In the South, London Plane Tree has many problems but is thought to be resistant to the anthracnose, making it superior to the American Plane Tree. There are also cultivars that have even more resistance to insects and diseases, but in my opinion there is still little reason to plant any of the Plane Trees.

Purple Leaf Plum
Prunus cerasifera cultivars

HEIGHT: 15–25 feet.

HABIT: Rounded head which may develop almost like an umbrella.

GROWTH RATE: Fast.

BEST USE: Small specimen tree where the wine-red-to-purple foliage blends rather than clashing with other plants in the landscape.

LEAF COLOR: Dark red to almost purple.

FALL COLOR: None.

FLOWERS: Pink and profuse in the early spring.

Purple Leaf Plum is really a misnomer for *Prunus cerasifera*, since the leaves of most commonly grown cultivars are more deep red than purple, which, to me, is a blessing.

I grew up in the days when Purple Leaf Plums were the rage, though my family never thought very much of them and we had only one in the landscape for a while. "Bilious pink thrift and Purple Leaf Plums are trashy," my mother would snort. "Some people think they are beautiful," my father pontificated, perhaps because our nursery outfitted the South with these plants.

When we moved to Sweet Apple over 30 years ago, both pink thrift and Purple Leaf Plum were common, but the newcomers decided that pink thrift really is bilious so there is only one big patch left. Purple Leaf Plums are still popular and are all over the place.

Beware though – Purple Leaf Plums grow rapidly and can be attractive for a number of years, but get pretty ratty-looking when old. I would estimate that they last about 40 years, then begin to die from all sorts of problems like borers and leaf spot.

I learned a lesson about fruit worms in plums when I was growing up. My father harvested a bunch of nice plums on our only Purple Leaf Plum tree, which he proudly gave us for breakfast one morning. I will never forget the look on my sister's and mother's faces when we cut them open and found a large fruit worm or two staring at us. Never again did we have homegrown plums for breakfast, and the Purple Leaf Plum disappeared soon after.

If you like wine-red and want a hot spot in the landscape, Purple Leaf Plum is a better choice than Crimson King Maple because it grows faster, the color is a better red, and it doesn't always look stunted.

Cultivars

The only way to have a Purple Leaf Plum is to choose a cultivar since its parent, Cherry Plum, has green leaves. Cultivars are numerous, some with white flowers. The best way to choose a cultivar is to see it in leaf (usually a bad time to plant) since they have different shades of red and purple. The more commonly grown in the South are *Atropurpurea*, with light pink flowers and red foliage that darkens to purple by summer; Newport, with pale pink flowers and deep purple foliage; and Thundercloud, with pink, somewhat fragrant flowers, and dark purple foliage.

Spring flowers of Purple Leaf Plum

Redbud
Cercis sp.

I am prone to dismiss our native Redbud as a useless tree because I grew up in a family that disliked its purplish pink flowers and my wife Betsy not only dislikes the color but hates the seedlings that sprout all over the place. Not even the glassy eyes of my Woody Plant Materials professor when he spoke of its spring beauty could overcome my genetic aversion to this plant. It might be something worth having in Ithaca, New York, where snow covers the ground so much of the time, but in the South there are too many other spring-flowering trees that don't make you want Pepcid AC after seeing them in bloom. But differences of opinion are what make the world go around, so ignore my bad-mouthing if you like its color and don't mind its seeds sprouting in every nook and cranny.

White Judas Tree, a name I prefer to the nonsensical White Redbud, is a different story and a great addition to any garden. I have also seen some fabulous Chinese Redbuds growing throughout the South. Their flowers are much brighter in the beginning, though a bit purple as they mature.

Common Redbud

Common Redbud
Cercis canadensis

HEIGHT: Usually 20 feet in the landscape but may be 30 or more in the wild.

HABIT: Upward spreading with an almost flat top. May have several large upward branches from near the ground.

GROWTH RATE: Medium but often fast in a fertilized landscape.

BEST USE: Specimen flowering tree.

FLOWERS: A purple-pink that evokes an "ughhh" from some people and an "ahhh" from others. Flowers are profuse.

LEAF COLOR: Dark green.

FALL COLOR: Usually not much, though I have seen yellow leaves in occasional cool autumns.

I admit that Redbuds look nice in our woods when their lavender-pink flowers are muted by the sur-

rounding green leaves emerging from dormant native trees, but we cut down the only one growing in our landscape when we arrived many years ago.

For those of you who like lavender-pink flowers, Redbud may be great in your landscape. It grows rapidly and flowers when young. It does have an interesting shape with upward-arching limbs. The seeds are numerous and can be a problem, sprouting easily in all the worst places, like Vinca minor, English Ivy, and Liriope.

White Redbud
Cercis canadensis 'Alba'

HEIGHT: The oldest tree I have ever seen was only about 15 feet tall, though its height is listed as more in some publications.

HABIT: More blocky in appearance than the species, but still upward spreading.

GROWTH RATE: Slow to medium.

BEST USE: Small specimen flowering tree.

FLOWERS: Masses of small pure white flowers up and down twigs, branches, and even trunks.

LEAF COLOR: Dark green.

FALL COLOR: None.

White Judas Tree is a more appropriate common name than White Redbud, which seems self-contradictory. I tend to praise White Judas Tree as much as I tend to disparage common Redbud. This is a lovely tree when it is filled with pristine white flowers in the spring. Ed Daugherty, the landscape architect I have mentioned several times, has used White Judas Tree several times at All Saints' Episcopal Church in Atlanta, and these trees, though small, look fantastic when blossoming each spring. Their pure appearance when life is renewed each spring seems most appropriate in a churchyard.

Cultivars

Several cultivars can be found in retail nurseries. Forest Pansy is a purple-leaf cultivar that I've seen growing in botanical gardens. The dark purple leaves seem to hold their color well into the summer. I have not seen it in flower.

Since color is a personal feeling, choose a cultivar that fits your taste, not mine.

Forest Pansy Redbud

Chinese Redbud

'Royal White' is a cultivar with larger and more profuse white flowers.

Chinese Redbud
Cercis chinensis

HEIGHT: 12 feet.
HABIT: Multistemmed. More of a shrub than a tree.
GROWTH RATE: Medium.
BEST USE: Large specimen shrub or small tree.
LEAF COLOR: Rich green.
FALL COLOR: None.
FLOWERS: Masses of pink to lavender-pink blossoms in the spring.

More correctly, Chinese Redbud should be in a book on shrubs rather than one on trees. I depart from form and list it with the redbuds because I have seen a planting on a bank at Kew Gardens in England that looked sort of like small trees and a planting at Sweet Apple

that also seemed treelike. I also wanted to show that something good can come out of the genus besides White Judas Tree.

Chinese Redbud hold its pink color longer, and lots of years it never becomes a sickening lavender. In a mass planting, it can be quite lovely.

Flowers of Chinese Redbud

Sourwood changes color before most other trees.   *Sourwood in flower*

Sourwood
Oxydendrum arboreum

HEIGHT: Usually around 30 feet in cultivation, but I have seen native trees in the mountains which were double that size.

HABIT: Pyramid when young, much more irregular when older.

GROWTH RATE: Slow.

BEST USE: Specimen tree, especially near other hardwood trees.

LEAF COLOR: Shining green.

FALL COLOR: Bright red, sometimes with orange or yellow.

FLOWERS: Long racemes of white flowers hang out of the green leaves. The flowers and resulting seed formations are showy from mid-summer into the fall.

Sourwoods are native throughout the South and often overlooked as a landscape tree, but once you've seen it used a specimen tree, the sight will linger until you find one to plant. Though they grow large in the wild, up to 60 feet or more, I have seldom seen a planted one over 25 or 30 feet high – a great size for most lots. For more than 30 years I have been watching a beautiful specimen in front of an older country home. The white panicles of small flowers nestling against the rich green leaves make a fantastic show during the mid-summer every year. The panicles remain showy after the seed are set and are attractive when the leaves turn red in September.

Sourwood is one of the earliest trees to color in the fall. The ones in our woods are usually red by early September. An added benefit of sourwood is the extraordinary honey that bees make from their flowers. If you find some sourwood honey for sale, grab it up and be ready for a delightful treat.

Norway Spruce

Spruce
Picea sp.

Not all spruce do well in the South, but those that do can be effective evergreens in the landscape. The most often used is Norway Spruce, *Picea abies*, which grows quite well in the upper piedmont and mountains. The two most coveted – Koster Blue Spruce, *Picea pungens 'Koster'* and White Spruce, *Picea glauca* – do rather poorly in the piedmont and aren't worth planting in the heat of the lower South.

Spruce start out in a tight pyramidal form with limbs brushing the ground, but change appearance as they become older. In other words, they start out like a tightly formed Christmas tree and end up more graceful sentinels in the landscape.

You may see large specimens of Norway Spruce and Colorado Blue Spruce growing in older areas of Birmingham, Charlotte, Richmond, and Atlanta, where narrowleaf evergreen trees were more popular in the first half of the century than after World War II, when broadleaf evergreens became the plants of choice.

I do not dismiss spruces as unworthy candidates for the landscape. I have a 50-year-old Norway Spruce growing on the edge of my lawn that's just beautiful, especially in contrast with an adjacent Sugar Maple.

Colorado Blue Spruce
Picea pungens 'Koster'

Koster Blue Spruce is the best-known of all white cultivars, though new ones like 'Hoopsii' may be better. It is really a moot point since none do well except in higher elevations of the South. Yet people seem to want a silvery-blue spruce in their landscape and keep trying to have one.

There may be an old beautiful Koster Blue Spruce somewhere in the mid-South, but it has escaped me. I always thought one might be nice here at Sweet Apple, but the challenge seemed formidable.

When Betsy and I were in Ireland in 1996 at the beginning of the Irish economic leap forward, we were amazed to see so many new Irish homes with a Bradford Pear and a Koster (or other) Blue Spruce in the landscape. Frankly it was getting really boring by the time we left and my enthusiasm for accepting the challenge to grow one vanished.

When young, Koster Blue Spruce is even more formal and Christmas tree–like than Norway Spruce. In old age, it never attains the softness and grace of Norway Spruce. Your landscape may call for something formal, so give Koster Blue Spruce a try if you live in places like Asheville, North Carolina, or in upper Virginia, West Virginia, or Kentucky.

Norway Spruce
Picea abies

HEIGHT: 40 feet or more.
HABIT: Tight, thick pyramid when young; graceful, loose pyramid when old.
GROWTH RATE: Medium.
BEST USE: Evergreen specimen in the lawn.
LEAF COLOR: Dark green.

Balsam Fir and Fraser Fir are much more beautiful in the landscape than Norway Spruce, but are almost entirely restricted to the higher elevations of the upper piedmont and the mountains of the South.

I keep seeing negative remarks about Norway Spruce being overplanted and not being all that good-looking anyway. Perhaps that's true above Washington, where they have been used in landscapes for so many years. But I find Norway Spruce very pleasing as a relief to the monotony of so many cookie-cutter land-

Young Norway Spruce

scapes. It is a plant for the upper piedmont, doing well in mid-South cities and the mountains. I can understand some negativism if you merely look at a young tree and don't like a Christmas tree growing in a front yard, since that is what a young Norway Spruce looks like. Give it a few years to lose its tightly pruned look and become a graceful addition to a landscape.

Norway Spruce does poorly in the shade, developing best in part sun. There are several nice 10- to 15-year-old specimens on our road that have done well in almost full sun.

White Spruce
Picea glauca

White Spruce seems much happier in the South than Blue Spruce and is found in many mid-South cities. Its color is more muted and blends easily into our typical landscapes. However, it isn't always happy in our heat and humidity, and older plants tend to lose their appeal when not in the best growing conditions.

If you live in the upper South, you should have good results. In the mid-South cities like Birmingham, Atlanta, and Charlotte, you can try, but expect only minimal success after they reach old age.

White Spruce

Stewartia

Stewartia sp.

In my memoir, *Rich Harvest*, I told of my father's sudden interest in Stewartia after an old-timer on Georgia's Pine Mountain asked him to drive down from Atlanta to see a "summer-flowering dogwood." Once he saw the flowers on the tree, Dad knew immediately that it wasn't a dogwood and recognized it as *Stewartia malacodendron*. The news didn't set too well with the old-timer, who thought Dad was trying to cheat him out of his place in horticultural history. Dad's story tweaked my interest, but in those days we knew of no Southern nurserymen growing Stewartia.

My first sighting of a Stewartia was when I was trout fishing in North Georgia and came across a number of fallen flowers lying in the path. Looking up, I saw a small tree filled with blossoms, as beautiful a sight as you will ever see. The flowers' purple stamens helped me identify it as *Stewartia ovata var. grandiflora*, the name I have used ever since – even though recently I understand from some plantsmen that it may be a purple stamens cultivar and not a distinct species. Later I asked a Park Ranger in the Great Smoky Mountain National Park if he knew of any colonies, and he said yes, but when I told him I was a nurseryman, he backed off and became as uncooperative as the man on Pine Mountain, Georgia. My youth must have made him suspicious that I was going to dig seedlings because he spent a lot of time finger-wagging and lecturing on the dire consequences of removing plant material from the park.

You seldom see any of the Stewartias in landscapes, though Callaway Gardens has some growing. I have seen *Stewartia pseudo-camellia* for sale in retail nurseries but have never been able to keep one alive in my garden for long, though I keep trying.

None of the Stewartias grow large, ranging only 10 to 20 feet. However, they are exceptional, and if you are lucky enough to find a good specimen in a nursery, snap it up. All Stewartias do best in the sun but not middle-of-the-day sun. When planting, use plenty of sphagnum peat moss to imitate acid forest soil.

The following are Stewartias listed in nursery trade lists, but they may be difficult to find in your local retail nursery outlet. None are easy to grow in a home landscape.

Stewartia malacodendron
Stewartia monadelpha
Stewartia ovata
Stewartia ovata var. grandiflora
Stewartia pseudocamellia

Sweet Gum

Liquidamber styraciflua

HEIGHT: 60-plus feet.

HABIT: Usually pyramidal when young, but varied from upright oval to round when older.

GROWTH RATE: Starts growing rapidly when first planted but slower when older.

BEST USE: Specimen tree. Also excellent in front of other hardwood trees.

LEAF COLOR: Glossy and deep green in the summer.

FALL COLOR: Red to shades of yellow. May have both red and yellow on one leaf.

FRUIT: A round ball (gum ball) which can be a nuisance in a lawn, especially to bare feet.

Left and Middle: *Sweet Gum.*   *Sweet Gum is tough and strong.*

The site of my family's home south of Atlanta where I grew up, which I have mentioned several times, was a hardwood-covered hill with fine specimen trees. My boyhood favorite was a large sweet gum back of the house which I climbed to escape reality and to perch high up in a world of my own fantasies and dreams. To this day, I am very partial to sweet gum. While driving here and there taking pictures for this book, I couldn't help stopping over and over to photograph yet another beautiful specimen, more as an excuse to dream a bit about the good old days than to use within these pages.

I don't know why landscapers don't call for this tree more often. Maybe they think it is too common since it grows so easily in the wild, or they consider the gum balls falling in a lawn to be a problem, but the same ones readily recommend Willow Oak, Chinese Elm, and other trees with far fewer merits and far more problems as a lawn tree.

Sweet gum grows moderately fast and has a beautiful pyramid form when young and a neat oval head when older. Its branches are strong; at least none ever broke when I ascended into its top. The leaves are deep glossy green and the fall color is outstanding, most often deep burgundy red, though some years you may see orange to yellow on the same tree.

Many cultivars are being propagated – and more will certainly come – that have no fruit and consistent fall color. Cultivars have a distinct advantage over seedlings since many are grown in containers that hold the fleshy roots, rather than their being cut when dug, balled, and burlapped. However, be sure the cultivars are from Southern nurseries since many Northern and Western selections may not be as suitably tolerant of our heat.

Tamarisk, Salt Cedar

Tamarix ramosissima

HEIGHT: 20–25 feet. Larger in Southern coastal areas.
HABIT: Irregular and wide. Pruning off lower limbs and tipping its branches help make it a more attractive tree.
GROWTH RATE: Very fast.
BEST USE: Background ornamental tree.
LEAF COLOR: Light green with feathery texture.
FALL COLOR: Insignificant.
FLOWERS: Late-April in the mid-South, later in the upper South and mountains, until mid-summer.

Tamarisk is an interesting plant noted for its cedarlike foliage and rosy-pink flowers from spring into the summer. It is most often grown as a windbreak near the sea, where it withstands salt air, though its wispy form and pink flowers make a nice contrast in a well-drained part of an upland garden. It is kin to the biblical Tamarisk tree, *Tamarix aphylla*, which Abraham is said to have planted and which is mentioned several times in the Old Testament.

Our tamarisk, *Tamarix ramosissima*, does best in heavy sun and can withstand the drier parts of the landscape where many plants do poorly. Though often kept as a large shrub by pruning severely, it also makes an attractive 20- to 25-foot tree.

We planted a tamarisk at our garden center in Atlanta many years ago, and it performed well on a dry bank, confirming the horticulturists' view that it does better in well-drained soil. After several years, the small tree became gnarled and unattractive, so we started a program of drastic pruning every two or three years to force more fresh growth and better blossoms.

Tulip Poplar, Tulip Tree, Yellow Poplar
Liriodendron tulipifera

HEIGHT: Very often over 75 feet. Old trees may be 150 feet.
HABIT: Younger trees may be pyramidal to oval while older trees vary from narrow upright to conical.
GROWTH RATE: Fast.
BEST USE: Large specimen shade tree.
LEAF COLOR: Bright green.
FALL COLOR: Yellow.
FLOWER: Interesting, relatively small tulip shape.

Because names can be so confusing, it is important always to know the botanical name of a plant to be sure the common descriptive name is what you really want. When I was a nurseryman many years ago, all our salesmen were instructed to be extra careful when selling *Liriodendron tulipifera* as Tulip Tree, which is also the name given to the spectacular spring-flowering magnolias. After all, when a customer wants to grow one of the most beautiful flowering trees on the block, they don't want to end up with a 75-foot shade tree. By the way, it is in the Magnolia family and is not even a poplar.

I have a special feeling for Tulip Poplar, the name I grew up with, because our home at Lovejoy was framed by two of these magnificent trees. As a small boy, I thought they were so tall that they touched the sky. They had sprouted in the Civil War trench that at one time cut across our front yard, so they were mature and at least 75 years old when I proclaimed that I saw an angel sitting on top. One of the pair was hit and killed by lightning fifty years ago while the other has survived until the new millennium, despite small lightning strikes, high winds, droughts, and my using its trunk for target practice with my .22 rifle (for which I received a really good scolding). I'm not sure which one I saw the angel on top of since I was only three or four years old at the time, but hope it was the tree that survived.

I have seen many admonitions against planting Tulip Poplar except in very large expanses, yet the best development in our area preserved existing trees in an exceptional way. Among those most often left alone were Tulip Poplars, which less enlightened developers would have cut while slashing and grading, then would have replaced with sorry Willow Oaks, which grow almost as tall and much broader.

Tulip Poplar's fall color may be lacking in seedling trees, which is what you see in forests. But there are a number of cultivars being sold that are noted for their consistent yellow fall color. In addition, there are cultivars with different forms which may also be better in your landscape.

Tulip Poplar is a tree you should leave if possible when grading for a new house, as well as a tree to plant if a fast-growing tree would solve sun problems or fulfill some other landscaping need.

A negative feature of the tree is its tendency to drop its leaves in early fall when growing in poor soil and after a dry summer. Aphids may also attack the foliage, resulting in a sooty fungus that lives on their honeydew. However, none of the native trees on our place are particularly bothered nor were the Tulip Poplars I grew up with.

A young pyramid-shaped Tulip Poplar

Flower of Tulip Poplar

Vitex, Chaste Tree
Vitex agnus-castus

HEIGHT: 15 feet.
HABIT: More or less rounded top.
GROWTH RATE: Fast.
BEST USE: Small flowering tree.
LEAF COLOR: Bluish green.
FLOWERS: Lavender with a spicy fragrance.

Chaste Tree originally came from southern Europe, but it has been with us for so many years and it is so common through the South, it might as well be a native. I remember recommending it as a large shrub that should be drastically pruned to encourage fresh growth on which the spicy-scented lavender blooms would appear during the summer. I was wrong, at least partly. I realized my error after seeing it grown as a tree along with tree-form crape myrtles at Callaway Gardens. Since then, I have noticed a number of tree-form Vitex around country homes and abandoned home sites. Landscapers are also using them on new home properties.

Do not discount Vitex as a shrub, since it is a lovely plant when grown that way. I am sure I'll proclaim its virtues if I ever write a book on Southern shrubs. But I also recommend it where space is restricted and you need a tree to give color, fragrance, and nice form.

Cultivars

There are a number of cultivars, including a more shrubby white form that we once sold. Be sure cultivars purchased to make trees are heavy, upright forms.

Chaste Tree flowers have a delightful fragrance.

Walnut

Juglans sp.

Black Walnut

Our native Black Walnut, *Juglans nigra*, and the English or Persian Walnut, *Juglans regia*, from southeast Europe and western Asia are the only species of the genus *Juglans* grown in the South. Both species are prized for their delicious nuts as well as for timber. Neither are easy to transplant and their use in landscape plans is restricted. English walnuts are available as bare root-plants from nursery catalogs. These young plants seem to survive fairly well, though I have planted several and all have died in a year or two.

Black Walnuts are native to most of the South, and if you have one already growing, thank your lucky star since it is a beautiful, long-lived tree. I must say, though, that it took me many years to overcome the all-too-many spankings I got over the stained clothes resulting from boyhood wars using walnuts as missiles. But eventually I developed a love for these trees and have discovered many fine Black Walnut specimens growing in older landscapes and in the wild.

Black Walnut
Juglans nigra

HEIGHT: 50-plus feet.
HABIT: Oval to broad-rounded when mature. May be loose with wide-spaced limbs when growing with other hardwoods close by.
GROWTH RATE: Medium.
BEST USE: Specimen, free from competition.
LEAF COLOR: Dull green to lustrous green.
FALL COLOR: Usually poor.

Black Walnuts are prize trees in a landscape. Few are ever planted for the purpose, but because they are handsome long-lived trees, most discerning homeowners demand their preservation when building their homes.

"Stately" is a good description of a massive Black Walnut standing uninhibited in a large lawn. Its fruit is four inches across with a thick fleshy layer covering a ridged two-inch walnut seed which is edible. A fresh-fallen walnut has an identifying aroma and the fleshy covering contains a stain.

Walnut wood is prized for making fine furniture, and a large tree is worth a small fortune, which has brought about a new group of rustlers — walnut tree thieves. Be careful if you have a fine tree growing in an isolated spot or you might be in for a horrible loss while you are on vacation.

People used to drive nails into Black Walnut trunks for good luck. I don't know how much luck it brought, but it was bad luck for any sawmill operator whose saw blade ran into an unseen nail, ripping off its teeth.

English Walnut
Juglans regia (Carpathian strain)

HEIGHT: 50-plus feet, but not as tall as Black Walnut under similar conditions.
HABIT: Open and spreading head.
GROWTH RATE: Medium.
BEST USE: Lawn specimen, especially as a dual shade tree and nut tree.
LEAF COLOR: Medium green.
FALL COLOR: None.
FRUIT: Delicious nuts, widely used in cooking.

The hardy strain of English (Persian) Walnut grows through the South and once was recommended for commercial crops. However, the production moved to California and Oregon where conditions are better for high-quality nut production.

Carpathian English Walnut makes a beautiful tree, a bit more refined than our native. Walnut tree lovers should consider planting a more readily available cultivar of Carpathian English walnut instead of Black Walnut, which is seldom seen in a nursery.

Wax Myrtle, Bayberry
Myrica sp.

Two species of wax myrtles are known in the South, *Myrica pennsylvanica* and *Myrica cerifera*. However, *Myrica pennsylvanica* is lower growing and more dense, making it less suitable for a tree. Also *Myrica cerifera* is almost entirely evergreen, whereas *Myrica pennsylvanica* loses its leaves during most very cold winters.

The waxy berries of both species were used for making fragrant candles, hence the alternate name, bayberry. Many years ago a Lockheed Electra prop-jet airliner taking off from the airport in Boston crashed when flocks of birds flew up from the many wax myrtles at the end of the runway and were sucked into the engines, causing them to fail.

Southern Wax Myrtle
Myrica cerifera, tree form

HEIGHT: 20 feet or over.
HABIT: Flat rounded, usually broader than tall.
HARDINESS: 0 degrees.
GROWTH RATE: Fast until near maturity.
BEST USE: Evergreen for a restricted spot.
LEAF COLOR: Dark green.

I have seen wax myrtle on the coast as long as I can remember, where the huge bushy plants are used as windbreaks and large landscape shrubs. Suddenly, they are being planted on many of the freeways in Metro Atlanta, where they withstand our hideous pollution and thrive in impossible combinations of direct sun and poor soil.

I discovered several tree-form wax myrtles at a motel adjacent to a small office park on Sea Island where we were staying while attending a wedding. I don't know who the developer and the landscape designer were, but both should receive crowns in heaven. A divided drive filled with American Plane Trees swept through a Centipede grass lawn connecting two ponds with banks of huge azaleas.

The office buildings were landscaped with Pittosporum foundation plants accented with tree Loquat, *Eriobotrya japonica*. But what really caught my eye were several 25-foot wax myrtle trees whose dark green foliage made the light smooth trunks stand out superbly. Since then, I observe office parks all over the mid- and lower South using tree-form wax myrtles in narrow spots between parking areas in front of buildings.

We now have many wax myrtles growing at Sweet Apple, which we started from seed harvested on trips to the coast, and we'll soon have some nice little evergreen trees in our landscape.

Wax myrtle and Carolina Cherry Laurel are two native Southern plants, long used as shrubs, which make excellent evergreen trees with a bit of judicious pruning.

Southern Wax Myrtle berries

Weeping Willow

Willow

Salix sp.

Most gardeners are familiar with willow trees. We see their limber branches hanging from interesting trees next to streams. Spring is announced by the sight of their fuzzy buds, and in the heat of summer, we feel cooled by their long branches weeping down to a green lawn. It's not surprising that the adjective *willowy* derives from these graceful trees.

Willows are also mentioned many times in the Bible, but the passage we especially remember and which is most associated with Weeping Willows is found in Psalms 137:1–2: "By the rivers of Babylon, there we sat down, yea, we wept when we remembered Zion. We hung our harps upon the willows in the midst of it" (New King James Version).

Even though the plants described were probably not willows, but some other tree, the name Weeping Willow and the botanical name *Salix babylonica* are certainly appropriate, even if botanically incorrect.

Willows are fast-growing trees that are seldom around as long as we would like. They are attacked by a number of insects and diseases like aphids and cankers, which, added to the short-life problem, limit their use in the garden. There were two large Pussy Willows in our landscape when we bought our place many years ago, which lasted until they finally outgrew their spots and I had to remove them. Betsy missed them; she loved to cut twigs to force buds inside during the winter. The boys, on the other hand, were glad that a convenient source of switches had suddenly dried up.

In the olden days, nurserymen bound bundles of fruit trees with willow branches and placed them in their moisture-laden holding bins. One innovative grower told me that the willows became so heavily rooted in the holding bins, he made them into cuttings and sold them as new willow plants.

Willows have been grown in Europe and the United States for centuries, and their nomenclature has become confusing, especially given the fact that willow descriptions in European publications vary tremendously from those used in American publications. Some scientists doubt if the Weeping Willow of earlier days is the one grown today, and there has certainly been a crossover between what was once sold as Pussy Willow, *Salix discolor*, and the one sold today, *Salix caprea*. Who knows for sure? I'll just do the best I can.

If you buy a Pussy Willow labeled *Salix discolor* and a taxonomist tells you it is some other plant, smile and say, "Maybe so, maybe not." Weeping Willow, Fantail Willow, and Corkscrew Willow have similar problems. Buy what you like, grow them into beautiful plants, and enjoy them. Your nomenclature may be wrong, but visually you are on firm ground. Willow names may seem to disprove my contention earlier in the book that Latin names clarify instead of confuse.

Though there are several hundred cultivated willow species, cultivars, and crosses, only a few are widely grown in Southern gardens and landscapes. The list below includes the ones we most often grow.

Pussy Willow
Salix caprea, Salix discolor

Salix discolor was once the predominantly grown willow species for the fuzzy buds that have been a part of Southern gardens since early times. Because it is more adapted to wetlands than the drier uplands, it has been largely displaced with *Salix caprea,* which is better adapted to conditions in the landscape. *Salix discolor* is also more prone to willow problems and therefore is not as easily grown.

Pussy Willow (I use the common name to discuss both of the above plants) is an interesting small tree with a maximum height of 20 to 25 feet after 10 years or so. There is a Pussy Willow tree in a well-landscaped property near us. When its buds shed their winter coats and look like little fuzzy kittens, it is a beautiful sight and worth driving to see.

Weeping Willow
Salix babylonica

Weeping Willow is as graceful tree as you will ever see. The long limber branches hang almost to the ground, looking like an umbrella dripping streams of water. Water and Weeping Willow are like a happily married couple. They aren't the same, but they live together in peace and contentment.

Though Weeping Willows are most often used near a pond or stream, I have seen many growing in quite different environments. I often pass one on top of an ugly bank next to a road. It grows quite well and does a great job of taking your eyes away from the exposed red clay on the bank. They also grow quite well in large lawns.

Weeping Willows seem to be less prone to insects and diseases when growing in the open. I planted one near the exit stream of our small lake, where it thrived happily for several years. But then every pest known to willows seemed to attack, and it died. I believe the spot was much too sheltered by the surrounding woods, causing dead air to hang over my willow like a blanket, trapping the heat and humidity conducive to insects and diseases.

You may find a Weeping Willow listed as Golden Weeping Willow, *Salix alba* 'Tristis,' which is said to be hardier and larger. I got interested in it many years ago, but since the strain being propagated at the time did not conform to the graceful ideal that customers had in mind, we discontinued its sale.

Confusion often arises when homeowners find the native White Willow, *Salix alba*, growing on their property. My nursery friend Milton Nardin best described the native willow to a customer who wondered why its branches weren't longer: "You have one that will never weep a tear." Milton, by the way, believed that anyone who could produce an almost-black Weeping Willow could make a fortune selling it to widows and widowers to plant near the grave of their loved one.

The ideal situation for a Weeping Willow is where there is ample moisture, but the soil is not tight and sticky. I also find it is better to plant smaller ones, rather than large balled trees. Smaller five- to six-foot trees seem to adjust more quickly to new soil conditions and quickly catch up to and pass larger trees. In the end, they seem to develop into better specimens.

Other Willows:

The two willows described below are specialty plants best used to give an entirely different effect in the landscape.

Corkscrew Willow
Salix matsudana 'Tortuosa'

Corkscrew Willow has twisted, contorted branches that are still limber enough to be less stark and much more pleasing than *Corylus avellana 'Contorta,'* often called Harry Lauder's Walking Stick, which looks like a plant more suited to a circus than a landscape.

Though Corkscrew Willow is reputed to be better suited to the upper South, I remember a beautiful specimen at Callaway Gardens that was 30 feet tall or taller with a graceful, interesting head. I keep forgetting to look for it when visiting Callaway Gardens in Pine Mountain, Georgia, and don't know whether it is still growing, but look for it if you visit there.

Corkscrew Willow can grow into a good tree of up to 50 feet high, but it has all the pests that attack other willows.

Japanese Fantail Willow
Salix sachalinensis 'Sekka'

Fantail Willow is a real specialty plant with its strange, flattened branches. Though it is more of a shrub than a tree, it can be tree-form when pruned properly. Flower arrangers delight in using its branches in their creations. We planted one at Lovejoy for my mother, who was well-known for her arrangements. It grew quite well but never attained much size since her enthusiasm for cutting its branches canceled out its impetus for growth.

Weeping Willow

Zelkova serrata

Zelkova

Zelkova serrata

HEIGHT: 50 feet.

HABIT: Upright, rather wide vase shape.

GROWTH RATE: Fast when young, medium after several years.

BEST USE: Medium-size tree for lawns, streets, and parks.

LEAF COLOR: Deep green.

FALL COLOR: May be bronze or skip coloring altogether.

Zelkova is touted as a replacement for the now-gone American Elm, *Ulmus americana*, as well as Siberian Elm (incorrectly listed in the nursery trade as Chinese Elm, *Ulmus pumila*). Zelkova is a fast-growing tree, especially when young, with a pleasant upright, vase-shaped form. Its ultimate height is 50 feet or more, evidence that most are planted too close to each other and to other trees. A large specimen at the Atlanta Botanical Garden certainly proves the point to me, and I urge landscapers and arborists to take note of mature trees before planting a line of Zelkovas like soldiers in formation.

I am not too impressed with younger trees, but middle-aged ones have good form, and the smooth, dark gray bark is very attractive. The bark of mature trees may exfoliate, which to me looks trashy. The leaves are larger than either the Siberian Elm, *Ulmus pumila*, or the true Chinese Elm, *Ulmus parvifolia*.

It is not pest-free as often advertised, being subject to Elm Leaf Beetle attacks as well as leaf spots. It may become subject to Dutch Elm Disease in the future since reports from Great Britain indicate its susceptibility there. Another disturbing possibility is a sensitivity to ozone, which might curtail its future as a street tree.

I do not want to alarm you too much about reports of diseases on trees since most are neither life threatening nor visibly detracting. However, in the case of such devastating diseases as Dutch Elm Disease and Chestnut Blight, I feel it wise to make special note of any tree's potential susceptibility.

Large numbers of Zelkova are being planted as street trees, but fortunately not as many as Bradford Pear. My preference for a street tree is Sawtooth Oak, but that will change if every street becomes lined with them. Zelkova is definitely lower on my list than many other landscape trees, but opinions vary.

The loss of the American Elm affects all of us who have deep feelings for trees, and our desire to replace it with a similar tree is worthy. I was taught a long time ago and still believe that you must look at all of a tree's attributes, not just a few, when choosing which to plant in your landscape.

Trees for Special Purposes

I am not too fond of recommendations – opinions are fine, as you have undoubtedly discovered, but I think recommendations are imposing my tastes on you. Therefore, I offer the following lists with this caveat: Before planting any tree, whether in this or any other lists you have, read the descriptions in Chapter 3, then make your own decision which tree to plant. Not all the trees listed in each category will grow throughout the South. Live Oak is not hardy above the lower coastal plain. Fraser Fir is a mountain tree that won't grow in the middle piedmont or coastal plain. This is a further reason to be sure to read the descriptions in Chapter 3.

Outstanding Large Trees

Best Large Spreading Shade Trees Growing 50 Feet or Higher
Ginkgo
October Glory Red Maple
Sugar Maple
Chestnut Oak
White Oak

Ten Best Tall Specimens for Large Lawns
Ginkgo
Southern Magnolia
October Glory Red Maple

Sugar Maple

Chestnut Oak

Sugar Maple
Mississippi Hackberry
Common Horse Chestnut
Live Oak
White Oak
Dawn Redwood
Fraser Fir

Small-Growing Trees

Very Dwarf Trees
Under 10 Feet
Weeping Yaupon Holly
Japanese Maple, dwarf cultivars
Crape Myrtle (heavily pruned)
Wax Myrtle

Dwarf Trees
10 to 15 Feet
Japanese Maple
Wax Myrtle (heavily pruned)
Crape Myrtle (lightly pruned)

Small Trees
15 to 25 Feet
Texas Umbrella Chinaberry
Wax Myrtle, tree form
Crape Myrtle, tree form
Foster Holly
Yaupon Holly

Medium Trees
25 to 35 Feet
Loblolly Bay
Flowering Cherry
Flowering Crabapple
Flowering Dogwood

Savannah Holly
Red Buckeye
Halesia, Silverbell

Special Characteristics

Weeping Trees
Weeping Beech
Weeping Cherry
Weeping Yaupon Holly

Outstanding Bark
American Beech
River Birch
Fastigiata European Hornbeam
Crape Myrtle
Paperbark Maple
London Plane Tree
Zelkova

Multi-stem
River Birch
Crape Myrtle
Wax Myrtle

Umbrella Form
Texas Umbrella Chinaberry

Tight Vase Shape
Fastigiata European Hornbeam

Attractive Fruit or Seed
Red Buckeye
Flowering Cherry
Flowering Crabapple
Chinese Dogwood
Flowering Dogwood

Golden-rain Tree
American Holly
Savannah Holly
Bigleaf Magnolia
Southern Magnolia
Red Mulberry
Common Persimmon
Japanese Persimmon

Fruit or Seed Attractive to Birds
Black Cherry
Texas Umbrella Chinaberry
Flowering Dogwood
American Holly
Savannah Holly
Southern Magnolia
Red Mulberry

Edible Fruit
Callaway Flowering Crabapple
Chinese Chestnut
Pecan
Purple Leaf Plum
English Walnut

Fast-Growing
Dawn Redwood
Chinese Elm
Zelkova

Flowers

Showy Spring Flowers
Red Buckeye
Flowering Cherry
Flowering Crabapple
Chinese Dogwood
Flowering Dogwood
Halesia, Silverbell
Common Horse Chestnut
Lily Magnolia
Saucer Magnolia
Star Magnolia
White Bark Magnolia

Flowering Peach
Bradford Pear
Purple Leaf Plum
Redbud
White Judas Tree, White Redbud
Chinese Redbud
Pussy Willow

Showy Summer Flowers
Crape Myrtle
Golden-rain Tree
Sourwood
Tamarisk
Vitex, Chaste Tree

Fragrant Flowers
European Linden
Southern Magnolia
Tamarisk
Vitex, Chaste Tree

Trees for Tall Screens
Japanese Cedar, Cryptomeria
Leyland Cypress
Canadian Hemlock
American Holly (slow)
Savannah Holly (medium)
Loblolly Pine
Slash Pine

Foliage

Colorful Summer Foliage
Copper Beech, purple
Crimson King Maple, dark purple
  (upper South only)
Japanese Maple, red leaf cultivars
Purple Leaf Plum, wine red to purple

Good Fall Color
Black Gum
Black Cherry
Texas Umbrella Chinaberry
  (attractive to birds)

Flowering Dogwood
Ginkgo
Katsura Tree, yellow with pink
  and fragrant
Paperbark Maple
October Glory Red Maple
Red Sunset Red Maple
Sugar Maple
Pin Oak
White Oak
Bradford Pear
Persimmon
Sourwood
Sweet Gum

Large Leaves over 12 inches long
Bigleaf Magnolia
Fraser Magnolia
Cucumber Magnolia
White Bark Magnolia
Umbrella Magnolia

Broadleaf Evergreens
Loblolly Bay
Carolina Cherry Laurel
American Holly
Foster Holly
Savannah Holly
Yaupon Holly
Southern Magnolia
Japanese Evergreen Oak

Needle Evergreens
Atlas Cedar
Indian Cedar
Japanese Cedar
Cedar of Lebanon
Red Cedar
Leyland Cypress
Balsam Fir
Fraser Fir
China Fir
Hemlock
Spruce

Tree Planting and Culture

L ook at trees growing effortlessly in a forest, or at Water Oak, White Ash, Box Elder, and Catalpa sprouting in flower beds, Liriope borders, and other impossible places. I even saw a Tree of Heaven taking its name seriously by sprouting in a crevice on top of a six-story building. Nature seems optimistic when seeds fall, but only one or two out of thousands that fall in forests or strange places in the landscape ever take root and begin to grow. And of those that do sprout, few reach significant size. Nature overdoes tree seed production because it's the mechanism that ensures the survival of species — including such species as squirrels, chipmunks, and birds.

As homeowners, we count on better odds and plant more methodically than Nature. Once we've selected that maple or magnolia, we confidently expect it to grow into a magnificent addition in our landscape.

The first two decisions are the most important: the right tree and the right place. Perhaps you need shade to protect your home from sun. You will need a tree that grows broad and tall and has ample room to develop. If you want a gorgeous flowering cherry or dogwood, it might look lost in a large expanse of lawn, but beautiful closer to your house.

The next step is to plant it correctly. I may seem a bit old-fashioned, but I believe in planting at the right time and in a tried and proven way. I shiver and shake when I see a gorgeous four-inch diameter, 12-foot tree being planted in a recently graded field of clay soil during mid-summer. I know builders have deadlines and demand trees at any time of the year. Still, it makes my skin crawl to watch a handsome well-grown tree sit like a pitifully sick child for the first couple of seasons or simply dry up and die during the first or second year after planting. What a difference a four- to six-month wait would have made.

How to plant trees:
I have lived long enough to see several revolutions in

tree-planting techniques. My son Chris and I discussed quite a few that were being touted when he studied for his postgraduate degree. I know that landscape installers need to cut corners and use the quickest and easiest ways, especially when planting extremely large trees. However, I feel strongly that a homeowner who goes the extra mile while planting reaps the benefits of better-growing and faster-developing trees. A homeowner who insists that an installer do more than plop a tree in a hole which barely fits its ball of earth will reap similar benefits.

The following steps should help you get the best results when planting a tree.

When to plant:
Developers and homeowners are always in a hurry when planting trees is on the agenda. Developers want trees in the ground when residential or commercial structures are finished, no matter what time of the year it is, because a finished landscape helps sell homes and rent office space. What's more, a home buyer knows that it is next to impossible to get a developer to return and plant shrubs and trees at the best planting time, which could be several months later. New owners of older homes also get anxious, especially when hot sunlight blazes through a window, bleaching draperies and furniture.

But the fact is, tree-planting is seasonal, despite the dictates of economics. I know too many slash-and-grade commercial and residential developments where trees are still sickly and pitiful-looking two or three years after planting. For several years, I have been watching a summer planting of trees near where I live. To paraphrase an old country saying, "I'd rather *want* a tree than have a tree like that."

The correct time for planting trees is from November until early March in the mid-South. Specifically, plant shade trees when they are dormant and without leaves, unless of course the ground is frozen. Plant evergreen trees during the same months, though you can plant a bit earlier if they are freshly dug, balled and burlapped, or container-grown.

Most people wait as late as possible to plant everything, including trees, hoping for mild weather. But the best first-year growth comes with trees planted much earlier. The reason is simple: Tree roots need to start growing well before leaf buds open. The more the roots grow before buds open, the more water and nutrients are at the growth points, ready to be used by the new growth. Summer planting is dangerous because the expanded leaves need tremendous amounts of water to survive without drying up or dropping prematurely.

Choosing a good tree in a nursery:

Find the species or cultivar you have decided upon. Don't be in a hurry. If the nursery doesn't have exactly what you want, do not substitute, but try elsewhere before purchasing your second or third choice. I have seen too many people rush into a nursery and buy the first tree that looked good or blindly take the suggestion of a salesperson, only to find later that the tree did not grow to the right size and shape or have the specific qualities they were looking for. Be stubborn and particular.

When you find the right species or cultivar, inspect the tree carefully. First try to sway the top. Don't yank it; just try to move it around to make sure that it is being held securely in its ball or container. If it is loose, many unseen roots may be broken, reducing your chances of success.

Find the central trunk and inspect its top. If it is firm and unbroken and you can see a strong terminal bud, you have found a good tree. A tree with the top broken off may never develop the natural shape of the species.

Inspect the trunk for scars and broken bark and check to see if it is misshapen. Some species do not grow as straight and cleanly as others, but if you have a choice, take the one with clean smooth bark. Do not choose a badly scarred tree.

Inspect the branches. If a few are broken, never mind, but if most are damaged, look for another one of the same species and cultivar.

Have the tree carefully loaded into your vehicle. Do not let the loader pick the tree up by the trunk; this can break the roots very easily or break the top off the central trunk. If the tree is evergreen, do not let it hang out of a window or trunk. Cold wind will quickly dry the leaves and cause browning. If you can't get it in your car without it hanging out, ask for burlap or paper to wrap up the exposed area. I recommend wrapping bare branches also since they may be tender and prone to drying in cold wind.

If you cannot plant it immediately, place your tree in a sheltered area, out of the wind. Water a container-grown tree frequently, but do not water balled and burlapped plants. It is better to pile wet mulch over the ball if a week passes before planting.

What you will need to plant a tree:

- A strong spade or long-handle shovel. I find a short-handled spade the easiest to use, but either is satisfactory.
- Peat moss or finely ground bark. I prefer peat moss (not Michigan peat muck).
- A source of water.
- A wheelbarrow or ground cloth to mix the soil removed from the hole and to prepare the backfill. (Note: Use a slow-release, polymer-encapsulated – referred to as "prill-type" – fertilizer, like Osmocote, to mix in the backfill. This type of fertilizer lasts for many months, releasing fertilizer whenever moisture and weather conditions are right for growth. If you cannot find a prill-type fertilizer, use a slow-release, high-nitrogen fertilizer for lawns or shrubs. But do not use a lawn fertilizer with pre-emergence weed killers or broadleaf weed killers.)

Digging the hole:

With balled and burlapped and container-grown trees, measure the width and depth of the ball of earth. If you are planting a bare-root tree, measure the distance from the bottom root to the point where the top root comes from the trunk.

For balled and burlapped and container-grown trees, dig a hole one inch shallower than the depth and six to eight inches wider than the ball of earth. For bare-root trees, dig a hole wide and deep enough to accommodate the root system.

Place soil removed from the hole in a wheelbarrow or on a ground cloth.

Preparing backfill soil (what you use to pack around a tree's roots or ball):

Thoroughly mix together one part peat moss, finely ground, or well-rotted compost with two parts soil taken from the hole.

Add the recommended amount of slow-release prill-type fertilizer, mixing it thoroughly into the backfill.

Planting balled and burlapped and container-grown trees correctly:

Carefully place the ball of earth in the hole so that the top of the ball at the trunk is an inch above the level of the surrounding soil. If it isn't high enough, carefully add unmixed backfill under the ball until the top of the ball is at the correct level.

Adjust the ball so that the tree is straight, level, and facing the way you want it when you have finished. Do not try to remove the burlap covering of balled and burlapped trees. However, cut any ties around the burlap attached to the trunk, remove any pinning nails on top of the ball, then cut the burlap off of the top of the ball.

Use the prepared backfill soil to fill the hole completely, packing it firmly as you fill it. I use the end of the shovel's handle to tamp the soil.

Planting bare-root trees correctly:

When you are planting bare-root trees, place the roots in the hole. Adjust them so that the top ones are slightly below the surface of the surrounding soil. Fill the hole halfway with the mixed backfill, then, if necessary, adjust the position of the roots so they are neither too shallow nor too deep. After the tree is at the correct level, start tamping the mixed soil carefully and firmly around the roots until the hole is full and the tree stands without assistance.

Finishing planting balled and burlapped, container-grown, and bare-root trees:

After the mixed soil has been thoroughly and firmly

The last step is to slowly water your new tree to settle the soil around the roots and drive out any air pockets.

After planting your tree:

Mulch the tree with pine straw, cypress mulch, or some other long-lasting material.

Inspect the tree and remove any damaged or broken limbs. Do not cut the central shoot. Topping a tree can ruin its shape and hinder its development for many years. I have seen trees ruined forever by topping.

Soak your tree whenever it is dry, especially after the weather warms in the spring.

If you have not mixed the slow-release, prill-type fertilizer in the backfill, fertilize with a high-nitrogen slow-release fertilizer when buds start to swell or when forsythia blooms in the spring.

Stake large bare-root and heavily branched balled and burlapped and container-grown trees to prevent excessive swaying in the wind before anchor roots develop. I position three stakes around the tree and tie a heavy hemp string to a point on the trunk below the branches, or two-thirds up the trunk when there are no branches. Do not tie the strings too tightly to the trunk. A tree trunk develops girth more rapidly when it can move back and forth.

Post-planting tree care:

Immediately after planting, inspect the tree for any broken, bruised, or cracked limbs and prune them off. If the central shoot has been broken, prune it off an inch above the next lower side bud. Don't severely cut back the central trunk or you may ruin the shape of your tree – forever.

Soak a newly planted tree every week unless there is good rain. I like to soak trees and shrubs with a water breaker (a gardening device that's like a soft water nozzle on your sink's faucet) attached to the hose. Place the water breaker at the stem, turn on the water very slowly, then soak for an hour.

If you have mixed a slow-release prill fertilizer in the backfill, no other fertilizing is necessary. If you missed this application, wait until forsythia blooms, then apply a slow-release high nitrogen fertilizer with a 30-4-12 or similar formula at the rate of one-half pound per inch circumference of the trunk measured three feet above the ground.

After growth starts in the spring, watch for small shoots sprouting below the major branches and remove

packed around the tree's ball of earth, make a final check to be sure that the top of the ball is above the surface of the surrounding soil. Now, not later, is the time to make any adjustments since new roots develop soon after planting and should not be disturbed.

Tamp bare-root trees firmly so the soil holds the tree tightly in place.

Now take the remaining mixed or unmixed soil and make a circular dam or collar around the outer edge of the hole you dug. This collar will hold moisture when it rains or when you soak your plant. Make sure the collar is firmly tamped so it won't wash away.

them as soon as possible. Otherwise, allow as many shoots and leaves to develop as possible since they are manufacturing food for growth. (However, as I explain below, you may have to remove excess limbs the next winter after planting.)

Caring for Trees in the Landscape:

What to do after the first growing season:
After the leaves have fallen at the end of the growing season, inspect your tree to see how its branches are developing. A well-developing tree should have branches spaced one to two feet apart and growing outward in a wide angle with the trunk, which will help prevent their splitting off in wind, ice, or snow. Some very upright trees, like Fastigiata European Hornbeam, *Carpinus betulus fastigiata*, grow upward with rather tight crotches, yet their wood formation is not prone to splitting. Other trees, like Bradford Pear, develop narrow, weak crotches and, despite all efforts, are likely to grow this way. That is why so many crash to the ground in high wind or ice storms. As an aside, this is also the reason that I caution people against planting Bradford Pear trees.

Most other shade trees naturally develop limbs with strong angles. Generally, you should remove limbs spaced less than two feet apart. At the same time, however, you want to have limbs growing on all sides of the tree. My rule is not to leave a limb that's less than two feet directly above another one.

Fertilize trees in the early spring when Forsythia blooms or when you see buds showing color. Apply a slow-release prill-type fertilizer worked into the top inch of the soil at the outer edge of the hole you dug when planting. Use the recommended rates for the brand you buy.

You can also fertilize with a high-nitrogen, slow-release fertilizer with a 30-4-12 or similar lawn or shrub formula at the rate of one-half pound per inch circumference of the trunk, measured three feet above the ground, or one pound per inch of a 15-15-15 commercial grade fertilizer. Spread the fertilizer evenly in a circle on top of bare ground, or under mulch at the outer edge of the hole you dug when planting.

Continuing care of newly planted landscape trees:
Once newly planted trees are growing well in the landscape, only minimal maintenance is needed. Following

is a quick guide to help you keep young trees developing as they should.

- Make a close and critical inspection at least once a year before leaf buds begin to show.

- Remove broken or damaged branches, those making a sharp angle with the trunk, and those spaced too close to a better branch above or below.

- Remove awkward branches that grow across other branches, causing one to scar the other. Remove the weaker of the two. However, if a smaller, well-developed branch is growing in a better direction, remove the stronger one, within reason, of course.

- Never remove the tip of the central trunk of a shade tree or you may ruin its shape forever.

- Fertilize each year for at least three years when forsythia blooms or leaf or flower buds first show color. Apply one pound of a commercial grade 15-15-15 fertilizer per inch circumference of the trunk measured approximately three feet above the ground, or one-half pound of a high-nitrogen, slow-release fertilizer for shrubs or lawns with a 30-4-12 or similar formula. See details below under fertilizing shade and flowering trees.

- After three years, less pruning and fertilizing is required. Trees growing in regularly fertilized lawns may no longer need any additional fertilizer unless growth is weak, off-color, or slow.

- Be alert for insects and diseases that might be a problem on younger trees. Trees are susceptible to many different kinds of insects and diseases that are not damaging enough to warrant spraying. However, check out any sudden changes in the color or appearance of leaves or the tree's growth rate. Identify the culprit and ask your local supplier for the best control measure.

Fertilizing shade and flowering trees:
Unlike trees of the forest, trees in the landscape are not sustained by nutrients from decomposing leaves and other organic matter found on the forest floor. Your trees need applications of commercial fertilizer for the

first three years or until their growth is rapid and sustained. In general, tree roots start taking in fertilizer when the soil temperature at their depth is above 45 degrees, and rapid translocation upward begins when the temperature at root level is above 55 degrees. The best indicator I know is Forsythia, which blooms when the soil and air temperature is above 45 degrees. It is easy to miss a tree's first bud breaks so watch for blossoms on Forsythia to know when to fertilize trees in your location.

First, measure the circumference of a tree about three feet above the ground. For me, that is knee height. You need to apply one-half pound of a slow-release fertilizer per inch circumference.

Use a high-nitrogen, slow-release fertilizer with a 30-4-12 or similar formula like those used on lawns or shrubs. However, do not use a lawn fertilizer with a weed killer or weed preventer mixed in. An excellent alternative is a slow-release, polymer-encapsulated prill-type fertilizer like Osmocote, which gives more sustained growth over a longer period of time. Apply the amount recommended on the prill-type package. Prill-type fertilizers for trees are activated by moisture and temperature, making application possible anytime, even before Forsythia blooms.

I believe fertilizer is more effective when deposited into the ground rather than scattered on the surface where heavy rains can wash it away. Make a series of holes 18 inches apart and as deep as you can around the tree under the outer edge of the branches, or "drip line." Count the number of holes, then divide the amount of fertilizer needed by the number of holes and place it in each hole. Use the same method when using prill-type fertilizers, except use the amounts recommended on the bag.

If older trees exhibit stress from drought, slow growth, poor leaf development, or other indications that they aren't too happy, fertilize them also, as directed above. Continue a yearly application until the tree is growing well once again.

Pruning shade and flowering trees:

The art of pruning any plant, especially trees, is an important part of being a good gardener. Incorrect pruning can easily damage woody shrubs and trees. Correct pruning techniques can help plants remain attractive for many years.

Have the right tools before you prune. You will need hand pruning shears for small twigs and branches, a lopper for branches that won't fit in the opening of pruning shears, and a pruning saw for limbs too large for either. Pruning saws are curved, with the blade tapered at the end, allowing easy access in tight areas. Limbs too large for shears, loppers, or saws require a chain saw, which can be a dangerous instrument if you aren't experienced. Never use a chain saw when climbing in a tree or on a tall ladder. Let professionals tackle such jobs.

Use only knife-cut hand shears or loppers. These are shears with a sharp blade that slides snugly behind a holding bar. The bar holds the twig or limb while the knife blade cuts it off. Always cut with the blade side toward the trunk. The holding bar may bruise the bark of a limb, possibly causing dieback. When the blade is toward the tree trunk, it will remove the damaged tissue. If you are right-handed, work clockwise around the tree; if left-handed, work counterclockwise, which naturally positions the blade toward the trunk. I have heard some retail nursery salesmen refer to this type of pruner as a scissor-cut shear or lopper. They use the wrong term or could be misleading you, since both blades of a scissor make a cut, which is not true of the proper kind of shear or lopper. Just smile as you examine what they recommend, making sure there is a blade and a holding bar, not two cutting blades.

Most twigs and limbs are easy to remove. However, larger limbs may not be cut through in one or two bites. On these larger ones, make the first bite upward from underneath the branch, then make the subsequent bites downward from the topside. Otherwise, heavier limbs may break before they are cut through, leaving the underside attached. This may tear the bark away from the trunk or the remaining stub of limb, damaging the tree. Similarly, when sawing off a limb, first cut upward about one-fourth of the way through the limb; then cut downward the rest of the way.

Important: Find the point where the limb you are removing joins the larger limb or trunk. Look closely for a collar surrounding the branch being removed. It may be small and hard to see, but identifying it is important. Avoid cutting into this collar, which contains tissue that heals the wound. If you can't identify the collar, cut one-fourth of an inch away from the main stem or branch to reduce the possibility of damage.

Most cuts do not need painting over with any sticky or tarlike material. Recent studies show these materials inhibit healing, though they may do some good in the short term. In the long term, they tend to dry out and let water through. A better solution is to make a downward-slanting cut, which prevents water from standing on the end. However, watch for new developments in pruning paints that solve these inherent problems.

Care of older trees:

Trees more than 10 years old need very little help except when damaged by wind, ice, snow, insects, diseases, or some sudden growth problem. Depending on a damaged tree's size and age, most work should be done by a qualified arborist who is trained not to fall out of the top of a 30- or 40-foot tree. Trained arborists working for reputable companies are your best friends when removing or repairing a large shade tree.

Seasonal timing of tree activities:

Most garden activities are dictated by the seasons. Trees are planted, pruned, fertilized, and sprayed at particular times of the year. Chapter 5 provides a seasonal guide to specific, time-related activities to nurture your trees and ensure that they remain as beautiful and useful as you want them to be.

Season-by-Season Tree Activities

Trees are tough. In forests, they sprout and grow for many years even when conditions are not ideal. They may not develop into beautiful specimens because of competition from other trees, lack of nutrients in the soil, and lower-than-optimum moisture, but they still grow and perform well. Landscapes, of course, do not have or need the abundance of trees found in forests, so each tree planted in a landscape is expected to grow as well as it can and be as beautiful as possible. Some native trees in my woods were small when I arrived many years ago and have never grown as large as they are supposed to. Yet the maples I planted almost 30 years ago to shield my house from hot western sun are now over 50 feet high and 40 feet across, making my living room a delightful place on a hot summer afternoon. I spaced them far enough apart to prevent their competing with each other, and therefore they've developed rapidly and fulfilled my highest hopes.

Trees require different levels of nutrients and moisture for growth, depending on the time of the year and the weather. Plant and prune when trees are not actively growing. Fertilize when tree roots first begin to take up nutrients in the spring. Insect and disease populations rise in the spring, reach a peak in the late summer, and decline in the fall, so watch for them more carefully during the times when they are most likely to be active. In fact, most garden activities relate to the seasons.

The South covers a huge amount of territory and topography. Spring comes earlier and fall is later in the Deep South than in upper Virginia, West Virginia, Kentucky, and the Appalachian Mountains. If you live in Mobile or New Orleans, you will see azaleas blooming a long time before they blossom in Asheville, North Carolina, and Charlottesville, Virginia.

Plan winter activities after trees lose their leaves, wherever you are in the South. In the mountains, you will have a longer dormant period than on the coasts. Spring starts about the time forsythia blooms, summer when temperatures reach 80 degrees, and fall when days are noticeably shorter, the first leaves turn color, and nights are cool.

This is the gardening way in the South. We cannot garden successfully by adhering to the seasons in the almanac, which says winter starts on December 21, the shortest day of the year; spring on March 20, the vernal equinox when daylight hours and night hours are equal; summer on June 21, the longest day of the year; and fall on September 22, the autumnal equinox when day and night hours are equal once again.

Gardeners need to be keen watchers of weather news, but even more observant of what is happening in nature. Just because you see Red Maple blooming in late January, don't think winter is over, because that is their nature. Forsythia is a better indicator of the end of winter and the beginning of spring since it almost always blossoms after hard freezes. Another reliable signal is dogwood. Year after year, the height of the dogwood season in Atlanta is the weekend closest to April 10, a good date for Atlantans to keep in mind for mid-spring. Farmers in the mid-South used to plant beans and field corn after Good Friday, by which time they believed the danger of a late frost was over. Easter is almost always cool, or even cold, regardless of whether it comes in late March or late April. Some say the last cold is on the full moon after the spring equinox, which also coincides with Easter.

Gardeners need to be good record-keepers. The two best weather instruments they can have are a rain gauge and an indoor-outdoor thermometer (I hate to go outside on a very cold day to find out what the temperature is). Our weathermen in Atlanta might advise that a cold front will be coming through and the low temperature will be 25 degrees on Tuesday and 30 degrees on Wednesday. I have observed for many years that my little corner of this earth will be colder than predicted on the second night after a front comes through than on the first. Cold settles on top of my area like a blanket. You should learn the idiosyncrasies of your own piece of property and abide by them rather than depending exactly on what radio or TV weathermen predict.

This season-by-season guide corresponds to my area in the mid-South. Adjust according to your own seasonal patterns and local weather. The activities will then be correct for Mobile, Asheville, and Roanoke, even though the exact days on the calendar might be different.

Trees are dormant in the winter

Winter Tree Activities
The Dormant Season

Winter officially begins on the shortest day of the year, December 21, but the winter gardening season starts earlier when hard freezes kill perennial tops and tender annuals. Leaves drop from deciduous trees, indicating that they are now dormant, and evergreen tree growth slows to almost nothing.

Planting
See Chapter 4 for planting instructions.

Plant most evergreen and deciduous balled and burlapped, container-grown, and bare root trees anytime during the winter season, except when the ground is frozen or very wet.

If planting is necessary before the soil dries out, use dry peat moss as the soil amendment. It will absorb excess moisture and make it easier to prepare a good mixture to use in the backfill.

Plant marginally hardy deciduous trees, like fig trees, at the end of winter.

Plant the following evergreen trees close to the end of winter: Southern Magnolia, *Magnolia grandiflora*, Cherry Laurel, *Prunus caroliniana*, and Chinese Evergreen Oak, *Quercus myrsinifolia*.

Water newly planted trees to settle the backfill against the ball of earth.

Mulch newly planted trees with pine straw or cypress mulch. Do not use tree leaves, which shingle and reduce water moving downward into the root system. Never allow mulch to pack against the tree's trunk.

Stake newly planted shade and flowering trees, especially if they were purchased bare root. Attach three slightly taut strings to the trunk about four to five feet off the ground and run them to wooden stakes driven at intervals around the tree. Make a collar of a piece of an old watering hose or some other padding that won't hold moisture to prevent the strings from cutting into the trunks.

Rake fallen leaves away from trees. They do not make a good mulch and should not be allowed to pack on top of existing bark or pine straw mulches.

Pruning
See Chapter 4 for the best ways to prune.

The best time to prune most trees is when they are dormant, especially if you need to remove heavy limbs. Trees are less likely to be damaged when they are not actively growing.

Prune large or broken limbs anytime trees are dormant except when the wood is frozen.

Prune summer-flowering trees anytime they are bare except when the wood is frozen. Summer-flowering trees like Crape Myrtle and Chaste Tree may be pruned severely to force new spring shoots on which the summer blossoms will develop.

Do not prune winter and spring-flowering trees until after they finish blossoming, or else you will remove flower buds and reduce the number of flowers.

You may need to prune spring-flowering fruit trees, like flowering forms of crabapples, cherries, peaches, and pears, to remove dead, diseased, or bad branches, even though you will be removing flower buds yet to come out. Prune them if necessary, but do it sparingly and selectively by removing only problem wood. Remember that buds for spring blossoms are already present on the branches and twigs grown last summer, and any pruning of live limbs or twigs will reduce the number of flowers on the tree.

I have noticed a number of maintenance people severely topping tall-growing and more upright Bradford Pear, either to restrict its growth or to reduce the weight on bad crotches. Be aware that the results can be disastrous. Not only is the shape altered and in some cases ruined, but the excess amount of succulent new growth that results is highly susceptible to Fire Blight disease.

Prune shade trees carefully by removing weak growth, crossed branches, and limbs making a narrow "V" with the trunk. Never top a shade tree or you may ruin its shape forever.

Spraying
See Chapter 6 for information on insects and diseases.

Apply dormant sprays like lime sulfur and dormant oil when it is not freezing and is not likely to rain before the material dries on the tree. Lime sulfur is quite helpful to control a number of pests on flowering forms of many fruit trees like flowering peach, flowering cherry, and flowering crabapples.

Scale on most trees can be controlled with Cygon or Orthene. Use Cygon on all except hollies or ornamental trees that are sensitive and have a warning on the package.

Fertilizing

See Chapter 4 for information on fertilizing.

If you didn't fertilize when you planted with a slow-release, prill-type fertilizer, fertilize all newly planted trees with a 30-4-12 or similar formula of slow-release fertilizer when forsythia blooms. Use one-half pound per inch circumference of the tree measured three feet above the ground. Do not use a high-nitrogen slow-release lawn fertilizer with a weed preventer or weed killer added. Spread the fertilizer in a circle at the edge of the hole you dug. Water thoroughly after fertilizing unless rain is forecast.

Fertilize large shade trees when forsythia blooms. Use one-half pound of a 30-4-12 or similar formula slow-release fertilizer per inch circumference of the tree measured three feet above the ground. Do not use a lawn fertilizer with weed preventer or a weed killer added. Alternatively, you can use one pound per inch circumference of a 15-15-15 fertilizer or a slow-release prill-type fertilizer for trees at the rate recommended on the bag.

Fertilize summer-flowering trees with 5-10-15 formula fertilizer. Use one pound per inch circumference of the tree measured three feet above the ground.

Other Winter Tree Activities

Trees with very narrow crotches tend to be weak and subject to breaking in high wind, ice, and snow. You can help prevent splitting and breaking by removing the least important branch or by carefully wiring the two limbs or a trunk and limb together. Never wrap a wire around a limb or tree trunk. Use a heavy eye bolt screwed into each one. Then fasten a heavy wire to each eye bolt, tightening it enough to hold the limb or trunk in place, but not so tight that the limb or trunk can't move at all. If this job seems too difficult, contact a reputable tree service, like Bartlett to do it for you.

The sight of Forsythia blooming means it's time to start spring activities.

Spring

The spring gardening season lasts from the time when forsythia blooms and soil temperatures are above 45 degrees until air temperatures are in the 80s.

Planting

Plant Southern Magnolia, Chinese Evergreen Oak, and Cherry Laurel as early as possible in the spring. Make sure to plant in a well-prepared hole at the correct depth. Never cover the ball around a new plant's roots with soil.

For best results, plant B&B trees before they leaf out. After they leaf out, plant with extreme caution and be prepared to water when there has been no significant rain in a week.

Plant container-grown trees all spring, but plant carefully after they leaf out. Be prepared to water late-spring-planted trees when there is no significant rain in a week.

It is not recommended to plant bare-root deciduous trees after they leaf out.

Pruning

Prune spring-flowering trees immediately after they finish blooming but only if needed. Heavy structural pruning should have already been done in the winter.

Remove newly sprouting branches on smaller trees as quickly as possible when they sprout too close together or come out at bad angles.

Fertilizing

See Chapter 4 for more information on fertilizing.

When the forsythia blooms, fertilize Southern Magnolia, Chinese Evergreen Oak, and Cherry Laurel with a slow-release high-nitrogen, evergreen formula or a slow-release prill-type. Use one-half pound of an evergreen formula per inch circumference of the tree measured three feet above the ground or at the recommended rate for a prill-type fertilizer.

Spring is not the best time to fertilize shade trees, but do so if you didn't fertilize earlier. Use one-half pound of a 30-4-12 or similar formula slow-release fertilizer per inch circumference of the tree measured three feet

above the ground. Do not use a lawn fertilizer with weed preventer or a weed killer added. Alternatively, you can use one pound per inch circumference of a 15-15-15 fertilizer or a slow-release prill-type fertilizer for trees at the rate recommended on the bag. Be prepared to water newly fertilized trees in drought situations.

Fertilize spring-flowering trees like flowering crabapples, flowering cherries, flowering peaches, and flowering plums as the flower petals fall. Use one pound of 5-10-15 fertilizer per inch circumference of the tree measured three feet above the ground.

Spraying

Timing is crucial in the control of insects and diseases. Start in the early spring when a problem first rears its ugly head.

Spraying large trees is nearly impossible for the homeowner. The only sprayer I have had any sort of success with is a trombone type. However, protecting smaller trees is very important and easy to do with any normal pressure sprayer.

Control scale on trees with Cygon, but use Orthene on hollies or any specific tree for which Cygon has a label warning.

Watch out for worms and caterpillars eating the foliage of trees. Bacillus thuringiensis (BT) gives excellent safe control of soft worms. Two BT forms are available: Thuricide as a spray or Dipel as a dust.

Protect dogwood buds from petal blight by spraying with Daconil or Dithane. Apply the spray when the bud cracks open, and every ten days after until the petals have fallen. However, do not spray when flowers are at their peak. Be sure to spray opening leaves, then spray again when half their full size.

Holly leaf miners are also a problem in the spring. This is a gnatlike insect that you will see flying around hollies, especially American Hollies. The insect lays eggs in the leaves, which hatch into tiny worms. The worms tunnel inside the leaf, ruining its appearance and causing premature leaf drop. Use Orthene as a control when you first spot the gnats.

A grotesque-looking disease, Cedar Apple Rust, may cause yellow spotting of crabapple, apple, and pear leaves. The alternate host of the disease is Red Cedar. Large gelatinous orange bodies will form on the cedar. Try to find and remove those found on cedars growing close to crabapples and apples. Spray the foliage of crabapples, apples, and pears with Maneb or a complete home orchard spray.

Japanese Beetles attack a variety of trees, especially flowering forms of peaches, plums, and cherries. Spray infested trees with Sevin.

Watering

Develop a rainfall pattern for your area. The general pattern for the South is a wet March, April and early May, and a very dry May after Mother's Day. But the South is a huge area. Those of you in the upper South, especially in the mountains, may have very different patterns. Adjust watering practices to coincide with the probability of receiving rain.

Thoroughly water trees like Southern Magnolia immediately after planting, even if the ground is wet. This settles the soil around the roots and helps them develop faster. You will not need to water again until new growth starts, unless there is a week without rain. Watch the weather. Soak newly planted or recently fertilized trees when there is no significant rainfall for a week.

Other springtime activities

Be extremely careful when mowing or using a power trimmer around old and new trees. Do not hit or damage the bark. Even the slightest damage may make an entrance for borers or other damaging insects. This is true for all trees in the landscape or any natural area, including planted and natural trees.

Be extremely careful when applying herbicides – either spray or powder – underneath trees. Do not spray with 2-4-D type weed killers for weeds growing in bare areas underneath trees. Do not let the material drift onto leaves or fall on the ground where there are shallow roots. These materials can severely damage shallow-rooted trees like dogwoods.

During the summer, trees are in full leaf and need minimal care.

Summer

Summer is the hot, humid season in the South when temperatures are high in the daytime as well as at night.

Plant

It is too late to plant B&B and container-grown trees successfully unless extreme care is given and you promise to soak plants during hot dry weather.

Prune

Summer is not the best time to prune tree limbs. If there is a broken branch, however, remove the limb (including the jagged break or split) with a clean cut.

Spray

Look for damaging insects on evergreen trees like magnolias and hollies. Scale, spider mite, lacebug, leaf miner, spittle bug, and leaf hopper are the most prevalent in the summer. Use Cygon or Orthene to control them. Do not use Cygon on hollies.

Protect flowering trees like flowering peaches and flowering plums from Japanese Beetle damage by spraying with Sevin or putting traps downwind from the tree.

On occasion, insects and diseases may show up on all trees. If this happens, take a branch containing some of the infected area to your local nurseryman or Cooperative Extension Service agent for identification and suggested controls.

Flowering fruit trees are susceptible to borers. Borer control takes place in August and September. Two sprayings are needed. In the lower South, spray in mid-summer and again in early September. In the middle and upper South, spray on the first of August and the first of September. Thiodan is the recommended material to use.

Water

Soak newly planted trees once a week when there is no significant rainfall.

During periods of extreme drought, large trees may need watering. Watch for discoloration, drying, dieback, and premature leaf-fall as signs that the tree is being affected. Use a watering spike placed intermittently around the perimeter of the tree's roots, approximately under the edge of the farthest-reaching limbs. Soak thoroughly.

Other

Keep newly planted trees mulched well to conserve moisture when it is hot and dry. However, never allow mulch to pack against the trunk.

Be extremely careful when mowing or using a power trimmer around old and new trees. Do not hit or damage the bark. Even the slightest damage may make an entrance for borers or other damaging insects. This is true for all trees in the landscape or natural areas – natives as well as those you have planted. Dogwood, flowering peach, flowering cherry, and flowering plum are highly susceptible to borer attacks. Shade trees like pines are also attacked by various borers and bark beetles.

Many trees are filled with colorful leaves in the fall as they prepare for winter.

Fall

Fall brings cooler nights even though days may still be warm. Days become shorter and evenings longer until the first freeze ends the fall gardening season.

Plant

Wait until early winter to plant B&B and container-grown flowering and shade trees. The trees being sold this time of year are not as healthy because they have just endured a hot summer in a container or burlapped ball of earth. Trees sold in early winter will have been dug close to planting time.

Prune

Do not prune trees in the fall. The best time to prune shade trees is in the winter when they are dormant.

Spring-flowering trees have set their blossom buds for next year. Pruning now will remove many of next year's flowers. Wait until winter to prune summer-flowering trees, which set flower buds on new growth.

Fertilize

Do not fertilize trees in the fall. Just like pruning, fertilizing could force tender growth that might be killed by the first hard freezes.

Spray

Watch for insects like scale. Spray with Orthene for general control and Cygon for scale on all except hollies.

Finish Southern borer control on flowering peaches, flowering cherries, and flowering crabapples by spraying for the second time in early September. Thiodan is the recommended material to use.

Water

Slowly water trees if there has been no significant rain in a week. This is especially important for last spring's plantings.

The effects of a summer drought may be showing up on large trees. Watch for discoloration, drying, dieback, and premature leaf-fall as signs that the tree is being affected. Use a watering spike placed intermittently around the perimeter of the tree's roots, approximately under the edge of the farthest-reaching limbs. Water thoroughly.

Other

Keep newly planted trees well mulched to conserve moisture when it is hot and dry, especially in September and October before leaves fall. Do not pile mulch against the trunks.

Be extremely careful when mowing or using a power trimmer around old and new trees, especially dogwoods, flowering cherries, crabapples, flowering peaches, and flowering plums. Do not hit or damage the bark. Even the slightest damage may make an entrance for borers or other damaging insects.

CHAPTER 6

Introduction to Tree Problems

Several years ago my son Chris strongly suggested that I purchase the book *Insects That Feed on Trees and Shrubs,* by Warren T. Thompson and Howard H. Lyon, and a companion book *Diseases of Trees and Shrubs,* by Wayne A. Sinclair, Howard H. Lyon, and Warren T. Thompson, all of whom were professors at Cornell where he studied. I did as Chris suggested and waited anxiously for the books to arrive. When I turned the first pages, I wasn't sure I had done the right thing by buying these magnificent books. Every tree seemed to have some problem, and if you think horticultural names are bad, you haven't seen insect and disease names.

In no way am I belittling these fabulous, well-illustrated books, but I soon realized that the home-owner needn't be concerned with perhaps 75 percent of the possible problems described. I constantly watch plants in landscapes and in the wild and observe how well they grow. There are galls, leaf spots, blights, and beetles attacking them all the time, but few of us ever take notice – and neither do the trees. And that's generally okay, because few of these problems are ever serious. But the other side of the coin is that some are serious enough to cause severe damage and perhaps the death of the plant. Failure to act on a problem at the outset can result in the loss of a prize part of your landscape.

Many problems causing poor growth start with the choice of an inappropriate tree. Planting a good tree in a bad place or choosing a tree without knowing its ultimate characteristics can teach a painful and perhaps costly lesson. Other problems begin on planting day, when a hole to deep or too shallow can weaken a plant and invite all sorts of insect and disease attacks. Negligence can also be disastrous. Damage from lawn machinery to the bark of a tree opens a door underneath the tree's natural protective layer for insects and diseases to enter.

Fertilizer-starved plants become weakened and subject to insects and diseases. Improper pruning also invites pest problems. Heavy topping of crabapples and Bradford Pear forces masses of new succulent shoots, which are prime targets of fire blight. Making a bad cut may cause the bark to peel or may keep the wound from healing rapidly.

I have a hard time explaining the need to remove vines climbing up tree trunks because some people like green all the way to the top. But vines can kill trees by strangling them or by attaching themselves to the bark and opening the way for problems. Some vines like honeysuckle and kudzu can cover the green area of a tree, depriving the plant of necessary sunlight.

Parasitic plants like mistletoe are not strong enough to kill a tree but can weaken the branch on which they live, possibly resulting in breakage during wind or ice storms. (Saprophytic plants like Spanish moss, though, aren't harmful since they are just parking and not entering the tree to rob its food.)

Some problems are beyond our control, or so it would seem. No one can predict or prevent lightning strikes, except by installing grounding devices at great expense, but this is certainly worthwhile if you have a 200-year-old champion tree. Wind, ice, and snow are beyond our control, though breakage-prone trees like Bradford Pear should be avoided where such storms are common.

Common sense and a bit of detective work are all you need to have beautiful trees in your landscape. Choose tree types that aren't likely to develop problems, then watch for the occasional pest, bad branch, or soil problem and take immediate action to overcome it.

Kudzu must be kept under control or it will cover and ruin trees.

Planting/Growing Problems

PROBLEM: Tendency to break in ice, snow, and wind storms.

SOLUTION: Choose better types with strong wood and wide crotches.

PROBLEM: Plants pruned heavily by line crews.

SOLUTION: Plant lower-growing trees or plant away from power lines.

PROBLEM: Trees causing damage to buildings.

SOLUTION: Plant smaller-growing trees and plant away from structures.

PROBLEM: Trees ruining foundations.

SOLUTION: Never plant trees close to buildings.

PROBLEM: Tree roots rising and breaking pavement.

SOLUTION: Plant deep-rooted trees farther away from driveways and streets.

PROBLEM: Dieback in a row of screening plants.

SOLUTION: Space plants farther apart, even when they look lonesome when young.

PROBLEM: Plants slowly die.

SOLUTION: They may be planted too shallowly or too deeply. Leave the top of the ball of earth only an inch above the ground when planting. Do not cover the top of the ball with soil by planting too deeply. See Chapter 4.

PROBLEM: Soil washing away from the roots.

SOLUTION: Prevent further erosion by making a gentler grade or building a retaining structure outside the canopy of the tree. Do not cover the roots of old, healthy trees with soil.

PROBLEM: Grass won't live underneath or near trees.

SOLUTION: Plant a groundcover like dwarf Liriope.

Insect Problems

PROBLEM: Tent caterpillar.

SOLUTION: Best control is when you first see the tents. Open the tent with a stick, then spray with Orthene followed by a spray of Bacillus thuringiensis (BT).

PROBLEM: Bagworms on conifers.

SOLUTION: Pick off bags in winter if you can reach them. Spray in early summer with Orthene followed Bacillus thuringiensis (BT). Check every ten days and respray if new ones appear.

PROBLEM: Borers in flowering forms of peaches, cherries, and crabapples.

SOLUTION: Prune off infected limbs during the winter. Spray trunks of trees in mid-August with thiodan and a second time in early September.

PROBLEM: Borers in dogwood.

SOLUTION: Prevention is the best method of control. Be careful never to damage bark with lawn machines. Keep trees healthy and filled with leaves to prevent sun scalding, which causes bark damage. Clean any wounds by carefully cutting away loose bark to promote healing. Keep mulch away from trunk.

PROBLEM: Dogwood twig gall.

SOLUTION: This problem is seldom serious and is usually left untreated. However, it is easy to control by snipping off the galls when first seen. Don't confuse them with dogwood flower buds, which look like a turk's cap.

PROBLEM: Elm leaf beetle.

SOLUTION: Plant true Chinese Elm and Zelkova, neither of which is susceptible.

PROBLEM: Scale on evergreen trees.

SOLUTION: Treat only if serious. Use Cygon on all trees except those with a label warning. Use Orthene on hollies and others that Cygon is not recommended for,

PROBLEM: Pine engraver beetle.

SOLUTION: This pest enters pine trees through weakened or broken parts, often after ice or wind damage occurs. There is no cure, though state foresters recommend removing infested trees as soon as possible to reduce the danger of infesting other trees.

Disease Problems

PROBLEM: Fireblight on flowering pears, flowering cherries, and crabapples.

SOLUTION: Refrain from severe pruning, which forces large numbers of succulent (and highly susceptible) new spring shoots. There is no practical way for a homeowner to spray for this disease.

PROBLEM: Mimosa wilt.

SOLUTION: This problem is incurable, and once a tree is infected its death is inevitable.

A dying Mimosa tree.

Cankered wood of an infected Mimosa tree.

PROBLEM: Dogwood flower blight.

SOLUTION: Spray when flower buds first crack open, then as the petals fall and leaves begin to emerge. Check with your County Extension Office for recommended material to use in your area.

PROBLEM: Tar spot on maples.

SOLUTION: This disease is unsightly but seldom seems to harm the plant. If you have a serious problem that's causing harm to your tree, check with your state forestry office.

PROBLEM: Lichens.

SOLUTION: Lichens do not harm a plant and are seldom seen on trees until they are old. They occur in cool, shaded spots with high humidity. If you have a young tree with lichens, it may be an indication that your tree is not growing well and should be fertilized. (The first picture is of lichens on a 100-year-old champion Fraser Fir. The second is on a 50-year-old spruce.)

Natural Problems

PROBLEM: Lightning.

SOLUTION: You can't prevent lightning from striking and killing a tree. However, protect rare old irreplaceable specimens with grounding wires installed by a professional tree service.

PROBLEM: Damage from animals like deer and voles.

SOLUTION: It's hard to keep deer from eating leaves or stems and scraping a tree with their antlers. I have had fair success by placing partially used unlighted aroma candles in areas where I see deer tracks near young shrubs or trees. Prevent vole damage by keeping mulch away from tree trunks.

PROBLEM: Vines in trees (kudzu, poison ivy, English ivy).

SOLUTION: Kudzu, the worst offender, must be kept clear of trees. Rogue out Kudzu often. Spray with a brush killer or Roundup in the early spring and again in August. With poison ivy, wait till winter when it is less noxious, then cut a two-foot plug out of the main vine to kill it. Use the same method to kill English ivy, which is harmless to us but can be fatal to trees.

Parasites and Saprophytes

PROBLEM: Mistletoe.

SOLUTION: Mistletoe is a parasitic plant that inserts its roots into a limb (usually very high up) and extracts its sustenance from the tree. It is seldom dangerous since the branches where it lives are usually young and seldom break. But it should be removed from larger limbs that can come crashing down in a storm.

PROBLEM: Spanish moss.

SOLUTION: Spanish moss does no harm since it resides among a tree's limbs without taking anything from the tree. Don't worry about it – just be happy you have it to enjoy.

REFERENCES

Diseases of Trees and Shrubs, by Wayne A. Sinclair, Howard H. Lyon, and Warren T. Johnson. Copyright 1987 by Cornell University. Published by Comstock Publishing Associates, a division of Cornell University Press, Ithaca and London.

Hortus Third, A Concise Dictionary of Plants Cultivated in the United States and Canada. Copyright 1976 by Cornell University for its L. H. Bailey Hortorium. Published by Macmillan Publishing Company, New York.

Insects That Feed on Trees and Shrubs, by Warren T. Johnson and Howard H. Lyon. Second Edition, Revised. Copyright 1991 by Cornell University. Published by Comstock Publishing Associates, a division of Cornell University Press, Ithaca and London.

Manual of Woody Landscape Plants, by Michael A. Dirr. Copyright Revised 1998. Stipes Publishing L.L.C., Champaign, Illinois.

The Royal Horticultural Society A-Z Encyclopedia of Garden Plants, Christopher Brickell, Editor-in-Chief. Copyright 1996 by Dorling Kendersley Limited, London.

The Travels of William Bartram, Naturalist's Edition, by Francis Harper, 1958. Yale University Press, New Haven.

INDEX

English Names

Ash ix, **19–21**
  Green Ash **19**, **20**
  Marshall Seedless Ash **20**
  White Ash 19, 20, **21**, 174

Baobab 1

Beech ix, 11, **23–25**
  American Beech x, **xi**, 11, **23**, **24**, 79, 172
  Copper (Purple) Beech **25** , 173
  European Beech 23, **25**
  Purple Beech 25
  Weeping Beech **25**, 172

Birch **26–28**
  European White Birch 26, 28
  Paperbark Birch **26**, 27, 28
  River Birch 26, 27, **28**, 172
  Sweet Birch 28
  White Birch 26

Black Gum (Black Tupelo) 11, 16, **29–30**, 173

Black Locust 102, 132

Bradford Pear **31–32**, 121, 171, 173, 179

Catalpa 11, 12, **33–34**, 70, 174
  Common (Southern) Catalpa **33**, 34
  Western (Northern) Catalpa 33, **34**

Cedar **35–39**
  Atlas Cedar **36**, 37, 173
  Cedar of Lebanon xii, 1, 4, 35, 37, 42, 173
  Gray Atlas Cedar **36**
  Indian Cedar 9, 13, **35**, 36, 37 , 173
  Japanese Cedar 10, 35, **38**, 39, 173
  Red Cedar 35, **39** , 173, 189

Chaste Tree (Vitex) 9, **162–163** , 173, 185

Cherry **40–45**
  Black Cherry, Wild Cherry 40, **41**, 42, 173
  Carolina Cherry Laurel 9, 40, **42**, 166, 173, 185, 188
  Cherry Plum 148
  Flowering Cherry xii, 9, 172, 173, 186, 188
  Kwanzan Cherry 40, **43**, 44

Mt. Fuji (Shirotae) Cherry 43, 44
Okame Flowering Cherry 12, **43**, 44
Shirofugen Cherry 44
Sweet Cherry 41
Taiwan Flowering Cherry 44

Yoshino Cherry **40**, 44, **45**, 52
Weeping (Weeping Higan) Cherry 25, **44**, 45, 172

Chestnut **46–47**
  American Chestnut 46, 47, 120
  Chinese Chestnut 13, **46**, 47 , 173

Chinaberry **48–49**
  Texas Umbrella Chinaberry 48, **49**, 172, 173

Flowering Crabapple 9, 45, **50–52**
  Almey Flowering Crabapple 51, **52**
  Callaway Flowering Crabapple 50, **51**, 173
  Dolgo Crabapple 51, 52
  Eleyi Flowering Crabapple 51, 52
  Floribunda (Japanese Flowering)

Crabapple **50**, 52
  Flowering Crabapple 50, 172, 173, 186, 188
  Hopa Flowering Crabapple 51, **52**
  Southern Crabapple 51
  Sweet Crabapple 51

Crape Myrtle xii, **9**, 16, **53–54**, 172, 173, 185
  Red Crape Myrtle 54
  Natchez Crape Myrtle **53**, 54
  White Crape Myrtle **54**

Cypress 1, **55–57**
  Bald Cypress 2, 8, **55**, **56**, 107
  Leyland Cypress 10, 38, 39, 55, **56–57**, 82, 142, 173

Dawn Redwood 8, 15, **58–59**, 172, 173

Dogwood ix, xii, 2, **9**, **11**, 40, **60–65**, 172, 173
  Bloodtwig Dogwood 60
  Cherokee Chief Dogwood 63, 90
  Chinese Dogwood 12, 14, 60, 64, **65**, 172, 173
  Cloud 9 Dogwood 52, 62–**63**
  Flowering Dogwood ix, xii, 2, 14, 40, 60, 172, 173
  Pagoda Dogwood 14
  Pink Flowering Dogwood 2, **63**

Red Osier Dogwood 14, 60
White Flowering Dogwood **60–62**

Eastern Sycamore (American Plane Tree) **145**, 146

Elm 8, **66–68**
  American Elm 66, 67, 171
  Chinese (Siberian) Elm 11, 66, 67, **68**, 95, 96, 171, 173, 200
  True Chinese Elm 66, 67

Empress Tree 5, 8, 12, **69–70**

Fir **71–73**
  Balsam Fir 9, 71, 72, 173
  China Fir (Monkey Tree, Cunninghamia) 72, **73** , 173
  Douglas Fir 1
  Fraser Fir (Southern Balsam, Double Balsam) 1, 16, **71**, 72, 172, 173, **183**
  Ginkgo (Maidenhair Tree) xii, 1, 4, 11, 16, **74–75**, 172, 173

Golden-rain Tree 9, **76–77**, 173

Hackberry **78–79**
  Common Hackberry 72
  Mississippi Hackberry, Sugar Hackberry 79, 172

Halesia (Silverbell) **80–81**, 172, 173
  Carolina Silverbell 81
  Two-winged Silverbell 81

Hemlock **82–83**, 173
  Canadian Hemlock 82, **83** , 173
  Carolina Hemlock 83

Hickory ix, x, xii, 11, 18, **84–85**
  Bitternut 84
  Pignut 84
  Shagbark Hickory **84**, 85
  Swamp Hickory 84

Holly **86–90**, 172, 173, 186
  American Holly 87, 88, 89, 173
  Boxleaf Holly 90
  Burford Holly 87, 142
  Chinese Holly 87
  Croonenberg Holly 89
  East Palatka Holly 90
  Foster Holly 87, **89**, 128, 172, 173
  Hoskins Shadow Holly 90
  Nellie R. Stevens Holly 83, 87
  Savannah Holly **86**, 89, 90, 172, 173
  Weeping Yaupon Holly 87, **90**, 172

Yaupon Holly 87, 128, 172, 173

Hornbeam (Ironwood) **95–96**
  American Hornbeam **95**
  European Hornbeam **95**
  Fastigiata European (Upright) Hornbeam 10, **96**, 172, 179

Horse Chestnut and Buckeye 1, **91–94**
  Bottlebrush Buckeye 91
  Common (European) Horse Chestnut **91**, 92, 93, 172, 173
  Red Buckeye 91, 93, **94**, 172, 173
  Red Horse Chestnut 93, 94

Huon 1, 4

Katsura Tree 11, **97–99**, 173

Kauri 1

Linden 1, **100–101**
  American Linden (Basswood) 100
  European Linden 10, 100, 101
  Lime Tree 100, **101**
  Little Leaf Linden 100, **101**

Loblolly Bay 22, 172, 173

Lost Gordonia 22, 46

Magnolia ix, xii, 3, **102–112**
  Alexandrina Magnolia **111**, 112
  Bigleaf Magnolia 7, 11, 104, **107**, **108**, 109, 110, 173
  Bracken's Brown Beauty Magnolia **106**
  Cucumber Magnolia or Cucumber Tree 10, 173
  Fraser Magnolia 107, 109, 173
  Kobus Magnolia 111
  Lily Magnolia 110, **111**, 112, 173
  Little Gem Magnolia 106
  Loebner Magnolia 111
  Saucer Magnolia 110, 111, 173
  Skunk (Umbrella) Magnolia 109, **110**, 173
  Southern Magnolia (Bull Bay) xii, 2, **9**, 39, 87, 92, **103**, **104**, **105**, 106, 108, 172, 173, 185, 188, 189
  Star Magnolia (Tulip Tree) 14, 110, **112**, 173
  Swamp Magnolia 109, **110**
  Sweet Bay (Virginia) Magnolia 22, 104, **106**, 107, 108
  Virginia Magnolia 22, 104, **106**, **107**, 108
  White Bark Magnolia 110, 173
  Yulan Magnolia 111

Malee 1, 4

Maple 3, 6, 8, 11, **113–121**, 182
  Bloodgood Japanese Maple **115**
  Box Elder 114, 174
  Burgundy Lace Japanese Maple **115**
  Cut Leaf Japanese Maple **115**
  Japanese Maple 14, **114**, **115**, 116, 172, 173
  Legacy Sugar Maple **121**
  Crimson King Maple 16, 114, **116**, 117, 148, 173
  Norway Maple 114, 116, 117
  October Glory Red Maple **118**, **119**, 172, 173
  Paperbark Maple 113, 114, **117**, 172, 173
  Red Maple 7, **8**, **10**, 11, **12**, 14, 15, 16, 21, 30, **113**, 114, 117, **118**, 120, 182
  Red Sunset Maple 118, 173
  Silver Maple 114, **119**, 120
  Sugar Maple **4**, 8, **10**, 113, 114, 116, **120**, 121, 153, **172**, 173
  Trident Maple 113, 114, 121
  Yellow Cut Leaf Japanese Maple **115**

Mimosa **122–123**

Moraine Locust 102

Mulberry **124–125**
  American Mulberry 124
  Common (White) Mulberry **124**, 125
  Red Mulberry **125** , 173
  White (Common) Mulberry **124**, 125

Oak ix, x, xii, 3, 6, 8, 11, **126–134**
  Black Jack Oak 126
  Chestnut Oak 7, 13, 127, **128**, 1
  Chinese Evergreen Oak 128, **129**, 185, 188
  Japanese Evergreen Oak 129, 173
  Live Oak ix, 2, 3, 16, **126**, **127**, **129**, 130, 133, 172
  Middleton Oak 1, 15, **126**, **127**, 129, 130
  Northern Red Oak 130, 131
  Pin Oak **10**, **130**, 132, 173
  Red Oak 7, 16, 126, 127, 130–131
  Sawtooth Oak 131, **132**, 171
  Scarlet Oak 130, 131
  Scrub Oak 126
  Southern Red Oak 130, **131**
  Water Oak 8, 13, 16, 24, 126, 127, 130, **132**, 133, 137, 174
  White Oak 1, 3, 7, **10**, 11, **17**, 126, 127, **133**, 134, 172, 173

Willow Oak 8, 13, 126, 127, 130, 132, **134**, 137, 161, 172

Peach, Flowering 135, 173, 186, 188
  Double Pink Flowering Peach 135
  Double Red Flowering Peach 135
  Double White Flowering Peach 135

Pecan 3, 84, **136–137** , 173

Persimmon **138–140** , 173
  Common Persimmon 139–140, 173
  Japanese Persimmon 139, 140, 173

Pine **141–144**
  Bristlecone Pine 4, 142
  Loblolly Pine 142, 173
  Longleaf Pine 142
  Japanese Black Pine 143
  Slash Pine 142–143, 173
  Virginia Pine **143**
  White Pine **142**, **143–144**

Plane Tree (Sycamore) 3, **145**
  American Plane Tree (Eastern Sycamore) **145**, 146, 166
  London Plane Tree 145, 146, 172
  Oriental Plane Tree 146

Poplar 3, 14

Purple Leaf Plum 16, **147–148** , 173
  Newport 148
  Thundercloud 148

Redbud **149–151**, 173
  Chinese Redbud 149, **151**, 173
  Common Redbud **150**
  Forest Pansy Redbud **150**
  White Redbud (White Judas Tree) 149, 150, 151, 173

Salt Cedar (Tamarisk) 159

Sequoia 4

Shademaster Locust 102

Sherman Redwood 1

Silverbell 80–81

Silver-dollar Tree 30

Sourwood **152** , 173

Spruce **153–155**, 173

Colorado (Koster) Blue Spruce 153, 154
Norway Spruce 9, **153**, **154**
White Spruce 153, 154, **155**

Stewartia 156

Sweet Gum 2, 3, 6, 30, **157–158**, 173

Tamarisk (Salt Cedar) 159, 173

Thornless Honey Locust 102

Tree of Heaven 119

Tulip Poplar (Tulip Tree, Yellow Poplar) x, 1, 2, 3, 6, 7, 10, 14, 111, **160–161**

Vitex (Chaste Tree) 9, **162–163** , 173, 185

Walnut **164**, 173
Black Walnut **164**
English (Persian) Walnut 164, 173

Wax Myrtle (Bayberry) **165–166**, 172
Bayberry (Wax Myrtle) 165–166
Southern Wax Myrtle 165, 166, 172

Willow 14, **167–169**
Corkscrew Willow 168, 169
Golden Weeping Willow 168
Japanese Fantail Willow 168, 169
Pussy Willow 168, 173
Weeping Willow **167**, 168–**169**
White Willow 168

Yellow Poplar (Tulip Poplar, Tulip Tree) x, 1, 2, 3, 6, 7, 10, 14, 111, 160–161

Yew 1

Zelkova 66, **170–171**, 172, 173, 200
Japanese Zelkova 95, 96

Latin Names

Abies, sp. (Fir) 71
Abies balsamea (Balsam Fir) 71, 72, 173
Abies fraseri (Fraser Fir) 16, 71, 72, 172, 173
Cunninghamia lanceolata (China Fir, Monkey Tree, Cunninghamia) 72, 73, 173

Acer sp. (Maple) 3, 6, 8, 11, 113–121
Acer buergerianum (Trident Maple) 113, 114
Acer griseum (Paperbark Maple) 113, 114, 117–118, 172, 173
Acer negundo (Box Elder) 114, 174
Acer palmatum (Japanese Maple) 14, 114, 115, 116, 172, 173
Acer palmatum atropurpureum dissectum (Red Cutleaf Japanese Maple) 115, 173
Acer platanoides (Norway Maple) 114, 116
Acer platanoides (Norway Maple 'Crimson King') 16, 114, 116, 117, 148, 173
Acer rubrum (Red Maple) 7, 8 (picture), 10 (picture), 11, 12, 15, 113, 114, 117, 118, 120, 182
Acer rubrum 'October Glory' (October Glory Red Maple) 118, 119, 172, 173
Acer rubrum 'Red Sunset' (Red Sunset Maple) 118, 173
Acer saccharinum (Silver Maple) 114, 119, 120
Acer saccharum (Sugar Maple) 4, 8, 10, 113, 114, 116, 120 (pic), 121, 172, 173
Acer saccharum 'Legacy' (Legacy Maple) 121

Aesculus sp. (Horse Chestnut and Buckeye) 91–94
Aesculus glabra (Ohio Buckeye) 91, 93
Aesculus hippocastanum (Common or European Horse Chestnut) 91, 92, 93, 172, 173
Aesculus parviflora (Bottlebrush Buckeye) 91
Aesculus pavia (Red Buckeye) 91, 93, 94, 172, 173
Aesculus x carnea (Red Horse Chestnut) 93, 94

Albizia julibrissin (Mimosa) 122–123

Betula, sp. (Birch) 26–28

Betula lenta (Sweet Birch) 28
Betula nigra (River Birch) 26, 27, 28, 172
Betula papyrifera (Paperbark Birch) 26, 27, 28
Betula pendula (European White Birch) 26, 28

Carpinus sp. (Hornbeam, Ironwood) 95–96
Carpinus betulus (European Hornbeam) 95
Carpinus caroliniana (American Hornbeam) 95
Carpinus betulus 'Fastigiata' (Upright or Fastigiata European Hornbeam) 10, 96, 172, 179

Carya illinoinensis (Pecan) 3, 84, 136–137, 173

Carya sp. (Hickory) ix, x, xii, 11, 18, 84–85
Carya ovata (Shagbark Hickory) 85

Castanea, sp. (Chestnut) 46
Castanea dentata (American Chestnut) 46, 47
Castanea mollissima (Chinese Chestnut) 13, 47

Catalpa, sp. 11, 12, 33–34, 70, 174
Catalpa bignonioides (Common Catalpa) 33, 34
Catalpa speciosa (Western Catalpa) 33, 34

Cedar (Various Genera) 35–39
Cedar, sp. (True Cedar) 36
Cedrus atlantica (Atlas Cedar) 36, 37, 173
Cedrus atlantica 'glauca' (Gray Atlas Cedar) 36
Cedrus deodara (Indian Cedar) 9, 13, 35, 36, 37 , 173
Cedrus libani (Cedar of Lebanon) xii, 1, 4, 35, 36, 37, 42, 173
Cryptomeria japonica (Japanese Cedar) 10, 35, 38, 39, 173
Juniperus virginiana (Red Cedar) 35, 39, 173, 189

Celtis, sp. (Hackberry) 78–79
Celtis laevigata (Mississippi Hackberry, Sugar Hackberry) 79, 172
Celtis occidentalis (Common Hackberry) 72

Cercidiphyllum japonicum (Katsura Tree) 11, 97–99, 173

Cercis sp. (Redbud) 149–151

Cercis canadensis (Common Redbud) 150, 173

Cercis canadensis 'alba' (White Redbud, White Judas Tree) 149, 150, 151, 173

Cersis chinensis (Chinese Redbud) 149, 151, 173

Cornus, sp. (Dogwood) 60–65
Cornus florida (White Flowering Dogwood) 2, 40, 60, 61, 62, 172, 173
Cornus florida 'Cherokee Chief' (Cherokee Chief Dogwood) 63
Cornus florida 'Cloud 9' (Cloud 9 Dogwood) 62–63
Cornus florida 'plena' (Double floweringDogwood) 64, 172
Cornus florida rubra (Pink Flowering Dogwood) 2, 63, 172
Cornus kousa var. chinensis (Chinese Dogwood) 60, 64, 172, 173
Cornus sanguinea (Bloodtwig Dogwood) 60

Corylus avellana 'Contorta' (Harry Lauder's Walking Stick) 169

Cupressus, sp. (Cypress) 55–57
x Cupressocyparis leylandii (Leyland Cypress) 56–57, 82, 142, 173

Diospyros sp. (Persimmon) 138–140
Diospyros virginiana (Common Persimmon) 139–140, 173
Diospyros kaki (Japanese Persimmon) 139, 140, 173

Eriobotrya japonica (Tree Loquat) 166

Eucalyptus, sp.
Eucalyptus cinerea (Silver-dollar Tree) 30

Fagus, sp. (Beech) ix, 11, 23–25
Fagus grandiflora (American Beech) x, xi, 11, 23, 24, 79, 172
Fagus sylvatica (European Beech) 23
Fagus sylvatica 'Atropunicea' (Copper, or Purple, Beech) 25 , 173
Fagus sylvatica 'Pendula' (Weeping Beech) 25, 172

Franklinia alatamaha (Lost Gordonia) 22, 46

Fraxinus, sp. (Ash) ix, 19–21
Fraxinus americana (White Ash) 19, 21, 174

Fraxinus pennsylvanica (Green Ash) 19, 20, 21

Ginkgo Biloba (Ginkgo, Maidenhair Tree) xii, 1, 4, 11, 16, 74–75, 173

Gleditsia triancanthos var. inermis (Thornless Honey Locust) 102

Gordonia lasianthus (Loblolly Bay) 22, 172, 173

Halesia, sp. (Silverbell) 80–81, 172, 173
Halesia tetraptera (Carolina Silverbell) 81
Halesia diptera (Two-winged Silverbell) 81

Ilex sp. (Holly) 86–90
Ilex x 'Nellie R. Stevens' (Nellie R. Stevens) 87
Ilex vomitoria (Yaupon Holly) 87, 128, 172, 173
Ilex x attenuata 'Foster' (Foster Holly) 87, 89, 128, 172, 173
Ilex cornuta 'Burfordii' (Burford Holly) 87, 142
Ilex cornuta (Chinese Holly) 87
Ilex opaca (American Holly) 87, 88, 89, 173
Ilex crenata (Boxleaf Holly) 90
Ilex opaca 'Croonenberg' 89
Ilex x attenuata 'Savannah' (Savannah Holly) 86, 89, 90 , 172, 173

Juglans sp. (Walnut) 164
Juglans nigra (Black Walnut) 164
Juglans regia (English or Persian Walnut) 164, 173

Koelreuteria paniculata (Golden-rain Tree) 9, 76–77, 173

Lagerstroemia indica (Crape Myrtle) 53–54, 172, 173, 185

Liquidambar styraciflua (Sweet Gum) 2, 3, 6, 30, 157–158, 173

Liriodendron tulipifera (Tulip Tree, Tulip Poplar, Yellow Poplar) x, 1, 2, 3, 6, 7, 10, 14, 111, 160–161

Magnolia sp. (Magnolia) ix, xii, 3, 102–112
Magnolia a cuminata (Cucumber Magnolia or Cucumber Tree) 109, 173
Magnolia denudata (Yulan Magnolia) 111
Magnolia fraseri (Fraser Magnolia) 107, 109, 173

Magnolia glauca (Virginia Magnolia) 22
Magnolia grandiflora (Southern Magnolia, Bull Bay) xii, 2, 9 (picture), 39, 87, 92, 103, 104, 106, 108, 172, 173, 185, 188, 189
Magnolia hypoleuca (White Bark Magnolia) 110, 173
Magnolia kobus (Kobus Magnolia) 111
Magnolia liliflora 'Nigra' (Lily Magnolia) 110, 111, 112, 173
Magnolia macrophylla (Bigleaf Magnolia) 7, 11, 104, 107, 108, 109, 110, 173
Magnolia stellata (Star Magnolia) 14, 110, 112 , 173
Magnolia tripentala (Umbrella, Skunk or Swamp Magnolia) 109, 110 , 173
Magnolia virginiana (Sweet Bay or Virginia Magnolia) 22, 104, 106, 107 (pic), 108
Magnolia x loebneri (Loebner Magnolia) 111
Magnolia x soulangeana 'Alexandrina' 111, 112
Magnolia x soulangeana (Saucer Magnolia) 110, 111, 173

Malus sp. (Flowering Crabapple) 50–52, 172, 173
Malus augustifolia (Southern Crabapple) 51
Malus 'Callaway' (Callaway Flowering Crabapple) 50, 51 , 173
Malus coronaria (Sweet Crabapple) 51
Malus floribunda (Japanese Flowering Crabapple) 50, 51, 52

Melia azederach (Chinaberry) 48–49
Melia azederach 'Umbraculiformis' (Texas Umbrella Chinaberry) 48, 49, 172, 173

Metasequoia gliptostroboides (Dawn Redwood) 8, 15, 58– 59, 172, 173

Morus sp. (Mulberry) 124–125
Morus alba (White or Common Mulberry) 124, 125
Morus rubra (Red Mulberry) 125 , 173

Myrica sp. (Wax Myrtle or Bayberry) 165–166, 172
Myrica pennsylvanica (Bayberry) 165
Myrica cerifera (Southern Wax Myrtle) 165, 166, 172

Nyssa sylvatica (Black Gum, Black Tupelo) 11, 16, 29, 30, 173

Oxydendrum arboreum (Sourwood) 152 , 173

Paulownia tomentosa (Empress Tree) 8, 12, 69–70

Picea sp. (Spruce) 153–155, 173
Picea abies (Norway Spruce) 9, 153, 154
Picea glauca (White Spruce) 153, 154, 155
Picea pungens 'Koster' (Koster or Colorado Blue Spruce) 153, 154

Pinus sp. (Pine) 141–144
Pinus elliottii (Slash Pine) 142–143, 173
Pinus palustris (Longleaf Pine) 142
Pinus strobus (White Pine) 142, 143–144
Pinus taeda (Loblolly Pine) 142, 173
Pinus thunbergii (Japanese Black Pine) 143
Pinus virginiana (Virginia Pine) 143

Platanus sp. (Plane Tree, Sycamore) 145
Platanus occidentalis (American Plane Tree, Eastern Sycamore) 145, 146
Platanus x acerifolia (London Plane Tree) 146, 172

Prunus cerasifera cultivars (Purple Leaf Plum) 147–148, 173

Prunus persica (Flowering Peach) 135, 173, 186, 188

Prunus sp. (Cherry) 40–45
Prunus avium (Sweet Cherry) 41
Prunus caroliniana (Carolina Cherry Laurel) 9, 40, 42, 166, 173, 185, 188
Prunus campanulata (Taiwan Flowering Cherry) 44
Prunus cerasus (Sour Cherry) 41
Prunus serotina (Black Cherry, Wild Cherry) 40, 41, 42 , 173
Prunus serrulata 'Kwanzan' (Kwanzan Cherry) 40, 41, 43, 44
Prunus serrulata 'Shirofugen' (Shirofugen Cherry) 44
Prunus serrulata 'Shirotae' (Mt. Fuji or Shirotae Cherry) 43, 44
Prunus subhirtella var. pendula (Weeping or Weeping Higan Cherry) 44, 45, 172
Prunus x Okame (Okame Flowering Cherry) 12, 41, 43, 44
Prunus x yedoensis (Yoshino Cherry) 40, 41, 44, 45, 52

Pyrus calleryana 'Bradford' (Bradford Pear) 31, 32 , 173, 179

Quercus sp. (Oak) 126–134
Quercus acuta (Japanese Evergreen Oak) 129, 173
Quercus acutissima (Sawtooth Oak) 131, 132, 171
Quercus alba (White Oak) 1, 3, 7, 10, 11, 17, 126, 127, 133, 134, 172, 173
Quercus coccinea (Scarlet Oak) 130, 131
Quercus falcata (Southern Red Oak) 130, 131
Quercus myrsinifolia (Chinese Evergreen Oak) 128, 129, 185, 188
Quercus nigra (Water Oak) 8, 13, 16, 24, 126, 127, 130, 132, 133, 137, 174
Quercus palustris (Pin Oak) 10, 130, 132, 173
Quercus phellos (Willow Oak) 8, 13, 126, 127, 130, 132, 134, 137, 161
Quercus primus (Chestnut Oak) 7, 13, 127, 128, 172
Quercus rubra (Northern Red Oak) 130, 131
Quercus virginiana (Live Oak) 1x, 2, 3, 129, 130, 133, 172

Robinia pseudoacacia (Black Locust) 102, 132

Salix sp. (Willow) 167–169
Salix alba (White Willow) 168
Salix alba 'Tristis' (Golden Weeping Willow) 168
Salix babylonica (Weeping Willow) 167
Salix caprea, salix discolor (Pussy Willow) 168, 173
Salix matsudana 'Tortuosa' (Corkscrew Willow) 168, 169
Salix sachalinensis 'Sekka' (Japanese Fantail Willow) 168, 169

Stewartia sp. (Stewartia) 156
Stewartia malacodendron 156
Stewartia monadelpha 156
Stewartia ovata 156
Stewartia ovata var. grandiflora 156
Stewartia pseudocamellia 156

Tamarix ramosissima (Tamarisk, Salt Cedar) 159, 173
Tamarix aphylla 159

Taxodium, sp. (Cypress) 55, 56
Taxodium distichum (Bald Cypress) 2, 8, 55

Tilia sp. (Linden) 1, 100–101
Tilia cordata (European Linden, Little Leaf Linden, Lime Tree) 100, 101, 173

Tsuga sp. (Hemlock) 82–83, 173
Tsuga canadensis (Canadian Hemlock) 83 , 173
Tsuga caroliniana (Carolina Hemlock) 83

Ulmus sp. (Elm) 8, 66–68
Ulmus americana (American Elm) 66, 67, 171
Ulmus parvifolia (True Chinese Elm) 66, 67, 171, 173, 200
Ulmus pumila (Chinese or Siberian Elm) 66, 67, 68, 171, 173

Vitex agnus-castus (Vitex, Chaste Tree) 9, 162–163, 173, 185

Zelkova serrata (Zelkova) 66, 170, 172, 173, 200